ALFA ROMEO GIULIA

TECHNICAL MANUAL FOR 1962 AND ONWARDS CARBURETED MODELS

© 2019 Veloce Enterprises Inc., San Antonio, Texas USA
All rights reserved. This work may not be reproduced or transmitted in any form without the express consent of the publisher

Introduction

Welcome to the world of digital publishing ~ the book you now hold in your hand, was printed using the latest state of the art digital technology. The advent of print-on-demand has forever changed the publishing process, never has information been so accessible and it is our hope that this book serves your informational needs for years to come. If this is your first exposure to digital publishing, we hope that you are pleased with the results. Many more titles of interest to the classic automobile and motorcycle enthusiast, collector and restorer are available via our website at www.VelocePress.com. We hope that you find this title as interesting as we do.

Note from the Publisher

The information presented is true and complete to the best of our knowledge. All recommendations are made without any guarantees on the part of the author or the publisher, who also disclaim all liability incurred with the use of this information.

Trademarks

We recognize that some words, model names and designations, for example, mentioned herein are the property of the trademark holder. We use them for identification purposes only. This is not an official publication.

Information on the use of this Publication

This manual is an invaluable resource for those interested in performing their own maintenance. However, in today's information age we are constantly subject to changes in common practice, new technology, availability of improved materials and increased awareness of chemical toxicity. As such, it is advised that the user consult with an experienced professional prior to undertaking any procedure described herein. While every care has been taken to ensure correctness of information, it is obviously not possible to guarantee complete freedom from errors or omissions or to accept liability arising from such errors or omissions. Therefore, any individual that uses the information contained within, or elects to perform or participate in do-it-yourself repairs or modifications acknowledges that there is a risk factor involved and that the publisher or its associates cannot be held responsible for personal injury or property damage resulting from the use of the information or the outcome of such procedures.

Warning!

One final word of advice, this publication is intended to be used as a reference guide, and when in doubt the reader should consult with a qualified technician.

NOTES ON THE USE OF THIS MANUAL

Page Numbering

As each of the individual publications in this manual have their own index, the page numbers corresponding to that index are printed to the top corner of each page. The number printed to the center bottom of the page is the page number within the book.

Contents

It should be noted that Alfa Romeo never published an 'all inclusive' manual for the individual models of Giulia automobiles. Instead, they produced a number of 'Technical' publications that provided model specific technical information plus individual 'Mechanical Repair' publications that were focused on the overhaul and service of various mechanical and electrical components. The intention was that these two separate publications were to be used in conjunction with each other in order to provide both technical and mechanical data for a particular model.

This manual is a compilation of the factory 'Technical' publications listed below and, while the list is not inclusive, the publications were selected as being representative for the 1300cc, 1600cc and 1750cc series of carbureted Alfa Romeo Giulia models.

Models	Publication date / Number		Book Pages
1300 GT Junior	March 1967	1226	Pages 1 - 20
1300 Spider Junior	July 1968	1366	Pages 21 - 42
Spider Junior Supplement	January 1969	1461	Pages 43 - 48
1300 Giulia TI	November 1969	1206-R1	Pages 49 - 84
1600 Giulia Ti 1600 Spider 1600 Sprint	October 1963	955	Pages 85 - 104
1600 Spider	August 1966	1212	Pages 105 - 124
1600 Sprint GT Veloce	October 1966	1210	Pages 125 - 144
1600 Giulia Super	April 1970	1133-R1	Pages 145 - 178
1750 Berlina 1750 GT Veloce 1750 Spider Veloce	February 1968	1321	Pages 179 - 208

Giulia Model Designations

To aid in better understanding the Alfa Romeo Giulia model designations GT, GTV and Sprint refer to 2 door coupes, Spider to 2 door convertibles and Berlina, Super and Ti to the 4 door sedans. The individual model types within each of these designations may (or may not!) include the engine capacity (1300, 1600, 1750 & 2000) before, after or somewhere within the particular model designation. The identification of a particular body style by the model designation plus the random positioning of the engine size within the model description often creates confusion among those unfamiliar with the Alfa Giula model line.

Measurements & Values

The metric system is the primary measurement method used in both the manufacture of these vehicles and in the production of the factory 'Mechanical Repair' and 'Technical' publications. As such, the reader is urged to verify that the conversion of those metric measurements to other forms of measurement is correct. All measurements and values contained within this compilation of the factory publications are made without any guarantees on behalf of the publisher, who also disclaims any and all liability incurred with the use of this manual.

The importance of using the Alfa Romeo 'Mechanical Repair' publications in conjunction with this Manual

As noted previously, Alfa Romeo also issued 'Mechanical Repair' publications that that were focused on the overhaul and service of various mechanical and electrical components. As these 'Mechanical Repair' publications were meant to be used in conjunction with the 'Technical' publications, we feel it is important that the reader is made aware of the associated Workshop Manual that compliments this Technical Manual.

Alfa Romeo Giulia Workshop Manual 1962-1975 All Models 1300cc, 1600cc, 1750cc & 2000cc
ISBN 9781588502254

This 338 page manual was compiled using data from seven of those individual factory 'Mechanical Repair' publications plus a number of additional pages of maintenance, repair, overhaul and wiring diagrams that were not included in the original factory publications. Consequently, it provides a generic 'Workshop Manual' for the repair and overhaul of the 1965-1971 Giulia series of automobiles. However, as the 1962-1975 series of Alfa models shared many of the same mechanical components, these 'Mechanical Repair' publications are also of use to owners of both the earlier and later models. For example, even though the engines were of four different capacities they are sufficiently alike for a single set of instructions to suffice for their maintenance and overhaul. The combination of the manual above, when used in conjunction with this Technical Manual, will provide a comprehensive 'Workshop Manual' for the carbureted series of Alfa Giulia.

The additional pages in this manual include maintenance and repair information on:

Drum brakes, hydraulic braking system, Dunlop disc brakes and additional information on ATE disc brakes. Front hubs, shock absorbers and stabilizer rod, ZF steering box, Burman steering box, steering linkage and steering adjustments. Electrical components including control box, regulator, generator, starter motor, windscreen wiper motor (both Bosch & Marelli), lamps and lighting and wiring diagrams for 14 different models.

The factory 'Mechanical Repair' publications included in this compilation are:

(1) **Engine, Clutch & Gearbox Manual for the 1600 Giulia TI, Sprint GT & TI Super.**
(First printed October 1964 this is the third printing dated December 1968 Publication No. 1008-R2).

(2) **Propeller Shaft, Rear Axle & Suspension for the Giulia 1300, 1300TI the Giulia 1600 TI Super, Sprint GT, GTC, TI, Super, Sprint GT Veloce & Spider 1600.**
(First printed October 1966 this is the fourth printing dated April 1971 Publication No. 1222-R3).

(3) **ATE Disc Brakes all Models, as appropriate.**
(First printed July 1966 this is the second printing dated November 1969 Publication No. 1202-R1).

(4) **Wheel, Suspension & Front End Geometry, for all Giulia and 1750 Models plus 2000 models amendment.**
(This May 1970 Publication No.1507 includes the October 1977 printing of the December 1971 amendment No. 1838-R2 for the 2000 models - Only sections that are 'owner appropriate' are included).

(5) **Electrical for the 1600 Giulia Super, 1750 Berlina, 1750 GT Veloce & 1750 Spider Veloce.**
(September 1969 Publication No. 1384 - Only sections that are 'owner appropriate' are included).

(6) **Air Conditioning all Models, as appropriate.**
(October 1972 Publication No.1969).

(7) **Body, for all Giulia and 1750 Models** - Only sections that are 'owner appropriate' are included.
(September 1970 Publication No.1570).

Alfa Romeo Giulia Technical Manual for 1969 and onwards SPICA Fuel Injected Models
ISBN 9781588502278

Owners of the 1750cc and 2000cc SPICA fuel injected cars are directed to the above publication which combines a selection of the appropriate factory 'Technical' publications into a single publication for the 1750cc & 2000cc series of SPICA fuel injected Giulia models.

GT 1300 Junior

**technical characteristics
and
principal inspection specifications**

C o n t e n t s

############# **T E C H N I C A L   C H A R A C T E R I S T I C S** #############

P r i n c i p a l   c h a r a c t e r i s t i c   d a t a . . . . Page 3

    Performance . . . . " 3
    Tires . . . . " 4
    Refillings . . . . " 4
    Prescribed oils and lubricant . . . . " 4
    Carburetion . . . . " 5
    Idling adjustment . . . . " 5
    Float level adjustment . . . . " 6
    Valve timing . . . . " 7
    Electrical equipment . . . . " 8
    Bulb's wattage . . . . " 8
    Tightening torque specifications . . . . " 9

######## **M A J O R   I N S P E C T I O N   S P E C I F I C A T I O N S** ########

    Camshafts . . . . Page 10
    Valves and valve guides . . . . " 10
    Valve seats . . . . " 10
    Valve cups . . . . " 11
    Valve springs . . . . " 11
    Connecting rods . . . . " 11
    Piston pins . . . . " 11
    Piston pin holes . . . . " 11
    Pistons and piston rings . . . . " 12
    Cylinder barrels . . . . " 12
    Crankshaft . . . . " 13
    Clutch . . . . " 14
    Gearbox . . . . " 14
    Rear axle and suspension . . . . " 15
    Front suspension . . . . " 16
    Brakes . . . . " 17

W h e e l   a l i g n m e n t

    Checking of wheel angles and car trim under static load . . . . Page 18

############ T E C H N I C A L   C H A R A C T E R I S T I C S ##############

Principal characteristic data

Number of cylinders	4
Bore	74 mm (2.913")
Stroke	75 mm (2.953")
Total cylinder capacity	1290 cc
Max. power at 6,000 rpm	SAE 103 CV
Front track	1310 mm (4'3")
Rear track	1270 mm (4'2")
Wheelbase	2350 mm (7'8½")
Min. turning circle	10700 mm (35')
Overall length	4080 mm (13'4 5/8")
Overall width	1580 mm (5'2 1/4")
Overall height (unladen)	1315 mm (4'4")
Dry weight, with tools and jack	930 kg (2020 lbs)
Number of seats	4
Fuel consumption for 100 Km (CUNA standard)	9.8 lt
For best engine performance, the use of premium-grade fuel is advised.	(28.8 mpg.GB) (24.0 mpg.US)

With 41 : 9 final drive

Gear	Max. Speeds					
	Running in				After running in	
	up to 1000 km (600 mi.)		1000 to 3000 Km (600 to 1900 mi.)			
	Km/h	mph	Km/h	mph	Km/h	mph
1st	30	18	38	24	44	27
2nd	49	30	62	38	74	46
3rd	72	45	91	56	108	67
4th	98	60	123	76	146	91
5th	114	71	143	92	over 170	105
Rev.	-	-	-	-	48	30

Oil pressures with hot engine
{ min. pressure at idling speed: .5-1 Kg/cm2 (7-14 psi)
  min. pressure at top speed: 3.5 Kg/cm2 (50 psi)
  max. pressure at top speed: 4.5-5 Kg/cm2 (65-70 psi)

<u>Warning</u>: Check that generator warning light goes off as soon the engine exceeds 1,100 rpm.

TIRES

Inflation pressures (cold tires)

	Front wheels		Rear wheels	
	Kg/cm2	psi	Kg/cm2	psi
PIRELLI 155 x 15 Cinturato S	1.7 *	24.1	1.8 *	25.6
	1.8 **	25.8	2.1 **	29.8
MICHELIN 155 x 15 X	1.7 *	24.1	1.7 *	24.1
	1.9 **	27.0	1.9 **	27.0

* Inflate to the lower pressure for use with low load and short bursts to top speed.
** Inflate to the higher pressure for use with full load and top speed (highways).

Refillings

		G.B.	U.S.
Water (engine & radiator) .... about	7.5 lt	1.65 gals	1.98 gals
Fuel (reserve 7 lt/1.5 gals GB / 1.8 gals US) .... about	46 lt	10.1 gals	12.1 gals
Oil — Engine (pan & filter) — to max. level * about	5.0 Kg	4.95 qts	5.95 qts
Oil — Engine (pan & filter) — to min. level about	3.25 Kg	3.2 qts	3.8 qts
Oil — Gearbox .... about	1.650 Kg	3.2 pts	3.8 pts
Oil — Differential .... about	1.250 Kg	2.5 pts	3.0 pts
Oil — Steering box .... about	.250 Kg	.5 pt	.6 pt

(*) This quantity is that needed for regular changing; the total amount of oil in the circuit (sump, filter, passages) is 5.75 Kgs. (5.7 qts G.B.) (6.8 qts U.S.).

Prescribed oils and lubricants

	API - SAE - NLGI Number	Recommended commercial equivalent	
		AGIP	SHELL
Engine (*)	SAE 20 W/40 API MS	F.1 Supermotoroil Multigrade 20 W/40	X100 Multigrade 20W/40
Gearbox (for correct use of lubricant refer to footnote 1)	SAE 90 / SAE 90 EP	F.1 Rotra SAE 90 / F.1 Rotra Hypoid SAE 90	Dentax 90 / Spirax 90 EP
Steering box and differential	SAE 90 EP	F.1 Rotra Hypoid SAE 90	Spirax 90 EP
Propeller shaft universal joints and sliding yoke	NLGI 1	F.1 Grease 15	Retinax G
Front wheel bearings	NLGI 2/3	F.1 Grease 33 FD	Retinax AX
Brake fluid	Castrol Girling Brake Fluid Amber		

(*) For steady temperatures below 0° C (32°F) we advise the use of
AGIP F.1 Supermotoroil Multigrade 10 W/40
SHELL Super Motor Oil

N o t e 1 - AGIP F.1 Rotra Hypoid or SHELL Spirax should be used <u>exclusively in gearboxes as directed on the red transfer applied on them.</u>

SAE - Society of Automotive Engineers
API - American Petroleum Institute
NLGI - National Lubricating Grease Institute

In countries where the recommended lubricants are not available it is possibile to replace them with products of other leading Companies provided that in accordance with the prescribed specifications.

Carburetion
2 Carburettors WEBER 40 DCOE 28

Venturi	30 mm (1 3/16")
Main jet	112
Main air metering jet	220
Idling jet	50 F11
Idling air metering jet	120
Choke jet	65 F5
Acceleration pump jet	35
Travel of acceleration pump control rod	14 mm (.55")
Delivery of acceleration pump every 20 strokes (for each barrel)	5 ± 1 cc.
Needle valve seat dia.	1.50 mm (.06")
Float weight	26 grs
Distance of fuel level from float chamber flange (with a pressure of 2 mts (6'6") H_2O upstream the needle valve)	29 ± .5 mm (1.12 to 1.16")

Idling adjustment

F   Adjusting screw for minimum opening of throttle.

M   Idling mixture adjusting screw.

S   Screw for synchronizing throttles of the two carburettors.

T   Joint for control linkage (to pedal).

PREPARATORY STEPS

- Check the ignition timing and inspect the electric system (spark plugs, distributor, coil, etc.) for proper operation.
- Remove the air filter element and clean it thoroughly.
- Check the flexible mounts between carburettors and intake manifold for tightness.

ALIGNING THE THROTTLE VALVES

- Detach the control linkage "T" from carburettors.
- Slacken the screws "F" and "S" almost fully.
- Operate the throttles a few times to make sure there is no binding.
- Fully depress the trottle control lever of rear carburettor so that the throttles are fully closed; then screw in the screw "S" until contact is made.

IDLING

- Back up the screw "M" of half a turn.
- Tighten the screw "F" to contact, then screw it in one more turn to ensure feeding of engine.
- Connect the accelerator control linkage "T" to carburettors.
- Start the engine and warm it up.
- If necessary, back up the screw "F" very slowly until the engine runs at about 600 to 700 rpms.

Float level adjustment
WEBER 40 DCOE 28 carburettor

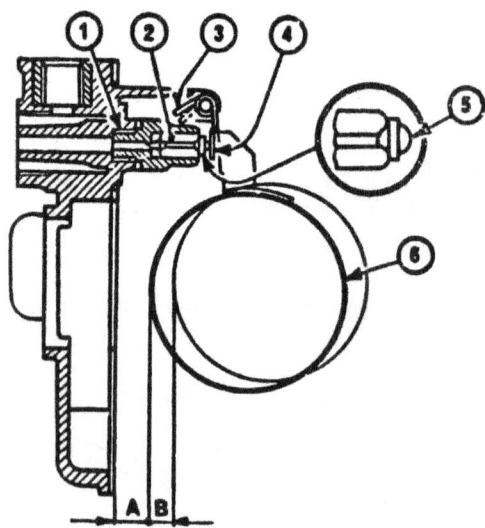

Check the level of fluid in float chamber as follows:

- Make sure the float weight is as specified (26 grs - .9 oz), that there are no leaks or indentations and that float can rotate freely about the pivot pin.

- The float weight must not be altered; consequently haphazard repairs (tinning, etc.) are detrimental to proper float operation.

- Check that needle valve (1) is well screwed into its seating and that the spring-loaded ball (5) part of the needle (2) is not jammed.

- Hold the carburettor cover in a vertical position as shown in the figure so that the float (6) does not depress the ball.

- With the cover vertical and the float tongue (4) in light contact with the ball, the two floats should be at a distance A=8.5 mm (.33") from the cover mating surface with the gasket fitted and well stuck to the cover.

- When the level has been set, check that the travel (B) of the float is 6.5 mm (.26"); if necessary, adjust the position of float pivot tail (3).

- The adjustment described above will correspond to a fuel level of 29 $\pm$ .5 mm (1.12 to 1.16") from the upper face of the float chamber (with a pressure of 2 mts - 6'6" H_2O upstream the needle valve).

- If distance (A) is not as specified, slightly bend the float tongue (4) until the correct distance is obtained; inspect the working surface of the float tongue for any sign of nicks which may restrict the free movement of needle (2).

- Then fit the carburettor cover and check that the float can move freely without rubbing against the walls of the float chamber.

C A U T I O N - The float level should be checked whenever the float or the needle valve has been changed. In the latter case it is also advisable to replace the gasket and make certain the new valve is securely screwed into its seating.

Valve timing

Checking of valve opening and closing angles

Clearance (with cold engine) between the unlobed profile of cams and the valve cup ceiling:
- intake . . . . .475 to .500 mm (.0187 to .0197")
- exhaust . . . . .525 to .550 mm (.0206 to .0216")

Opening of intake valve:
- lift of cup . . . . .20 mm (.008")
- corresponding to an angle . . . . before TDC of . . . . . 18° 30' ± 1° 30'

Closing of intake valve:
- lift of cup . . . . .20 mm (.008")
- corresponding to an angle . . . . after BDC of . . . . . . 42° 30' ± 1° 30'

Opening of exhaust valve:
- lift of cup . . . . .15 mm (.006")
- corresponding to an angle . . . . before BDC of . . . . . 42° 30' ± 1° 30'

Closing of exhaust valve:
- lift of cup . . . . .15 mm (.006")
- corresponding to an angle . . . . after TDC of . . . . . . 18° 30' ± 1° 30'

Angle values of the actual diagram of valve timing system with cold engine
(clockwise rotation direction of the crankshaft seen from the front side):

- opening of intake valve (before TDC) . . . . 36° 50'
- closing of intake valve (after BDC) . . . . 60° 50'
- opening of exhaust valve (before BDC) . . . . 54° 10'
- closing of exhaust valve (after TDC) . . . . 30° 10'
- induction stroke . . . . 227° 40'
- exhaust stroke . . . . 264° 20'

Ignition

Firing order: 1 - 3 - 4 - 2 (no. 1 cylinder is that at the fan side)

Values of advance of ignition distributor

Opening of contact points of ignition distributor . . . . S = .30 to .40 mm (.014 to .016")
The distributor is correctly fitted when the oiler is toward the engine.

Fixed advance F Before T D C	Maximum Advance M Before T D C
2° / 4°	40° / 43° at 5000 rpm

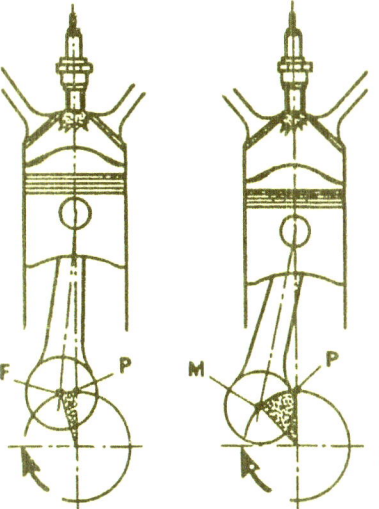

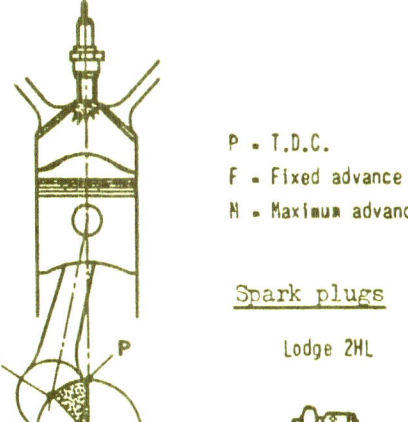

P = T.D.C.
F = Fixed advance
M = Maximum advance

Spark plugs

Lodge 2HL

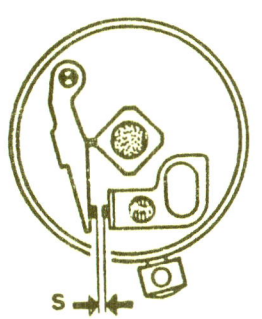

Electrical equipment

	BOSCH
Voltage	12 V
Battery	40 Ah
Generator	EG (R) 14 V 25 A 9
Voltage regulator	VA 14 V 25 A
Starting motor	EF (R) 12 V 0,7 PS
Coil	TK 12 A 19
Ignition distributor	JF 4
Windshield wiper	WS 13/11 T 1a

Bulb's wattage

Headlights (high and low beams)	45/50 asymmetric
Tail lights - parking & stop	5/20
Front lights - direction indicators Tail lights - direction indicators Back-up light	20
Front parking lights License plate light	5 globular
Engine compartment light Courtesy light inside the car	5 cylindrical
Side lights - direction indicators Instrument panel light Tell-tale for fuel reserve Tell-tale for high beams Tell-tale for parking lights Tell-tale for direction indicators Tell-tale for generator Tell-tale for blower	3 tabular

Tightening torque specifications

ENGINE-GEARBOX UNIT	Kgm.	lb. ft	Manner of tightening
Nuts of cylinder head — after repairing, when cold	6.2 to 6.4	44.8 to 46.3	Slacken and retighten without lube
Nuts of cylinder head — when hot	6.6 to 6.7	47.7 to 48.4	Lock without slackening the nut
Spark plugs	2.5 to 3.5	18.1 to 25.3	With graphite grease, when cold
Nuts of the camshaft caps	2 to 2.25	14.5 to 16.3	in oil
Nuts of the connecting rod caps	5 to 5.3	36.2 to 38.3	" "
Nuts of main bearing caps	4.7 to 5	33.9 to 36.1	" "
Screws of flywheel on crankshaft	4.2 to 4.5	30.4 to 32.5	" "
Nut of generator pulley	3 to 3.5	21.7 to 25.3	dry
Nut of gearbox main shaft yoke	12	86.8	"
Nut of gearbox layshaft	5	36.1	"
Nut of gearbox half-casing	1.8	13	"
Bolts joining gearbox output shaft yoke to prop. shaft yoke	4.5 to 5.5	32.6 to 39.7	"
Nut of gearbox inner swivel	325 to 365	23.6 to 26.4	"

REAR FRAME	Kgm.	lb. ft	Manner of tightening
Screws securing ring gear to differential case	4.5 to 5	32.6 to 36.1	dry
Ringnut securing yoke on final drive pinion shaft	8 to 14	58 to 101.2	"
Nuts securing bearing housing to real axle tubes	4.8 to 5.5	34.8 to 39.7	"
Nuts securing radius rods to body	10 to 11.5	72.4 to 83	"
Nuts securing radius rods to rear axle tubes	11.5 to 13	83 to 94	"
Nut securing reaction triangle to body	4.8 to 5.5	34.8 to 39.7	"
Nut securing reaction triangle to rear axle	11 to 15	79.6 to 108.5	"
Screws securing rear brake caliper to support (ATE brakes)	2.3 to 2.8	16.7 to 20.2	"
Nuts securing wheels	6 to 8	43.4 to 57.8	"
Bolts joining differential yoke to prop. shaft yoke	3.5 to 4	25.3 to 28.9	"

FRONT FRAME	Kgm.	lb. ft	Manner of tightening
Nut securing steering wheel to column	5 to 5.5	36.1 to 39.7	dry
Screws securing Burman steering box cover	2.3 to 2.5	16.7 to 18	"
Screws securing steering box & bellcrank bracket to body	4.8 to 5.5	34.8 to 39.7	"
Nuts of steering linkage ball joints	4.8 to 5.5	34.8 to 39.7	"
Nut securing steering arm to box	12.5 to 14	90.5 to 101.2	"
Screws securing upper attachment of shock absorber to body	2.3 to 2.8	16.7 to 20.2	"
Nut securing shock absorber to suspension arms	7.5 to 8.5	54.3 to 61.4	"
Screws securing upper wishbone front arm to body	2.3 to 2.8	16.7 to 20.2	"
Nut securing upper wishbone front arm to rear arm	4.8 to 5.5	34.8 to 39.7	"
Nut securing upper wishbone rear arm to body	11.5 to 13	83 to 94	"
Nuts securing lower wishbone shaft to cross-member	13 to 18	94 to 130	"
Nuts securing steering arm to steering knuckle	4.8 to 5.5	34.8 to 39.7	"
Nut securing upper wishbone rear arm to steering knuckle	7.5 to 8.5	54.3 to 61.4	"
Nut securing lower ball joint to wishbone	7.5 to 8.5	54.3 to 61.4	"
Nut securing lower ball joint to steering knuckle	7.5 to 8.5	54.3 to 61.4	"
Nuts securing caliper support to steering knuckle	4.8 to 5.5	34.8 to 39.7	"
Screws securing front brake caliper to support (ATE brakes)	7.5 to 8.5	54.3 to 61.4	"
Screws securing front brake discs	7.5 to 8.5	54.3 to 61.4	"
Nuts securing wheels	6 to 8	43.4 to 57.8	"

ATE BRAKES	Kgm.	lb. ft	Manner of tightening
Front brake bleed screw	.2 to .35	1.5 to 2.5	dry
Caliper joining bolts	2.9 to 3.4	21 to 24.6	"
Inlet fitting to caliper (without gasket)	.8 to 1.1	6 to 8	"

######### MAJOR INSPECTION SPECIFICATIONS #########

CAMSHAFTS

Diameter of journals: A	26.959 to 26.980 mm (1.0614 to 1.0622")
Diameter of journal bearings: B	27.000 to 27.033 mm (1.0630 to 1.0642")
Radial clearance between journals and bearings B-A	.020 to .074 mm (.0008 to .0028")
End play of camshaft in thrust bearing: C	.065 to .182 mm (.0026 to .0071")

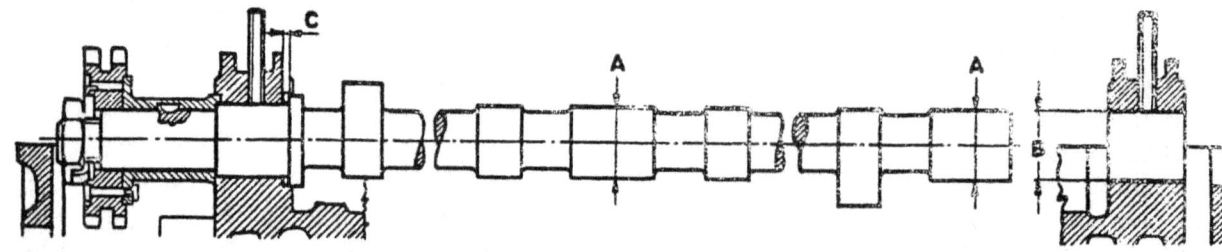

VALVES AND VALVE GUIDES

		Intake	Exhaust (sodium type)
		LIVIA H	LIVIA C
Valves	poppet dia. O	37.000 to 37.150 mm (1.4657 to 1.4625")	34.000 to 34.150 mm (1.3386 to 1.3838")
	stem dia. M	8.972 to 8.987 mm (.3532 to .3538")	8.935 to 8.960 mm (.3518 to .3527")
	Total length L	109 to 109.3 mm (4.2913 to 4.3131")	108.6 to 108.9 mm (4.2758 to 4.2874")

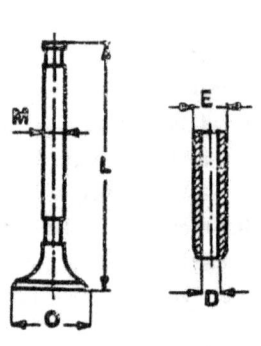

Valve guide { Outside diameter with guide removed E	14.033 to 14.044 mm (.5528 to .5529")
{ Inside diameter with guide assembled in cylinder head D	9.000 to 9.015 mm (.3544 to .3549")
Projection of intake valve guides from their recesses in cylinder head	13.800 to 14.000 mm (.543 to .551")
Projection of exhaust valve guides from their recesses in the cylinder head	16.800 to 17.000 mm (.662 to .669")
Clearance between guide assembled in cylinder head and valve stem { intake	.013 to .043 mm (..0005 to .0031")
{ exhaust	.040 to .080 mm (.0016 to .0031")

Valve seats

Diameter of valve guide seat in cylinder head F	13.990 to 14.018 mm (.5508 to .5518")
Interference between seat and valve guide E-F	.015 to .054 mm (.0006 to .0021")

		Intake	Exhaust
Outside diameter of the valve seat H	standard	38.597 to 38.532 mm (1.5196 to 1.5209")	35.422 to 35.457 mm (1.3946 to 1.3960")
	oversized	38.897 to 38.932 mm (1.5314 to 1.5327")	35.722 to 35.757 mm (1.4054 to 1.4077")
Diameter of recess in the cylinder head for valve seat G	standard	38.532 to 38.557 mm (1.5169 to 1.5179")	35.357 to 35.382 mm (1.3920 to 1.3930")
	oversized	38.832 to 38.857 mm (1.5288 to 1.5298")	35.657 to 35.682 mm (1.4038 to 1.4048")

Interference between valve seat and recess in cylinder head . . . . . . H-G   .100 to .040 mm (.0039 to 0016")

Valve cups

Diameter of cup . . . . A	standard	34.973 to 34.989 mm (1.3769 to 1.3775")
	oversized	35.173 to 35.189 mm (1.3848 to 1.3854")
Diameter of cup seat in cylinder head . . . . B	standard	35.000 to 35.025 mm (1.3780 to 1.3789")
	oversized	35.200 to 35.225 mm (1.3859 to 1.3868")
Clearance between seat and cup . . . . . . B-A		.011 to .052 mm (.0005 to .0020")

Valve springs

	Free length	Length under test load	Test load
Inner spring . . l	red mark 47.3 mm (1.87") green mark 46.5 mm (1.83")	l = 26 mm (1.02")	22.2 to 23.1 Kg. 48.9 to 51.1 lbs
Outer spring . . L	red mark 52.8 mm (2.08") green mark 51.3 mm (2.02")	L1 = 27.5 mm (1.08")	35.7 to 37.1 Kg. 78.6 to 81.8 lbs

Note - The RED-mark valve spring should be fitted with the color-marked coil downward.

Connecting rods

Length between ℄ of big end and ℄ of small end of connecting rod . D		147.955 to 148.045 mm (5.8250 to 5.8285")
Inside diameter of the big end of connecting rod . . . . E		53.695 to 53.708 mm (2.1140 to 2.1144")
Inside diameter of bushing in the small end of rod C		22.005 to 22.015 mm (.8664 to .8667")
Thickness of connecting rod bearings . . . . . . F	standard	1.822 to 1.829 mm (.0718 to .0720")
	1st oversize	1.949 to 1.956 mm (.0768 to .0770")
	3rd oversize	2.076 to 2.083 mm (.0817 to .0820")
Radial clearance between crankpins and bearing for big end of connecting rod		.025 to .064 mm (.0010 to .0024")
Maximum out of parallelism between ℄ of big end hole and ℄ of small end hole measured on piston pin overall length		.0317 mm (.0018")

PISTON PINS

O.D. of pin I	Black color	19.994 to 19.997 mm (.78777 to .78788")
	White color	19.997 to 20.000 mm (.78788 to .78800")
Clearance between piston pin and small end hole . .	Black color	.008 to .021 mm (.0003 to .0008")
	White color	.005 to .018 mm (.0002 to .0007")

Piston pin holes

	Black color	White color
Borgo piston	20.000 to 20.002 mm (.7874 to .78748")	20.003 to 20.005 mm (.78752 to .7876")
Mahle piston . . . . H	19.996 to 19.999 mm (.78784 to .78796")	19.999 to 20.002 mm (.78796 to .78808")
K.S. piston	20.000 to 20.0025 mm (.78800 to .78809")	20.0025 to 20.0050 mm (.78809 to .78819")

End play of the connecting rods on the crankpins G .200 to .300 mm (.0079 to .0118")

Pistons and piston rings

Diameter of pistons to be measured to square with the hole for piston pin and at a distance of L = 10-12 mm (.394 - .472) from the lower border of skirt.
For cylinder barrel classification purpose, use the minimum diameter recorded.

	Class A - BLUE	Class B - PINK	Class C - GREEN
Borgo piston	73.930 to 73.940 mm (2.9128 to 2.9132")	73.940 to 73.950 mm (2.9132 to 2.9136")	73.950 to 73.960 mm (2.9136 to 2.9140")
Mahle piston	73.925 to 73.935 mm (2.9126 to 2.9130")	73.935 to 73.945 mm (2.9130 to 2.9134")	73.945 to 73.955 mm (2.9134 to 2.9138")
K.S. piston	73.925 to 73.935 mm (2.9126 to 2.9130")	73.935 to 73.945 mm (2.9130 to 2.9134")	73.945 to 73.955 mm (2.9134 to 2.9138")

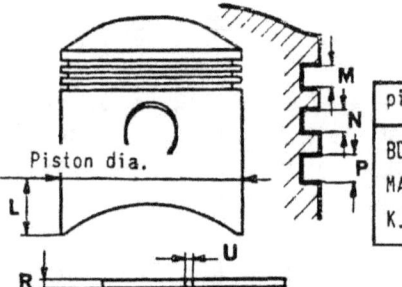

Height of grooves in piston for rings

piston	compression rings M and N	oil control ring P
BORGO	2.022 to 2.047 mm (.0797 to .0806")	4.006 to 4.031 mm (.1578 to .1588")
MAHLE	2.025 to 2.040 mm (.0798 to .0803")	4.015 to 4.030 mm (.1582 to .1587")
K.S.	2.022 to 2.047 mm (.0797 to .0806")	4.006 to 4.031 mm (.1578 to .1588")

Thickness of rings:
- compression (chromium-plated) R 1.978 to 1.990 mm (.0779 to .0784")
- compression (normal) S 1.978 to 1.990 mm (.0779 to .0784")
- oil control T 3.958 to 3.970 mm (.1559 to .1564")

Gap of rings to be checked in ring gauge or in cylinder barrels . . . . . U   .25 to .40 mm (.010 to .015")

End play of rings in grooves

Piston	Compression rings	Oil control rings
MAHLE	.035 to .062 mm (.0014 to .0024")	.045 to .072 mm (.0018 to .0028")
BORGO	.032 to .069 mm (.0013 to .0027")	.036 to .073 mm (.0014 to .0028")
K.S.	.032 to .069 mm (.0013 to .0027")	.036 to .073 mm (.0014 to .0028")

CYLINDER BARRELS

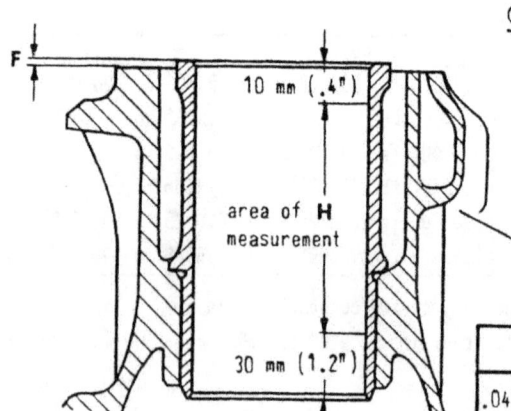

Cylinder barrel diameter

BLUE	PINK	GREEN
73.985 to 73.994 mm (2.9150 to 2.9153")	73.995 to 74.004 mm (2.9154 to 2.9157")	74.005 to 74.014 mm (2.9158 to 2.9161")

Clearance between cylinder barrel and piston

with Borgo piston	with Mahle piston	with K.S. piston
.045 to .064 mm (.0018 to .0025")	.050 to .069 mm	(.0020 to .0027")

Wear limit . . . . .120 mm (.0047")
Elongation and taper of barrels { new . . . . .010 mm (.0004")
{ wear limit . . . . .050 mm (.0019")
Projection of barrels from cylinder block . . . . F   .000 to .060 mm (.0000 to .0024")
Surface roughness . . . . 20 - 40 microinches RMS

CRANKSHAFT

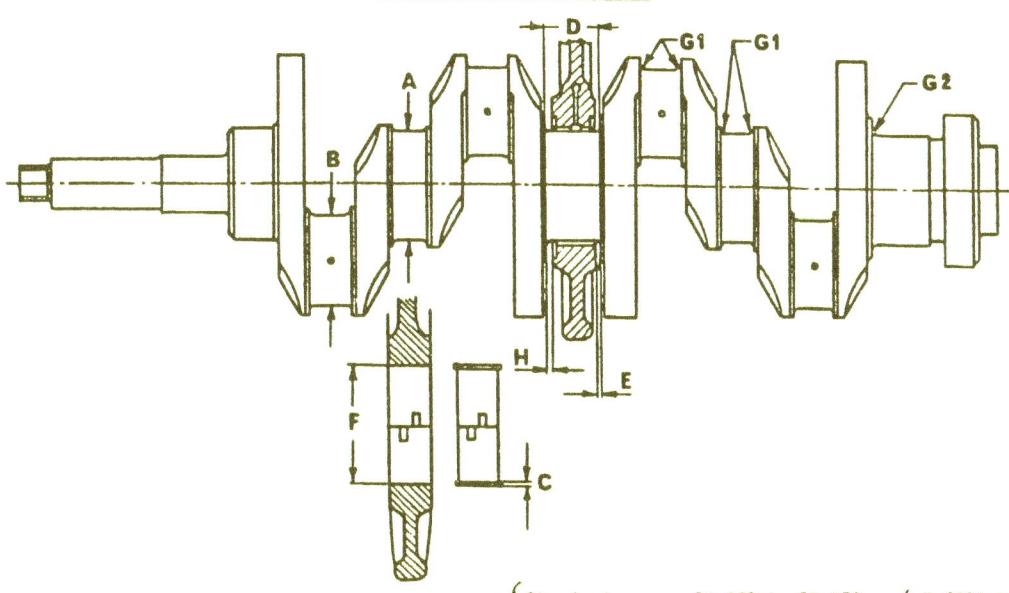

Diameter of main journals A	Standard	59.960 to 59.973 mm	(2.3606 to 2.3611")
	1st undersize	59.706 to 59.719 mm	(2.3506 to 2.3511")
	2nd undersize	59.452 to 59.465 mm	(2.3407 to 2.3411")
Diameter of crankpins B	Standard	44.963 to 44.975 mm	(1.77154 to 1.77201")
	1st undersize	44.709 to 44.721 mm	(1.76154 to 1.76200")
	2nd undersize	44.555 to 44.467 mm	(1.75133 to 1.75199")
Thickness of main bearings C	Standard	1.829 to 1.835 mm	(.0720 to .0722")
	1st oversize	1.956 to 1.962 mm	(.0770 to .0772")
	2nd oversize	2.083 to 2.089 mm	(.0820 to .0822")
Diameter of seat for main bearings in crankcase F		63.657 to 63.676 mm	(2.5062 to 2.5069")
Length of central journal D	Standard	30.000 to 30.035 mm	(1.1811 to 1.1824")
	1st oversize	30.127 to 30.162 mm	(1.1861 to 1.1874")
	2nd oversize	20.254 to 30.289 mm	(1.1911 to 1.1924")
Thickness of thrust rings for central journal E	Standard	2.311 to 2.362 mm	(.0910 to .0929")
	1st oversize	2.374 to 2.425 mm	(.0935 to .0954")
	2nd oversize	2.438 to 2.489 mm	(.0960 to .0980")
End play of crankshaft H		.076 to .263 mm	(.003 to .010")
Clearance between journals and main bearings (*)		.014 to .058 mm	(.0005 to .0022")

(*) Clearance = main bearing ID - (twice bearing thickness - journal OD).

Fillet radii	main journals and crankpins G1	1.7 to 2.1 mm	(.069 to .082")
	pin on flywheel side G2	3.7 to 4.1 mm	(.146 to .161")

Main journals & crankpins surface roughness	16 microinches
Maximum elongation of main journals and crankpins	.007 mm (.00027")
Maximum taper of main journals and crakpins measured on their full length	.01 mm (.00039")
Maximum error of parallelism of main journals and crankpins measured on their full length	.015 mm (.00059")
Maximum misalignment allowed between main journals	.01 mm (.00039")
Maximum misalignment between ℄ of the two pairs of crankpins and ℄ of main journals	.300 mm (.0118")

C L U T C H

Pedal free travel	23 mm (.9")
Distance between thrust ring and the reference sleeve of tool C. 6.0104 (red dot).	.75 to 1.25 mm (.029 to .053")
Squareness of the clutch driven plate assembled on gearbox direct drive shaft . . .	.50 mm (.019")
Wear limit of driven plate thickness	6 mm (.236")

Rating of Spring A =
- free length . . . . . . 43 to 46 mm (1.69 to 1.81")
- length under test load 29.2 mm (1.150")
- test load . . . . 44.5 to 49.5 Kg (98.1 to 109.1 lbs)

Rating of springs B =
- free length . . . . . 48.5 to 51.5 mm (1.91 to 2.02")
- length under test load 29.4 mm (1.157")
- test load . . . . 50 to 54 Kg (110 to 119 lbs)

G E A R B O X

Transmission ratios . . . .
- 1st gear   3.30 : 1
- 2nd gear   1.99 : 1
- 3rd gear   1.35 : 1
- 4th gear   1.00 : 1
- 5th gear   .86 : 1
- Reverse gear 3.01 : 1

Maximum eccentricity of main shaft . . . . .05 mm (.020")

End play between forks and sleeves . . . .
- assembly . . . . .15 to .34 mm (.006 to .013")
- wear limit . . . .85 mm (.033")

Calibration of spring for striking rod balls

Gear	1st - 2nd - 3rd	5th - Rev.
free length	15.2 mm (.600")	30.5 mm (1.2")
length under test load	10 mm (.390")	20 mm (.78")
test load	2.88 to 3.12 Kg (6.4 to 6.8 lbs)	4.32 to 4.68 Kg (9.5 to 10.3 lbs)

Maximum end play of the main shaft gears
- 1st speed gear   .170 to .245 mm (.0067 to .0096")
- 2nd & 3rd speed gear .130 to .205 mm (.0052 to .0081")
- 5th speed gear & Rev. .160 to .220 mm (.0063 to .0087")

Radial clearance between gear bushings and mainshaft
- 1st speed gear   .125 to .170 mm (.0049 to .0067")
- 2nd & 3rd speed gear .095 to .140 mm (.0038 to .0055")
- 5th speed gear   .065 to .107 mm (.0026 to .0041")

Distance between outer planes of the engaging teeth of 3rd and 4th gears   42 to 42.2 mm (1.65 to 1.66")

Distance, in neutral, of the rear band (propeller shaft side) of 5th speed
    sleeve from the rear edge of gear engaging teeth . . . .   12.9 mm (.508")

Rear axle and suspension

Transmission-axle overall ratios-with 41 :: 9 final drive
- 1st gear .... 15.049 : 1
- 2nd gear .... 9.055 : 1
- 3rd gear .... 6.172 : 1
- 4th gear .... 4.555 : 1
- 5th gear .... 3.918 : 1
- Rev. ...... 13.710 : 1

Maximum eccentricity of axle shafts .... .10 mm (.004")

Backlash of differential gears .... .05 mm (.002")

Backlash of bevel drive .... .05 to .10 mm (.002 to .004")

Reference dimension on tool C.6.0101 for pinion-to-ring gear fitting ...... 70 ± .0025 mm (2.7559 ±.0001")

Pre-load on pinion bearing .... 11.5 to 15.5 Kgcm (10 to 13.5 in. lbs)

Total preload bevel drive bearings .... 16.5 to 24.5 Kgcm (14.4 to 21.3 in. lbs)

Max. factory end play between reaction trunnion and attachment to body .... 1 mm (.04")

CHECKING OF SHOCK ABSORBERS ON TEST BENCH - Calibration data (when cold)

| | BIANCHI - ALLINQUANT ||
	Extension	Compression
High speed	135 to 190 Kgs (298 to 418 lbs)	50 to 80 Kgs (111 to 176 lbs)
Low speed	19 to 55 Kgs (42 to 121 lbs)	9 to 22 Kgs (20 to 48 lbs)

CHECKING OF SUSPENSION SPRINGS

Free length .... 437 mm (17.2")

Length under test load .... 252 mm (10")

Test load .... 268.7 to 285.3 Kgs (592 to 628 lbs)

Colored marks:
Blue-Blue
Blue-White

Front suspension

ADJUSTMENT OF CLEARANCE IN WHEEL BEARINGS

When performing regular servicing or whenever the removal of wheel hubs is required, adjust the bearing clearance as follows:

1) Screw in the nut and lock it to a torque of 2.5 Kgm (18 lb-ft) while at the same time revolving the wheel hub to set the bearings properly in their seats;
2) Unscrew the nut half a turn or more;
3) Lightly tap on the stub axle end with a mallet in order to return the outboard bearing in its proper position even in the case a slight interference between bearing cone and stub axle exists;
4) Lock the nut in place to 1.5 Kgm (10.8 lb-ft);
5) Unscrew the nut of a quarter turn;
6) If the hole in the axle is aligned with a slot in the castellated nut insert the cotter pin; if not, screw in the nut by the minimum angle needed to line up the hole and the next slot;
7) Again tap lightly on stub axle end to restore the same condition as under step 3;
8) The end play so obtained on stub axle should fall between .02 - .12 mm (.0008 - .0047")

WHEEL BEARING LUBRICATING INSTRUCTIONS

The quantity of lubricating grease should be about 65 grammes (2½ ozs) for each hub; do not exceed such a quantity to avoid bearing overheating, grease leakage, etc.
The grease should be well distributed inside the bearings and into side recesses.
Subsequently, at the regular schedule, remove the hub cover and pack the outboard bearing.

BALL JOINTS

End play of lower ball joint in its socket .... 1 mm (.04")

N o t e - Ball joints require no regular lubrication being provided with special grease seals which retain the grease in by factory on assembly - Only if strictly needed (joints squealing) grease with SHELL Retinax A or AGIP F. 1 Grease 30 (See I.S. 1.05.097/1).

CHECKING OF SUSPENSION SPRINGS

Free length .... 303 mm (11.9")
Length under test load .... 200 mm (7.8")
Test load .... 776 to 828 Kg (1720 to 1825 lbs)

Colored marks:

WHITE -WHITE - SKY BLUE

CHECKING OF SHOCK ABSORBERS ON TEST BENCH
Calibration data (when cold)

	GIRLING		ALLINQUANT	
	Extension	Compression	Extension	Compression
High speed	210 to 310 Kgs (463 to 683 lbs)	27 to 52 Kgs (60 to 114 lbs)	150 to 190 Kgs (331 to 418 lbs)	55 to 80 Kgs (121 to 176 lbs)
Low speed	30 to 52 Kgs (66 to 114 lbs)	9 to 22 Kgs (20 to 48 lbs)	25 to 55 Kgs (56 to 121 lbs)	9 to 22 Kgs (20 to 48 lbs)

BRAKES (ATE make)

Disc

When a brake disc is replaced it is necessary to check it for run-out after installation:

- use a dial indicator and the special tool A.2.0151 which is mounted to the caliper by means of the pad retaining pins.

Maximum permissible run out as measured at the swept surface should not exceed .22mm (.0086").

Note - run-out readings can be misleading if bearing clearance is not as specified; therefore, check and adjust if necessary, according to factory instructions.

If the disc is scored, see I.S. 0.00.055/3; the grinding of the surfaces is allowed providing not to exceed an undersize of 1 mm (.0394"), equalized on both faces, i.e. .5 mm (.0197") each face; disc wear limit: 8.5 mm (.335") thick.

Inspection specifications after regrinding of disc surfaces:
- Max. out of parallelism with disc mounting plane: .05 mm (.0020");
- Max. out of flat: .025 mm (.0010") and max. difference in thickness: .038 mm (.0015") as measured along any radial line;
- Max. out of flat: .025 mm (.0010") and max. difference in thickness: .015 mm (.0006") as measured along any circular line;
- The surface should show no sign of scoring or porosity.

The surface roughness should be:
- 26 microinches as measured circularly;
- 36 microinches as measured radially.

FRICTION PADS

	Front	Rear
Thickness when new	15 mm (.590")	
Wear limit	7 mm (.275")	

CALIPERS

On replacement of disc or caliper, measure the running clearance between caliper and disc on each side; the difference should not exceed .5 mm (.0197").

To centralize the caliper about the disc, insert shims between caliper and mounting flange as required.

HAND BRAKE

It is mechanically operated and acts on the rear wheels through suitable shoes which spread apart against a drum machined in the disc casting

For a brief description and repair and maintenance instructions refer to:

ATE DISC BRAKES Publication no. 1202.

Note - when reassembling the operating levers, a slight quantity of grease AGIP F1 Gr SM or SHELL Retinax AM is to be applied to the pivot pionts and rubbing surfaces of levers.

WHEEL ALIGNMENT AND CAR "TRIM"

Put the car under static load, with shock absorbers and stabilizer rod connected, with full tank or equivalent, with spare wheel, tool kit and the tires inflated as specified.

Before checking, slightly jolt the car so as to settle the suspensions.

Static load
- 2 weights of 45 Kgs (100 lbs) on front seats
- 2 weights of 25 Kgs (55 lbs) on flooring where feet rest

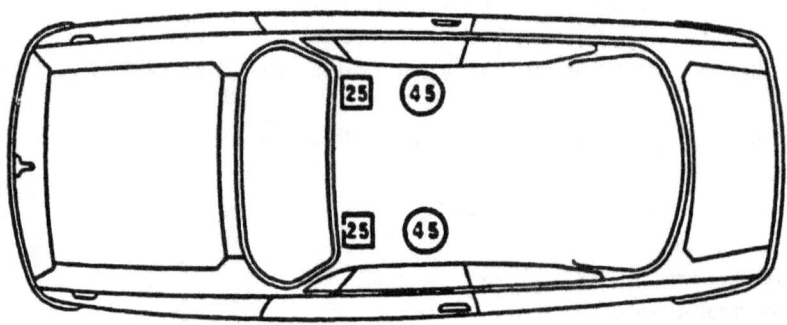

DISTANCE OF LOWER WISHBONE OF FRONT SUSPENSION FROM A REFERENCE LEVEL

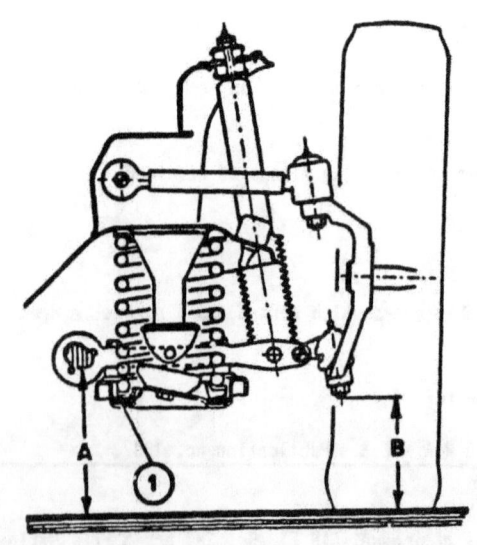

$A - B = 34 \pm 3$ mm ($1.34 \pm .12"$)

N o t e - for suspensions having the upper limiting bumper outside the spring, A-B should be: 14 ± 3 mm ($.55 \pm .12"$)

Dimension A must be measured in correspondence of the lower line of wishbone shaft as shown.

To adjust, add shims in (1).

Shims are available in the following thicknesses :
3.5 mm (.14") - 7 mm (.28") - 10.5 mm (.42")

DISTANCE OF REAR AXLE FROM RUBBER BUFFERS

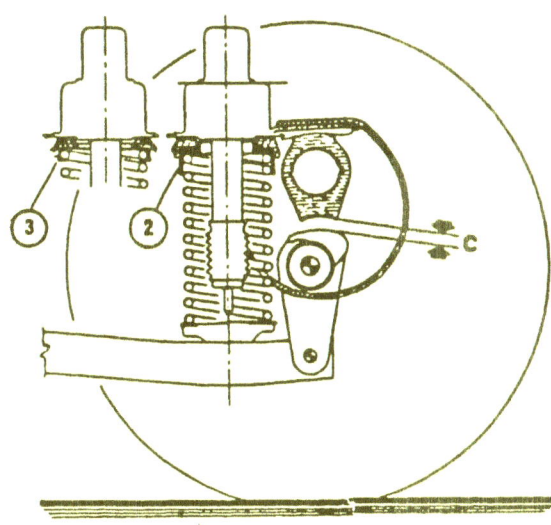

$C = 15 \pm 5 \text{ mm } (.59 \pm 2")$

Note - To adjust, remove the seat 3 and add shims in 2 as shown.

Shims are available in the following ticknesses

6.5 mm (.26")
11.5 mm (.45")
16.5 mm (.65")
21.5 mm (.85")

In the condition as specified check the wheel angles.

Caster angle

$\alpha = 1° \pm 30'$

The difference in caster angle between R.H. and L.H. wheel must not exceed 0°20'.

To adjust, loosen jam nut D and rotate rod E.

Small adjustments of the caster angle allow to correct slight drift tendency of the car.

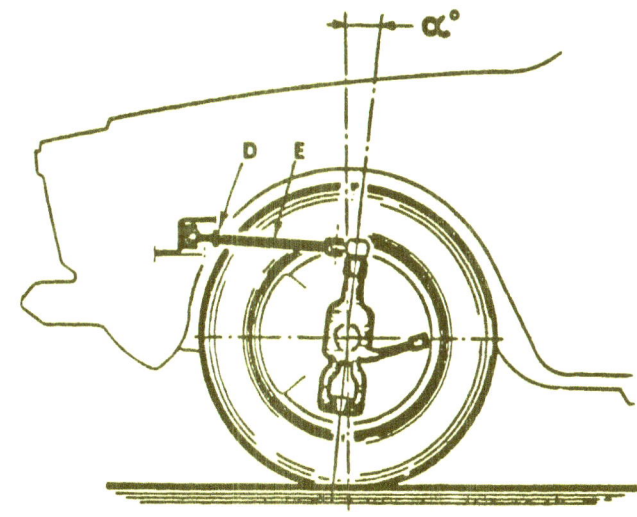

N.B. - Before checking the caster angle shake the front end of car in order to allow the rubber bushing on the front slanting arm to set properly.

FRONT WHEEL CAMBER

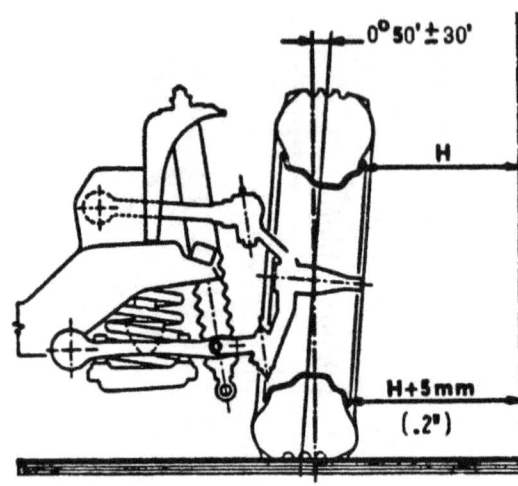

Difference in camber angle between
R.H. and L.H. wheel - 0° 40'

N o t e - Not adjustable. Check the chassis and suspension arms if necessary.

FRONT WEEL TOE-IN

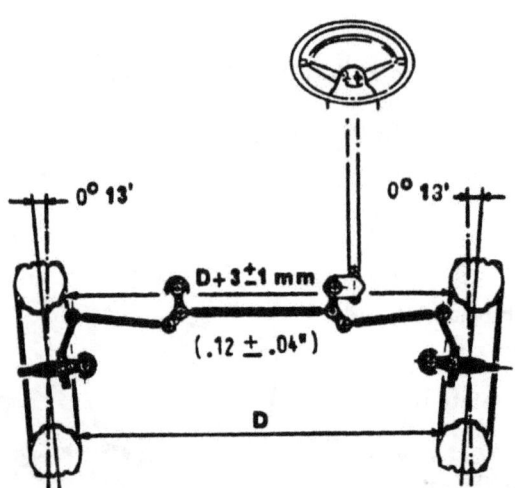

Rod length:
    side . . . . 272 to 288 mm (10.7 to 11.3")
    track . . . . 530 to 550 mm (20.86 to 21.66")

With the toe-in as specified, the length of rods as measured between ball joint centers should fall within the limits shown. If these values cannot be restored, the cause will probably be attributable to distortion of the body resulting from a collision.

SPIDER 1300 JUNIOR

technical characteristics
and
principal inspection specifications

C O N T E N T S

T E C N I C A L   C H A R A C T E R I S T I C S

PRINCIPAL CHARACTERISTIC DATA .... Page 2

   Performance .... " 2
   Tires .... " 3
   Refillings .... " 3
   Prescribed oils and lubricants .... " 3
   Carburetion .... " 4
   Idling adjustment .... " 4
   Float level adjustment .... " 5
   Valve timing .... " 6
   Ignition .... " 6
   Spark plugs .... " 6
   Electrical equipment .... " 7
   Bulb's wattage .... " 7
   Tightening torque specifications .... " 8

M A J O R   I N S P E C T I O N   S P E C I F I C A T I O N S

   Camshafts .... " 10
   Valves and valve guides .... " 10
   Valve seats .... " 10
   Valve cups .... " 11
   Valve springs .... " 11
   Connecting rods .... " 11
   Piston pins .... " 11
   Piston pin holes .... " 11
   Pistons and piston rings .... " 12
   Cylinder barrels .... " 12
   Crankshaft .... " 13
   Clutch .... " 14
   Gearbox .... " 14
   Rear axle and suspension .... " 15
   Front suspension .... " 16
   Brakes .... " 17

WHEEL ALIGNMENT

   Checking of wheel angles and car trim under static load .... " 18

TECHNICAL CHARACTERISTICS

Principal characteristic data

Number of cylinders	4
Bore	74 mm (2.913")
Stroke	75 mm (2.953")
Total cylinder capacity	1290 cc
Max. power at 6,000 rpm	SAE 103 HP
Front track	1324 mm (52.1")
Rear track	1274 mm (50.1")
Wheelbase	2250 mm (88.6")
Min. turning circle	10500 mm (413.4")
Overall length	4250 mm (167.3")
Overall width	1630 mm (64.2")
Overall height (unladen)	1290 mm (50.8")
Dry weight, with tools and jack	990 Kg (2182 lbs)
Number of seats	2
Fuel consumption for 100 Km (CUNA standard)	9.8 lt (28.8 mpg. GB) (24.0 mpg. US)

(For best engine performance, the use of premium-grade fuel is advised)

With 41 : 9 final drive

Gear	Max. Speeds					
	Running in				After running in	
	up to 1000 km (600 mi.)		1000 to 3000 km (600 to 1900 mi.)			
	Km/h	mph	Km/h	mph	Km/h	mph
1st	30	18	38	24	44	27
2nd	49	30	62	38	74	46
3rd	72	45	91	56	108	67
4th	98	60	123	76	146	91
5th	114	71	143	92	over 170	105
Rev.	-	-	-	-	48	30

Oil pressures with hot engine:
- min. pressure at idling speed .... .5-1 Kg/cm^2 (7-14 psi)
- min. pressure at top speed .... 3.5 Kg/cm^2 (50 psi)
- max. pressure at top speed .... 4.5-5 Kg/cm^2 (65-70 psi)

<u>Warning</u>: Check that generator warning light goes off as soon the engine exceeds 1,100 rpm.

Tires

Inflation pressures (cold tires)

	Front wheels		Rear wheels	
	Kg/cm^2	psi	Kg/cm^2	psi
PIRELLI 155 x 15 Cinturato S	1.7 *	24.1	1.8 *	25.6
	1.8 **	25.6	2.1 **	29.8
MICHELIN 155 x 15 X	1.7 *	24.1	1.7 *	24.1
	1.9 **	27.0	1.9 **	27.0

* Inflate to the lower pressure for use with low load and touring riding
** Inflate to the higher pressure for use with full load and sustained high speed

Refillings

		G. B.	U. S.
Water (engine & radiator) about	7.5 lt	1.65 gals	1.98 gals
Fuel (reserve 7 lt / 1.5 gals G.B. / 1.8 gals U.S.) about	46 lt	10.1 gals	12.1 gals
Oil — Engine (sump & filter) to max. level * about	6.0 Kg	5.95 qts	7.1 qts
Oil — Engine (sump & filter) to min. level about	4.0 Kg	3.95 qts	4.75 qts
Oil — Gearbox about	1.650 Kg	3.2 pts	3.8 pts
Oil — Differential about	1.250 Kg	2.5 pts	3.0 pts
Oil — Steering box about	.250 Kg	.5 pt	.6 pt

* This quantity is that needed for regular changing; the total amount of oil in the circuit (sump, filter, passages) is 6.5 Kgs. (6.5 qts G.B.) (7.8 qts U.S.).

Prescribed oils and lubricants

	API - SAE - NLGI Number	Recommended commercial equivalent AGIP	Recommended commercial equivalent SHELL
Engine	SAE 20 W/40￼ API MS	F.1 Supermotoroil Multigrade 20 W/40	X 100 Multigrade 20 W/40 Super Motor Oil "100"
Gearbox - Steering box and differential	SAE 90 API EP	F.1 Rotra Hypoid SAE 90	Spirax 90 EP
Propeller shaft universal joints and sliding yoke	NLGI 1	F.1 Grease 15	Retinax G
Front wheel bearings	NLGI 2/3	F.1 Grease 33 FD	Retinax AX
Brake fluid	ATE "Blau H"		

SAE - Society of Automotive Engineers
API - American Petroleum Institute
NLGI - National Lubricating Grease Institute

In countries where the recommended lubricants are not available it is possible to replace them with products of other leading Companies provided that in accordance with the prescribed specifications and grades.

Carburetion

2 Carburettors WEBER 40 DCOE 28

Venturi	28 mm (1.10")
Main jet	112
Main air metering jet	220
Idling jet (axial passage)	50 F11
Idling air metering jet	120
Choke jet	65 F5
Acceleration pump jet	35
Travel of acceleration pump control rod	14 mm (.55")
Delivery of acceleration pump every 20 strokes (for each barrel)	5 ± 1 cc.
Needle valve seat dia.	1.50 mm (.06")
Float weight	26 grs
Distance of fuel level from float chamber flange (with a pressure of 2 mts (6'6") H_2O upstream the needle valve)	29 ± .5 mm (1.12 to 1.16")

Idling adjustment

F   Adjusting screw for minimum opening of throttle

M   Idling mixture adjusting screw.

S   Screw for synchronizing throttles of the two carburettors

T   Joint for control linkage (to pedal)

PREPARATORY STEPS

- Check the ignition timing and inspect the electric system (spark plugs, distributor, coil, etc.) for proper operation.
- Remove the air filter element and clean it thoroughly.
- Check the flexible mounts between carburettors and intake manifold for tightness.

ALIGNING THE THROTTLE VALVES

- Detach the control linkage "T" from carburettors.
- Slacken the screw "F" and "S" almost fully.
- Operate the throttles a few times to make sure there is no binding.
- Fully depress the throttle control lever of rear carburettor so that the throttles are fully closed; then screw in the screw "S" until contact is made.

IDLING

- Back up the screw "M" of half a turn.
- Tighten the screw "F" to contact, then screw it in one more turn to ensure feeding of engine.
- Connect the accelerator control linkage "T" to carburettors.
- Start the engine and warm it up.
- If necessary, back up the screw "F" very slowly until the engine runs at about 600 to 700 rpms.

Float level adjustment

WEBER 40 DCOE 28 carburettor

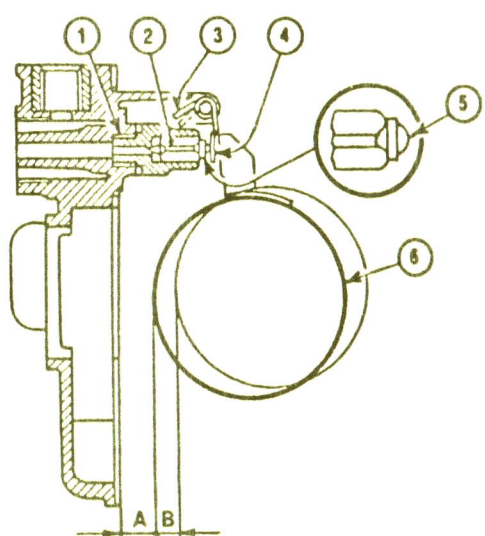

Check the level of fluid in float chamber as follows:

- Make sure the float weight is as specified (26 grs - .9 oz), that there are no leaks or indentations and that float can rotate freely about the pivot pin.

- The float weight must not be altered; consequently haphazard repairs (tinning, etc.) are detrimental to proper float operation.

- Check that needle valve (1) is well screwed into its seating and that the spring-loaded ball (5) part of the needle (2) is not jammed.

- Hold the carburettor cover in a vertical position as shown in the figure so that the float (6) does not depress the ball.

- With the cover vertical and the float tongue (4) in light contact with the ball, the two floats should be at a distance A = 8.5 mm (.33") from the cover mating surface with the gasket fitted and well stuck to the cover.

- When the level has been set, check that the travel (B) of the float is 6.5 mm (.26"); if necessary, adjust the position of float pivot tail (3).

- The adjustment described above will correspond to a fuel level of 29 + .5 mm (1.12 to 1.16") from the upper face of the float chamber (with a pressure of 2 mts - 6'6" H2O upstream the needle valve).

- If distance (A) is not as specified, slightly bend the float tongue (4) until the correct distance is obtained; inspect the working surface of the float tongue for any sign of nicks which may restrict the free movement of needle (2).

- Then fit the carburettor cover and check that the float can move freely without rubbing against the walls of the float chamber.

- C A U T I O N - The float level should be checked whenever the float or the needle valve has been changed. In the latter case it is also advisable to replace the gasket and make certain the new valve is securely screwed into its seating.

Valve timing

CHECKING OF VALVE OPENING AND CLOSING ANGLES

Clearance (with cold engine) between the unlobed profile of cams and the valve cup ceiling
- intake . . . . .475 to .500 mm (.0187 to .0197")
- exhaust . . . . .525 to .550 mm (.0206 to .0216")

Opening of intake valve
- lift of cup . . . . .20 mm (.008")
- corresponding to an angle . . . . . . before TDC of 18° 30' ± 1° 30'

Closing of intake valve
- lift of cup . . . . .20 mm (.008")
- corresponding to an angle . . . . . . after BDC of 42° 30' ± 1° 30'

Opening of exhaust valve
- lift of cup . . . . .15 mm (.006")
- corresponding to an angle . . . . . before BDC of 42° 30' ± 1° 30'

Closing of exhaust valve
- lift of cup . . . . .15 mm (.006")
- corresponding to an angle . . . . . after TDC of 18° 30' ± 1° 30'

ANGLE VALUES OF THE ACTUAL DIAGRAM OF VALVE TIMING SYSTEM WITH COLD ENGINE
(clockwise rotation direction of the crankshaft seen from the front side)

opening of intake valve (before TDC) . . . . 36° 50'
closing of intake valve (after BDC) . . . . 60° 50'
opening of exhaust valve (before BDC) . . . . 54° 10'
closing of exhaust valve (after TDC) . . . . 30° 10'
induction stroke . . . . 227° 40'
exhaust stroke . . . . 264° 20'

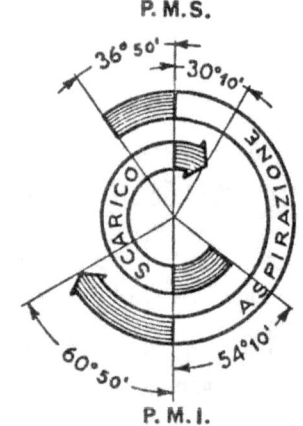

Ignition

Firing order: 1 - 3 - 4 - 2 (no. 1 cylinder is that at the fan side)

VALUES OF ADVANCE OF IGNITION DISTRIBUTOR

Opening of contact points of ignition distributor S = .35 to .40 mm (.014 to .016)
The distributor is correctly fitted when the oiler is toward the engine.

Fixed advance F Before TDC	Maximum advance M Before TDC
2° / 4°	40° / 43° at 5300 rpm

P = T.D.C.
F = Fixed advance
M = Maximum advance

Spark plugs

Lodge 2HL

Electrical equipment

Voltage	12 V
Battery	60 Ah

	BOSCH
Generator	EG (R) 14 V 25 A 29
Voltage regulator	VA 14 V 25 A
Starting motor	EF (R) 12 V 0,7 PS
Coil	TK 12 A 19
Ignition distributor	JF 4
Windshield wiper (2 speed)	WS 13/11 T 3 A

Bulb's wattage

Headlights (high and low beams)	45/50 asymmetric
Tail lights - parking & stop	5/21
Front lights - direction indicators	21
Tail lights - direction indicators	21
Back-up light	21
Front parking lights	5 globular
License plate light	5 globular
Engine compartment light	5 cylindrical
Courtesy light (rearview mirror)	5 cylindrical
Side lights - direction indicators	4 tubular
Instrument panel light	3 tubular
Tell-tale for fuel reserve	3 tubular
Tell-tale for generator	3 tubular
Tell-tale for blower	3 tubular
Tell-tale for high beams	1,2 tubular
Tell-tale for parking lights	1,2 tubular
Tell-tale for direction indicators	1,2 tubular

Tightening torque specifications

ENGINE - GEARBOX UNIT			Kgm.	lb. ft	Manner of tightening
Cylinder head nuts *	Inspection	when cold	6.2 to 6.4	45 to 46	Slacken in proper sequence, the nuts by one and one half turn and lubetorque
		when hot	6.6 to 6.7	47.7 to 48.5	Warm up the engine and when hot retighten without unscrewing
	After repairing	when cold	6.2 to 6.4	45 to 46	Retighten with lube
		when hot	6.6 to 6.7	47.7 to 48.5	Warm up the engine by actually driving the car and when hot retighten without unscrewing
		when cold	6.2 to 6.4	45 to 46	After tested the car, slacken, when cold and in proper sequence, the nuts by one and one half turn and lubetorque
Spark plugs			2.5 to 3.5	18.1 to 25.3	With graphite grease, when cold
Nuts of the camshaft caps			2 to 2.25	14.5 to 16.3	in oil
Nuts of the connecting rod caps			3.4 to 3.6	24.5 to 26.4	" "
Nuts of main bearing caps			3.2 to 3.5	23.5 to 25.3	" "
Screws of flywheel on crankshaft			4.2 to 4.5	30.4 to 32.5	" "
Nut of generator pulley			3 to 3.5	21.7 to 25.3	dry
Oil drain plug			7 to 8	51 to 57	"
Nut of gearbox main shaft yoke			12	86.8	"
Nut of gearbox layshaft			5	36.1	"
Nut of gearbox half-casing			1.8	13	"
Bolts joing gearbox output shaft yoke to prop. shaft yoke			4 to 4.5	29 to 32.5	"
Nut of gearbox inner swivel			3.25 to 3.65	23.6 to 26.4	"
REAR FRAME					
Screws securing ring gear to differential case			4.5 to 5	32.6 to 36.1	"
Ringnut securing yoke on final drive pinion shaft			8 to 14	50 to 101.2	"
Nuts securing bearing housing to real axle tubes			4.8 to 5.5	34.8 to 39.7	"
Nuts securing radius rods to body			10 to 11.5	72.4 to 83	"
Nuts securing radius rods to rear axle tubes			11.5 to 13	83 to 94	"
Nut securing reaction triangle to body			4.8 to 5.5	34.8 to 39.7	"
Nut securing reaction triangle to rear axle			11 to 15	79.6 to 108.5	"
Screws securing rear brake caliper to support (ATE brakes)			5.5 to 6.5	39.7 to 47.0	"
Nuts securing wheels			6 to 8	43.4 to 57.8	"
Bolts joining differential yoke to prop. shaft yoke			3.5 to 4	25.3 to 28.9	"
Nuts securing rear axle tubes to differential carrier			2.4	17.4	"

* **Warning:** in case of any repair work involving the removal of cylinder head, the gasket must be renewed at all times.

FRONT FRAME

	Kgm.	lb. ft	Manner of tightening
Nut securing steering wheel to column	5 to 5.5	36.1 to 39.7	d r y
Screws securing Burman steering box cover	2.3 to 2.5	16.7 to 18	"
Screws securing steering box & bellcrank bracket to body	4.8 to 5.5	34.8 to 39.7	"
Nuts of steering linkage ball joints	4.8 to 5.5	34.8 to 39.7	"
Nut securing steering arm to box	12.5 to 14	90.5 to 101.2	"
Nut securing shock absorber to suspension arms . .	8.2 to 9.2	59.3 to 66.5	"
Screws securing upper wishbone front arm to body .	2.3 to 2.8	16.7 to 20.2	"
Nut securing upper wishbone front arm to rear arm	4 to 4.5	29 to 32.5	"
Nut securing upper wishbone rear arm to body . . .	12.5 to 14	83 to 94	"
Nuts securing lower wishbone shaft to cross-member (To tighten these nuts use tool A.5.0161 and torque to 5.2 to 5.5 (37.6 to 39.7)	5.6 to 5.9	94 to 130	"
Nuts securing steering arm to steering knuckle . .	4 to 4.5	29 to 32.5	
Nut securing upper wishbone rear arm to steering knuckle	7.5 to 8.5	54.3 to 61.4	"
Nut securing lower ball joint to wishbone	8.2 to 9.2	59.3 to 66.5	"
Nut securing lower ball joint to steering knuckle	7.5 to 8.5	54.3 to 61.4	"
Nuts securing caliper to steering knuckle	7.5 to 8.5	54.3 to 61.4	"
Screws securing brake splash shields	.8 to 1	5.8 to 7.2	"
Nuts securing wheels & brake discs	6 to 8	43.4 to 57.8	"

ATE BRAKES

	Kgm.	lb. ft	Manner of tightening
Bleed screw	.2 to .35	1.5 to 2.5	"
Caliper joining bolt	2.9 to 3.4	21 to 24.6	"
Inlet fitting to caliper { with gasket	.8 to 1.1	6 to 8	"
{ without gasket . . .	1 to 1.5	7.2 to 10.8	"

MAJOR INSPECTION SPECIFICATIONS

Camshafts

Diameter of journals	A =	26.959 to 26.980 mm (1.0614 to 1.0622")
Diameter of journal bearings	B =	27.000 to 27.033 mm (1.0630 to 1.0642")
Radial clearance between journals and bearings	B-A =	.020 to .074 mm (.0008 to .0028")
End play of camshaft in thrust bearing	C =	.065 to .182 mm (.0026 to .0071")

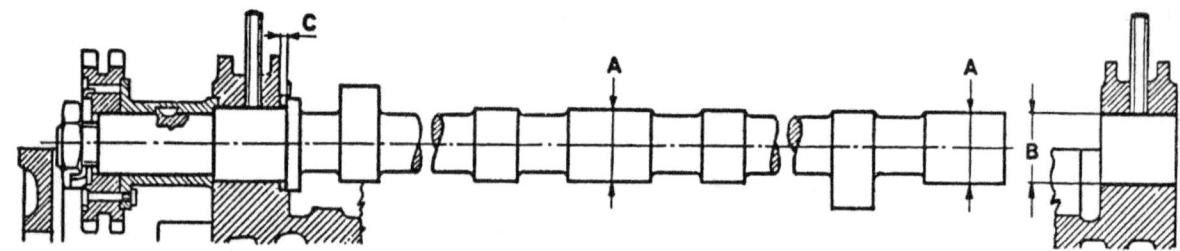

Valves and valve guides

	Intake	Exhaust (sodium cooled)	
	LIVIA H	LIVIA C	A T E
Valves — poppet dia. O	37.000 to 37.150 mm (1.4657 to 1.4625")	34.000 to 34.150 mm (1.3386 to 1.3838")	34.000 to 34.150 mm (1.3386 to 1.3838")
Valves — stem dia. M	8.972 to 8.987 mm (.3532 to .3538")	8.935 to 8.960 mm (.3518 to .3527")	8.935 to 8.960 mm (.3518 to .3527")
Valves — total length L	109 to 109.3 mm (4.2913 to 4.3131")	108.6 to 108.9 mm (4.2758 to 4.2874")	108.5 to 108.6 mm (4.2720 to 4.2758")

Valve guide — Outside diameter with guide removed	E =	14.033 to 14.044 mm (.5528 to .5529")
Valve guide — Inside diameter with guide assembled in cylinder head	D =	9.000 to 9.015 mm (.3544 to .3549")
Projection of intake valve guides from their recesses in cylinder head		13.800 to 14.000 mm (.543 to .551")
Projection of exhaust valve guides from their recesses in the cylinder head		16.800 to 17.000 mm (.662 to .669")
Clearance between guide assembled in cylinder head and valve stem — intake		.013 to .043 mm (.0005 to .0031")
Clearance between guide assembled in cylinder head and valve stem — exhaust		.040 to .080 mm (.0016 to .0031")

Valve seats

Diameter of valve guide seat in cylinder head	F =	13.990 to 14.018 mm (.5508 to .5518")
Interference between seat and valve guide		.015 to .054 mm (.0006 to .0021")

		Intake	Exhaust
Outside diameter of the valve seat H	standard	38.597 to 38.632 mm (1.5196 to 1.5209")	35.422 to 35.457 mm (1.3946 to 1.3960")
	oversized	38.897 to 38.932 mm (1.5314 to 1.5327")	35.722 to 35.757 mm (1.4054 to 1.4077")
Diameter of recess in the cilinder head for valve seat G	standard	38.532 to 38.557 mm (1.5169 to 1.5179")	35.357 to 35.382 mm (1.3920 to 1.3930")
	oversized	38.832 to 38.857 mm (1.5288 to 1.5298")	35.657 to 35.682 mm (1.4038 to 1.4048")

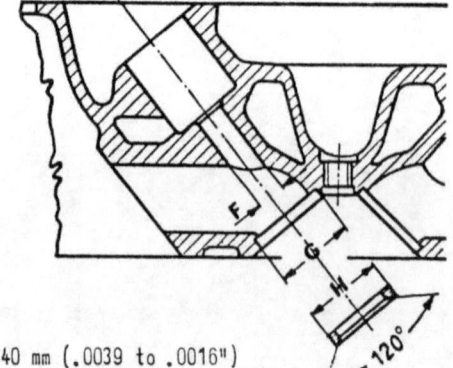

Interference between valve seat and recess in cylinder head   .100 to .040 mm (.0039 to .0016")

Valve cups

Diameter of cup A { standard ... 34.973 to 34.989 mm (1.3769 to 1.3775")
oversized ... 35.173 to 35.189 mm (1.3848 to 1.3854")
Diameter of cup seat in cy { standard. 35.000 to 35.025 mm (1.3780 to 1.3789")
linder head ..... B { oversized 35.200 to 35.225 mm (1.3859 to 1.3868")
Clearance between seat and cup .... .011 to .052 mm (.0005 to .0020")

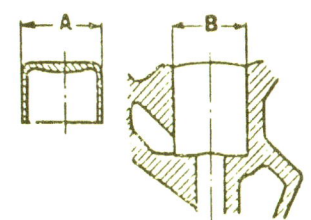

Valve springs

	Free length	Length under test load	Test load
Inner spring l	46.50 mm (1.83") 47.35 mm (1.88") 47.00 mm (1.85")	l1 - 26 mm (1.02")	22.3 to 23.1 Kg. 49.9 to 51.1 lbs
Outer spring L	51.30 mm (2.02") 52.80 mm (2.08") 52.00 mm (2.05")	L1 - 27.5 mm (1.08")	35.67 to 37.13 Kg. 78.6 to 81.8 lbs 35.87 to 37.33 Kg. 79.1 to 82.3 lbs

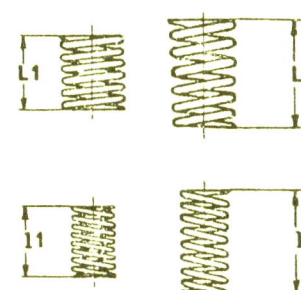

Connecting rods

Length between ℄ of big end and ℄ of small end of connecting rod .. D = 132.955 to 133.045 mm (5.239 to 5.242")
Inside diameter of the big end of connecting rod .... E = 48.658 to 48.671 mm (1.9172 to 1.9176")
Inside diameter of bushing in the small end of rod .... C = 20.005 to 20.015 mm (.7882 to .7886")
Thickness of connecting rod bearings F { standard .... 1.822 to 1.829 mm (.0718 to .0720")
1st oversize .... 1.949 to 1.956 mm (.0768 to .0770")
3rd oversize .... 2.076 to 2.083 mm (.0817 to .0820")
Radial clearance between crankpins and bearing for big end of connecting
rod .... .025 to .064 mm (.0010 to .0024")
Maximum out of parallelism between ℄ of big end hole and ℄ of small end
hole measured on piston pin overall length .... .0317 mm (.0018")

Piston pins

O.D. of pin I { Black color .... 19.994 to 19.997 mm (.78777 to .78788")
White color .... 19.997 to 20.000 mm (.78788 to .78800")
Clearance between piston pin and small end hole { Black color ..... .008 to .021 mm (.0003 to .0008")
White color ..... .005 to .018 mm (.0002 to .0007")

Piston pin holes

BORGO piston H { Black color .... 20.000 to 20.002 mm (.7874 to .78748")
White color .... 20.003 to 20.005 mm (.78752 to .7876")

End play of the connecting rods on the
crankpins G .200 to .300 mm (.0079 to .0118")

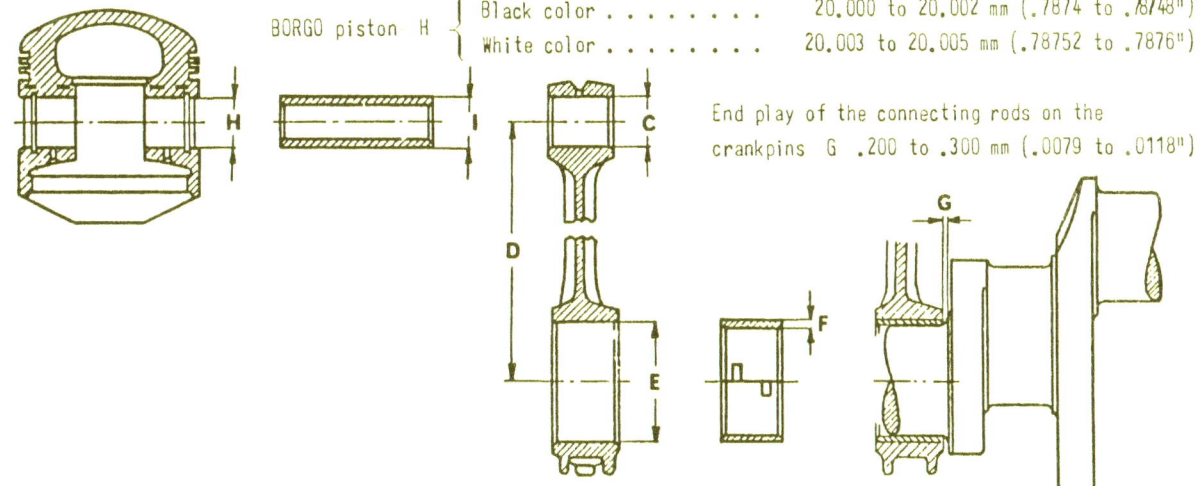

Pistons and piston rings

Diameter of pistons to be measured to square with the hole for piston pin and at a distance of L = 17 mm (.670") from the lower border of skirt.
For cylinder barrel classification purpose, use the minimum diameter recorded.

	Class A (Blue)	Class B (Pink)	Class C (Green)
BORGO piston	73.945 to 73.955 mm (2.9112 to 2.9115")	73.955 to 73.965 mm (2.9115 to 2.9119")	73.965 to 73.975 mm (2.9119 to 2.9123")

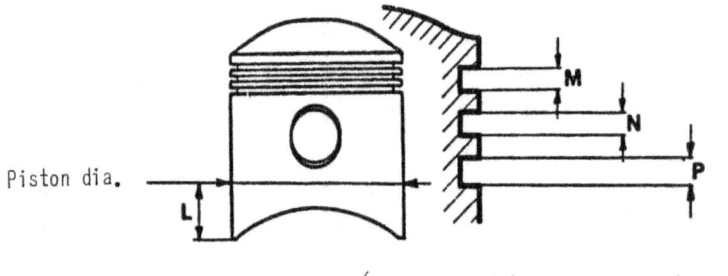
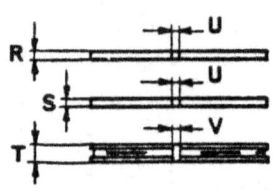

Piston dia.

Height of grooves in piston for rings:
- compression (chromium-plated) M = 1.535 to 1.556 mm (.0605 to .0613")
- compression (standard) N = 1.775 to 1.795 mm (.0699 to .0706")
- oil control P = 4.015 to 4.035 mm (.1581 to .1590")

Thickness of rings:
- compression (chromium-plated) R = 1.478 to 1.490 mm (.0582 to .0586")
- compression (standard) S = 1.728 to 1.740 mm (.0681 to .0685")
- oil control T = 3.978 to 3.990 mm (.1567 to .1571")

End play of rings in grooves:
- compression (chromium-plated) .045 to .077 mm (.0018 to .0030")
- compression (standard) .035 to .067 mm (.0014 to .0026")
- oil control .025 to .057 mm (.0010 to .0022")

Gap of compression rings to be inspected in ring gauge or in cylinder barrels U = .250 to .400 mm (.0100 to .0157")
Gap of oil scraper rings to be inspected in ring gauge or in cylinder barrels V = .200 to .350 mm (.0078 to .0138")

Cylinder barrels

	Blue	Pink	Green
Cylinder barrel diameter	73.985 to 73.994 mm (2.9128 to 2.9131")	73.995 to 74.004 mm (2.9132 to 2.9135")	74.005 to 74.014 mm (2.9136 to 2.9139")

Clearance between cylinder barrel and piston .... .030 to .049 mm (.0012 to .0019")

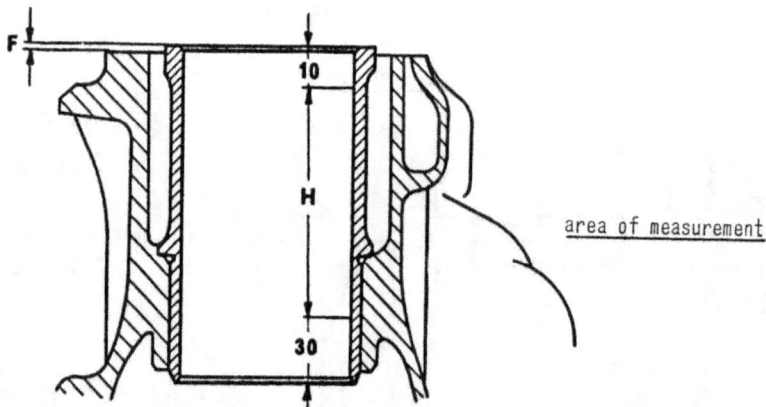

area of measurement

Wear limit .... .120 mm (.0047")
Elongation and taper of barrels:
- new .... .010 mm (.0004")
- wear limit .... .050 mm (.0019")

Projection of barrels from cylinder block .... F = .000 to .060 mm (.0000 to .0024")
Surface roughness .... 20 – 40 microinches RMS

Crankshaft

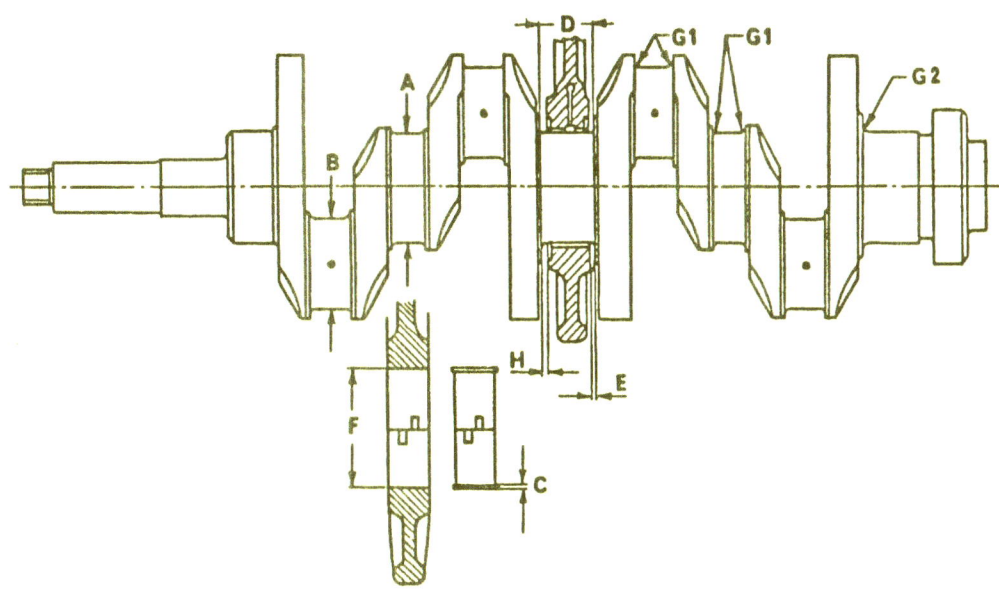

Diameter of main journals A	Standard	59.960 to 59.973 mm (2.3606 to 2.3611")
	1st undersize	59.706 to 59.719 mm (2.3506 to 2.3511")
	2nd undersize	59.452 to 59.465 mm (2.3407 to 2.3411")
Diameter of crankpins B	Standard	44.963 to 44.975 mm (1.77154 to 1.77201")
	1st undersize	44.709 to 44.721 mm (1.76154 to 1.76200")
	2nd undersize	44.555 to 44.467 mm (1.75133 to 1.75199")
Thickness of main bearings C	Standard	1.829 to 1.835 mm (.0720 to .0722")
	1st oversize	1.956 to 1.962 mm (.0770 to .0772")
	2nd oversize	2.083 to 2.089 mm (.0820 to .0822")
Diameter of seat for main bearings in crankcase F =		63.657 to 63.676 mm (2.5062 to 2.5069")
Length of central journal D	Standard	30.000 to 30.035 mm (1.1811 to 1.1824")
	1st oversize	30.127 to 30.162 mm (1.1861 to 1.1874")
	2nd oversize	30.254 to 30.289 mm (1.1911 to 1.1924")
Thickness of thrust rings for central journal E	Standard	2.311 to 2.362 mm (.0910 to .0929")
	1st oversize	2.374 to 2.425 mm (.0935 to .0954")
	2nd oversize	2.438 to 2.489 mm (.0960 to .0980")
End play of crankshaft H =		.076 to .263 mm (.003 to .010")
Clearance between journals and main bearings (*)		.014 to .058 mm (.0005 to .0022")

(*) Clearance = main bearing ID − (twice bearing thickness + journal OD)

Fillet radii	main journals and crankpins G1 =	1.7 to 2.1 mm (.069 to .082")
	pin on flywheel side G2 =	3.7 to 4.1 mm (.146 to .161")
Main journals & crankpins surface roughness		16 microinches
Maximum elongation of main journals and crankpins		.007 mm (.00027")
Maximum taper of main journals and crankpins measured on their full length		.01 mm (.00039")
Maximum error of parallelism of main journals and crankpins measured on their full length		.015 mm (.00059")
Maximum misalignment allowed between main journals		.01 mm (.00039")
Maximum misalignment between ₵ of the two pairs of crankpins and ₵ of main journals		.300 mm (.0118")

Clutch

Pedal free travel	23 mm (.9")
Distance between thrust ring and the reference sleeve of tool C.6.0104 (red dot)	.75 to 1.25 mm (.029 to .053")
Squareness of the clutch driven plate assembled on gearbox direct drive shaft	.50 mm (.019")
Wear limit of driven plate thickness	6 mm (.236")
Number of springs	9

Rating of spring A:
- free length .... 43 to 46 mm (1.69 to 1.81")
- length under test load . 29.2 mm (1.150")
- test load .... 44.5 to 49.5 Kg (98.1 to 109.1 lbs)

Rating of spring B:
- free length .... 48.5 to 51.5 mm (1.91 to 2.02")
- length under test load . 29.4 mm (1.157")
- test load .... 50 to 54 Kg (110 to 119 lbs)

Total spring load	432 to 480 Kg (952 to 1058 lbs)
Disengagement load	137 to 163 Kg (305 to 357 lbs)

Gearbox

Transmission ratios:
1st gear	3.30 : 1
2nd gear	1.99 : 1
3rd gear	1.35 : 1
4th gear	1 : 1
5th gear	.86 : 1
Reverse gear	3.01 : 1

Maximum eccentricity of main shaft	.05 mm (.020")
End play between forks and sleeves — assembly	.15 to .34 mm (.006 to .013")
End play between forks and sleeves — wear limit	.85 mm (.033")

Calibration of spring for striking rod balls:

	1st - 2nd - 3rd	5th - Rev.
free length	15.2 mm (.600")	30.5 mm (1.2")
length under test load	10 mm (.390")	20 mm (.78")
test load	2.88 to 3.12 Kg (6.4 to 6.8 lbs)	4.32 to 4.68 Kg (9.5 to 10.3 lbs)

Maximum end play of the main shaft gears:
1st speed gear	.170 to .245 mm (.0067 to .0096")
2nd & 3rd speed gear	.130 to .205 mm (.0052 to .0081")
5th speed gear & Rev.	.160 to .220 mm (.0063 to .0087")

Radial clearance between gear bushings and mainshaft:
1st speed gear	.125 to .170 mm (.0049 to .0067")
2nd & 3rd speed gear	.095 to .140 mm (.0038 to .0055")
5th speed gear	.065 to .107 mm (.0026 to .0041")

Distance between outer planes of the engaging teeth of 3rd and 4th gears	42 to 42.2 mm (1.65 to 1.66")
Distance, in neutral, of the rear band (propeller shaft side) of 5th speed sleeve from the rear edge of gear engaging teeth	12.9 mm (.508")

REAR AXLE AND SUSPENSION

Transmission-axle overall ratios - with 41 : 9 final drive
- 1st gear. — 15.049 : 1
- 2nd gear. — 9.055 : 1
- 3rd gear. — 6.172 : 1
- 4th gear. — 4.555 : 1
- 5th gear. — 3.918 : 1
- Rev. — 13.710 : 1

Maximum eccentricity of axle shafts . . . . .10 mm (.004")

Backlash of differential gears . . . . .05 mm (.002")

Backlash of bevel drive . . . . .05 to .10 mm (.002 to .004")

Reference dimension on tool C.6.0101 for pinion-to-ring fitting . . . . . 70 ± .0025 mm (2.7559 ± .0001")

Pre-load on pinion bearing . . . . 11.5 to 15.5 Kgcm (10 to 13.5 in. lbs)

Total pre-load bevel drive bearings . . . . 16.5 to 24.5 Kgcm (14.4 to 21.3 in. lbs)

Max. factory end play between reaction trunnion and attachment to body . 1 mm (.04")

Checking of shock absorbers on test bench - Calibration data (when cold)

	BIANCHI	
	Extension	Compression
High speed	135 to 190 Kgs (298 to 418 lbs)	50 to 80 Kgs (111 to 176 lbs)
Low speed	19 to 55 Kgs (42 to 121 lbs)	9 to 22 Kgs (20 to 48 lbs)

Checking of suspension springs

- Free length . . . . 429 mm (16.9")
- Length under test load . . . . 252 mm (10")
- Test load . . . . 257 to 273 Kg (565 to 600 lbs)

Colored marks:
White - white
Blue - white

FRONT SUSPENSION

Adjustment of clearance in wheel bearings

When performing regular servicing or whenever the removal of wheel hubs is required, adjust the bearing clearance as follows:

1) Screw in the nut and lock it to a torque of 2.5 Kgm (18 lb-ft) while at the same time revolving the wheel hub to set the bearings properly in their seats;
2) Unscrew the nut half a turn or more;
3) Lightly tap on the stub axle end with a mallet in order to return the outboard bearing in its proper position even in the case a slight interference between bearing cone and stub axle exists;
4) Lock the nut in place to 1.5 Kgm (10.8 lb-ft);
5) Unscrew the nut of a quarter turn;
6) If the hole in the axle is aligned with a slot in the castellated nut insert the cotter pin; if not, screw in the nut by the minimum angle needed to line up the hole and the next slot;
7) Again tap lightly on stub axle end to restore the same condition as under step 3;
8) The end play so obtained on stub axle should fall between .02 - .12 mm (.0008 - .0047").

Wheel bearing lubricating instructions

The quantity of lubricating grease should be about 65 grammes (2½ ozs) for each hub; do not exceed such a quantity to avoid bearing overheating, grease leakage, etc.

The grease should be well distributed inside the bearings and into side recesses.

Subsquently, at the regular schedule, remove the hub cover and pack the outboard bearing.

Ball joints

End play of lower ball joint in its socket 1 mm (.04").

N o t e - Ball joints require no regular lubrication being provided with special grease seals which retain the grease packed in by factory on assembly - Only if strictly needed (joints squealing) grease with SHELL Retinax A or AGIP F.1 Grease 30 (See I.S. 1.05.097/1).

Checking of suspension springs

Free length . . . . 317 mm (12.5")   Colored marks:
Length under test load . . . . 200 mm (7.8")   White - Blue
Test load . . . . 820.6 to 871.4 Kg (1810 to 1920 lbs)   Blue - Blue

Checking of shock absorbers on test bench

Calibration data (when cold)

	ALLINQUANT	
	Extension	Compression
High speed	150 to 190 Kgs (331 to 418 lbs)	55 to 80 Kgs (121 to 176 lbs)
Low speed	25 to 55 Kgs (56 to 121 lbs)	9 to 22 Kgs (20 to 48 lbs)

BRAKES (ATE make)

Disc

When a brake disc is replaced it is necessary to check it for run-out after installation:

- use a dial indicator and the special tool A.2.0151 which is mounted to the caliper by means of the pad retaining pins.

Maximum permissible run out as measured at the swept surface should not exceed .22 mm (.0086").

Note - run-out readings can be misleading if bearing clearance is not as specified; therefore, check and adjust if necessary, according to factory instructions.

If the disc is scored, see I.S. 0.00.055/3; the grinding of the surfaces is allowed providing not to exceed an undersize of 1 mm (.0394"), equalized on both faces, i.e. .5 mm (.0197") each face; disc wear limit: front 10 mm (.394") rear 8.5 mm (.335") thick.

Inspection specifications after regrinding of disc surfaces:

- Max. out of parallelism with disc mounting plane: .05 mm (.0020");
- Max. out of flat: .025 mm (.0010") and max. difference in thickness: .038 mm (.0015") as measured along any radial line;
- Max. out of flat: .025 mm (.0010") and max. difference in thickness: .015 mm (.0006") as measured along any circular line;
- The surface should show no sign of scoring or porosity.

The surface roughness should be:

- 26 microinches as measured circularly;
- 36 microinches as measured radially.

Friction pads

	Front	Rear
Thickness when new	15 mm (.590")	
Wear limit	7 mm (.275")	

Calipers

On replacement of disc or caliper, measure the running clearance between caliper and disc on each side; the difference should not exceed .5 mm (.0197").
To centralize the caliper about the disc, insert shims between caliper and mounting flange as required.

Hand brake

It is mechanically operated and acts on the rear wheels through suitable shoes which spread apart against a drum machined in the disc casting.
For a brief description and repair and maintenance instructions refer to:

ATE DISC BRAKES (Publication no. 1202)

Note - When reassembling the operating levers, a slight quantity of grease AGIP F.1 Gr SM or SHELL Retinax AM is to be applied to the pivot pins and rubbing surfaces of levers.

WHEEL ALIGNMENT AND CAR "TRIM"

Checking of wheel angles and car trim under static load

Put the car under static load, with shock absorbers and stabilizer rod disconnected, with full tank or equivalent, with spare wheel, tool kit and the tires inflated as specified.

Before checking, slightly move the car up and down so as to settle the suspensions.

Static load { 2 weights of 45 Kgs (100 lbs) on front seats
2 weights of 25 Kgs (55 lbs) on flooring where fest rest

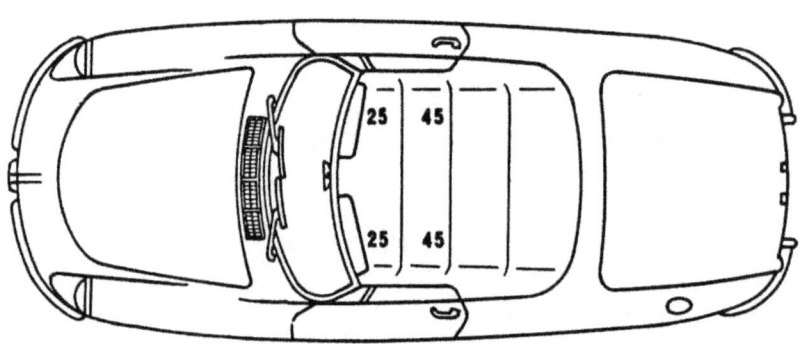

Distance of lower wishbone of front suspension from a reference level

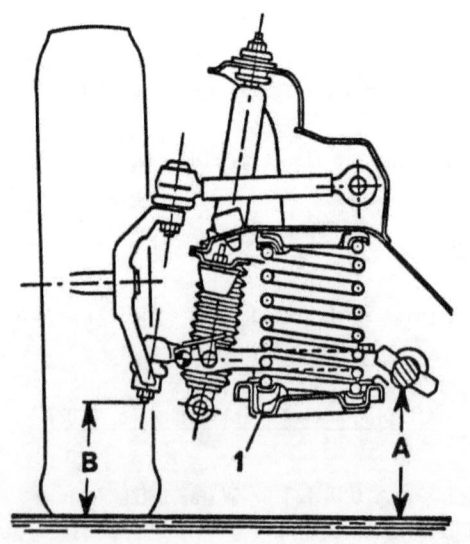

$A - B = 24 \pm 5$ mm ($.95 \pm .2"$)

Dimension "A" must be measured in correspondence of the lower line of wishbone shaft as shown.

To adjust, add shims in "1".

Shims are available in the following thicknesses:
3.5 mm (.14") - 7 mm (.28") - 10.5 mm (.42")

Distance of rear axle from rubber buffers

$$C = 33 \pm 5 \text{ mm} (1.30 \pm .20")$$

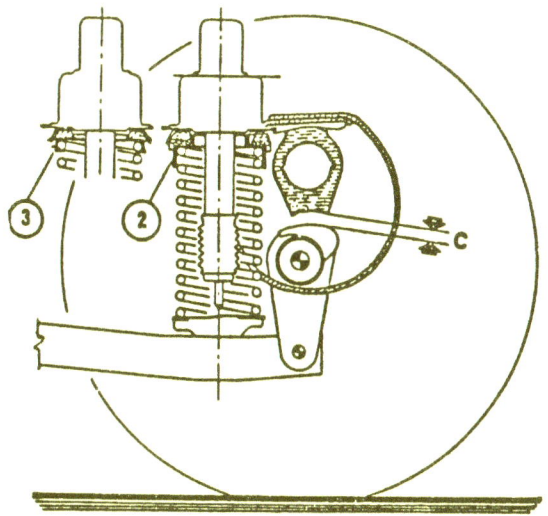

Note - To adjust, remove the seat 3 and add shims in 2 as shown.

Shims are available in the following ticknesses:

6.5 mm (.26")
11.5 mm (.45")
16.5 mm (.65")
21.5 mm (.85")

In the condition as specified check the wheel angles.

Caster angle: $\alpha = 1° 30' \pm 30'$

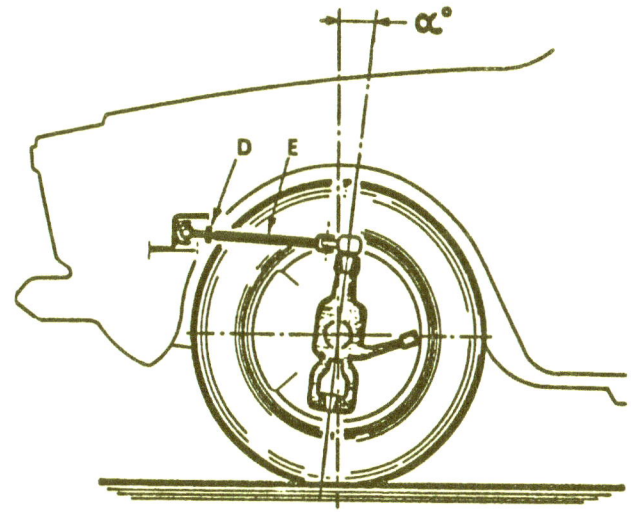

The difference in caster angle between R.H. and L.H. wheel must not exceed 0° 20'.

To adjust, loosen jam nut "D" and rotate rod "E"

Small adjustments of the caster angle allow to correct slight drift tendency of the car.

The caster angle should be checked under static load and alignment conditions as specified and with shock absorbers disconnected at one end.

N.B. - Before checking the caster angle shake the front end of car in order to allow the rubber bushing on the front slanting arm to set properly.

Front wheel camber

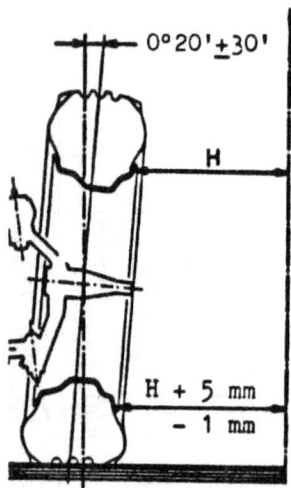

Difference in camber angle between R.H. and L.H. wheel = 0° 40'

N o t e - Not adjustable. Check the chassis and suspension arms if necessary.

Front wheel toe-in

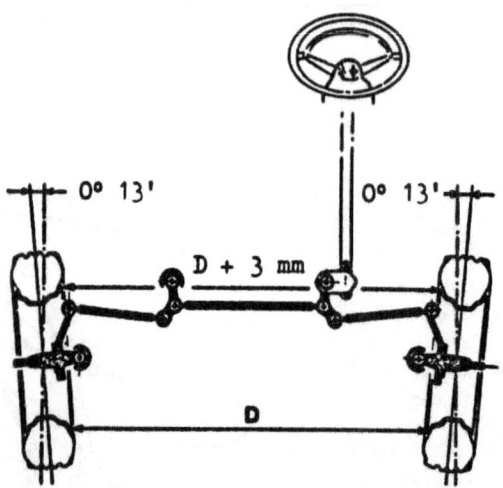

Rod length:

    side .... 264 to 280 mm (10.4 to 11.0")
    track .... 530 to 550 mm (20.86 to 21.66")

With the toe-in as specified, the length of rods as measured between ball joint centers should fall within the limits shown. If these values cannot be restored, the cause will probably be attributable to distortion of the body resulting from a collision.

NOTE: SUPPLEMENTS WERE ISSUED ON COLORED PAPER

January 1969

Supplement to " TECHNICAL CHARACTERISTICS " (Publ. N. 1366 dated 7/1968)

SPIDER 1300 JUNIOR

Variants from chassis no.	1571501 (L.H.D.)
	1695201 (R.H.D.)

TYRES – Inflation pressure (when cold) – Kg/cm²

		Front	Rear
155 × 15	Pirelli cinturato S	1.7 *	1.8 *
		1.8 **	2.1 **
	Michelin ZX	1.6 *	1.7 *
		1.7 **	1.9 **
	Kleber Colombes V 10 GT	1.6 *	1.7 *
		1.9 **	2.2 **
	Goat Drive D2 – Continental – Pirelli cinturato SR – Kleber Colombes V 10 (under all conditions)	1.7	1.8
	Michelin ZX (under all conditions)	1.4	1.7

* With reduced load and touring sizes
** With full load and top range of speed

REFILLINGS

Steering box	Burman	0.360 Kg
	ZF	0.120 Kg

ELECTRICAL EQUIPMENT

Bosch coil   K 12 V

Bosch windshield wiper   WS 4903 AR 2 A (0)

TIGHTENING TORQUE SPECIFICATIONS

	Kgm	Manner of tightening
Plug on oil filter	3.5 to 4	dry
Nut of gearbox layshaft	4.5 to 5.5	"
Bolts joining output shaft yoke to prop shaft yoke	5.5 to 5.7	"

REAR FRAME

	Kgm	Manner of tightening
Nuts securing radius rods to body	9 to 10	"
Nuts securing radius rods to rear axle tubes	12.5 to 14	"
Nut securing reaction triangle to rear axle	11.5 to 13	"
Nut securing link to radius rod bolt	3.3 to 3.5	"
Nut attaching the joining flange to the front shaft	9 to 11	"
Bolts joining flanges of front shaft and sliding yoke	3.2 to 3.5	"
Bolts joining differential yoke to prop. shaft yoke	3.2 to 3.5	"

CLUTCH

The clutch is of the hydraulically-operated single plate dry type. The clutch pedal acts on a master cylinder supplied with the same type of fluid as the brake system.

When the clutch pedal is depressed, the fluid under pressure actuates the piston in the cylinder "4" connected to the clutch disengagement lever "5".

The pressure plate is controlled by means of diaphragm spring "6".

The clutch pedal free travel "A" should be about 30 - 32 mm. When owing to wear on the clutch disc facing, the pedal free travel is reduced to 17 - 19 mm the free travel must be restored.

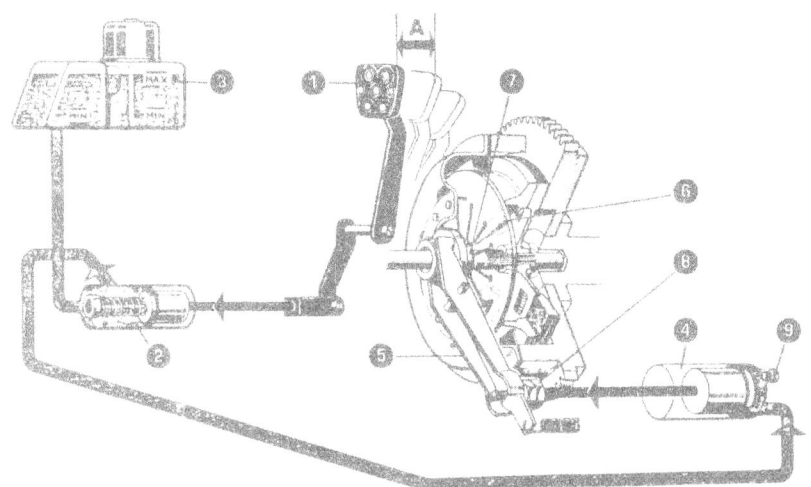

A Pedal free travel
B Disengagement lever free travel

1 Pedal
2 Master cylinder
3 Clutch & brake fluid reservoir
4 Slave cylinder
5 Disengagement lever
6 Diaphragm spring
7 Throwout bearing
8 Adjusting nuts
9 Air bleed screw

Adjustment

Measure with a rule the free travel "B" at the end of push rod of cylinder "4" depressing the clutch pedal until the throwout bearing "7" contacts the spring "6"; the travel "B" should be about 2 - 2.5 mm.

If the travel is shorter, act on the adjusting nut "8".

At the same time make sure that, by pressing the pedal as far as it will go, the push rod can move through a total travel of 13.5 - 14.2 mm. If any component of the system has been removed, thoroughly bleed the circuit. To check as specified use special tool no. C.6.0146 (see Tool Bulletin no. 135).

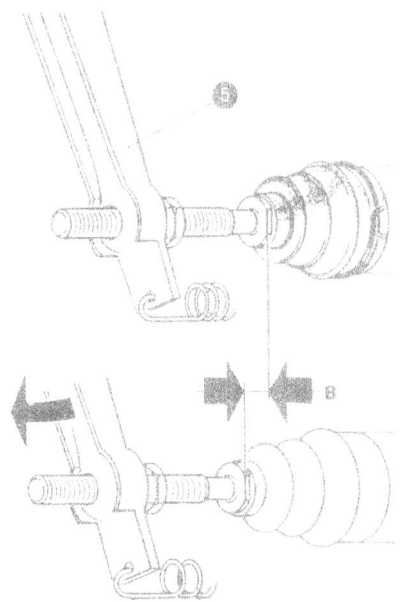

Inspection specifications

Wear limit of driven plate thickness . . . . 6.5 mm
Squareness of driven plate as mounted on gearbox output shaft . . . . 0.50 mm

GEARBOX

Calibration of striking rod ball springs
- free length . . . . 35.8 mm
- length under test load . . . . 17.2 mm
- test load . . . . 7.680 to 8.320 mm

BRAKE SYSTEM

The ATE brake system consists of four caliper type disc brakes operated by an assisted master cylinder. The friction pads of the front and rear brakes are directly actuated by the cylinders integral with the calipers.
The brakes are self-adjusting.

A pressure regulator controls the braking power to rear brakes. Such a regulator shall not be tampered with; specifically do not attempt to act on the adjusting nut as it is factory sealed.

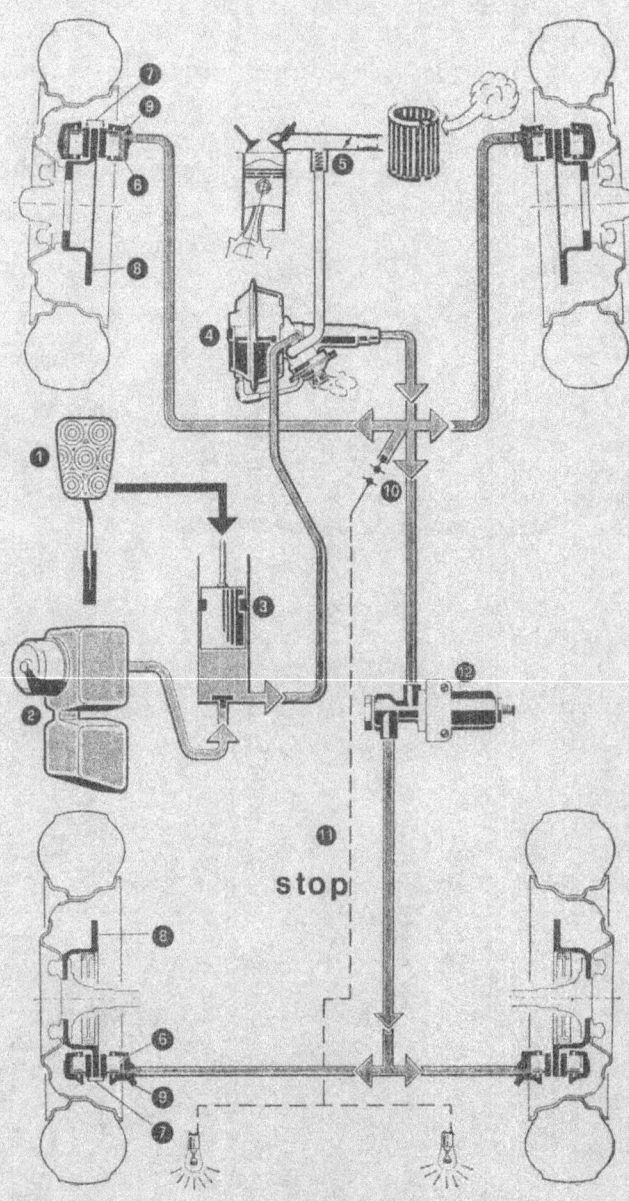

1. Brake pedal
2. Reservoir
3. Master cylinder
4. Vacuum servo
5. Vacuum connection
6. Pistons
7. Friction pads
8. Discs
9. Bleed screws
10. Stop light switch
11. Stop light cable
12. Pressure regulator

FRONT WHEEL TOE-IN (for L.H.D.)

Lock steering wheel in the central position i.e. with the spokes symmetrically disposed in relation to the vertical. Starting with the track rod "1" on the steering box side, place the corresponding wheel so that the toe-in is 1.5 mm. Measure the length thus obtained of the track rod and adjust the rod "2" on the other side to a length 5 mm shorter. Bring the first wheel to a 1.5 mm toe-in by adjusting the centre track rod "3".

$$A \begin{cases} \text{for 15" wheels} = 0° \ 13' \\ \text{for 14" wheels} = 0° \ 14' \end{cases}$$

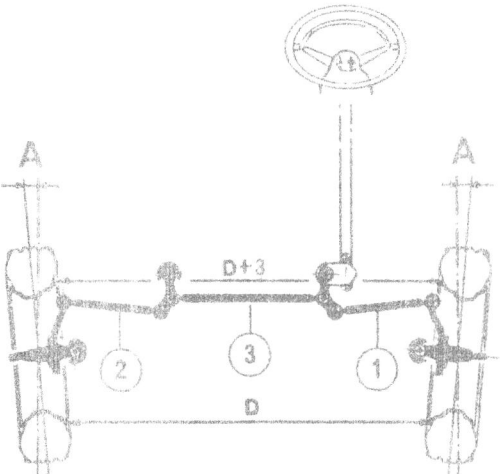

Rod length:

    side . . . . 264 to 280 mm
    track . . . . 530 to 550 mm

With the toe-in as specified, the length of rods as measured between ball joint centers should fall within the limits shown. If these values cannot be restored, the cause will probably be attributable to distortion of the body resulting from a collision.

Note - For R.H.D. the side rods maintain the same length (symmetrical adjustment).

NOTES

GIULIA 1300 ti

alfa romeo

technical characteristics and principal inspection specifications

CONTENTS

TECHNICAL CHARACTERISTICS

PRINCIPAL CHARACTERISTIC DATA .... Page 2

   Performances .... " 2
   Tires .... " 3
   Refillings .... " 3
   Prescribed oils and lubricants .... " 3
   Solex C 32 PAIA 7 Carburettor .... " 4
   Valve timing .... " 6
   Ignition .... " 6
   Spark plugs .... " 6
   Electric system .... " 7
   Tightening torque specifications .... " 8

MAJOR INSPECTION SPECIFICATIONS

   Camshafts .... " 9
   Valves and valve guides .... " 9
   Valve seats .... " 9
   Valve cups .... " 10
   Valve springs .... " 10
   Connecting rods .... " 10
   Piston pin .... " 10
   Piston and cylinder barrels .... " 11
   Compression and oil control rings .... " 11
   Crankshaft .... " 12
   Clutch .... " 13
   Gearbox .... " 13
   Rear axle and suspension .... " 14
   Front suspension .... " 15
   Brakes .... " 16
   Wheel alignment and car trim .... " 17

Variants from chassis no. { 645001 (L.H.D. cars) / 763001 (R.H.D. cars) } .... " 20

Variants from chassis no. { 1029001 (L.H.D. cars) / 765001 (R.H.D. cars) } .... " 26

TECHNICAL CHARACTERISTICS

PRINCIPAL CHARACTERISTIC DATA

Number of cylinders	4
Bore	74 mm (2.913")
Stroke	75 mm (2.953")
Total cylinder capacity	1290 cc
Max. power at 6.000 rpm .... DIN	82 CV
SAE	94 CV
Front track	1310 mm (51.6")
Rear track	1270 mm (50")
Wheelbase	2510 mm (99")
Min. turning circle	10.900 mm (429.1")
Overall length	4140 mm (463")
Overall with	1560 mm (61.5")
Overall height (unladen)	1430 mm (56.3")
Dry weight, with tools and jack	980 Kg (2.160 lbs)
Number of seats	5
Tires 155 x 15	PIRELLI cinturato S / MICHELIN X
Fuel consumption for 100 Km (CUNA standard)	9,8 lt
For best engine performance, the use of premium-grade fuel is advised.	(28.8 mpg. GB)
	(24.0 mpg US)

		Max. Speeds				
	Gear	Running in			After running in	
		up to 1000 Km (600 mi.)		1000 to 3000 Km (600 to 1900 mi.)		
		Km/h	mph	Km/h	mph	Km/h	mph
With 41 : 0 final drive	1st	26	16	32	20	40	25
	2nd	44	27	54	33	66	40
	3rd	64	39	79	49	97	60
	4th	87	54	107	66	131	80
	5th	110	68	135	83	over 160	100
	Rev.	-	-	-	-	44	27

Oil pressures with hot engine ....
- min. pressure at idling speed: .5 ÷ 1 Kg/cm2 (7-14 psi)
- min. pressure at top speed: 3.5 Kg/cm2 (50 psi)
- max. pressure at top speed: 4.5 ÷ 5 Kg/cm2 (65) 70 psi)

WARNING: Check that generator warning light goes off as soon the engine exceeds 1.100 rpm.

T I R E S

Inflation pressures (with tire cold)

Front wheels - 1.6 to 1.8 Kg/cm^2 (22.7 to 25.6 psi)

Rear wheels - 1.7 to 2.1 Kg/cm^2 (24.1 to 29.8 psi)

N.B. - Inflate to the lower pressure for use with low load and short peaks in speed.
Inflate to the higher pressure for use with full load and max. speeds (highways).

R E F I L L I N G S

		G. B.	U. S.
Water (engine & radiator) .... about	7.5 lt	1.65 gals	1.98 gals
Fuel (reserve 7 lt / 1.5 gals G.B. / 1.8 gals U.S.) .... about	46 lt	10.1 gals	12.1 gals
Oil — Engine (pan & filter) — to max. level* .... about	5.0 Kg	4.95 qts	5.95 qts
Oil — Engine (pan & filter) — to min. level .... about	3.25 Kg	3.2 qts	3.8 qts
Oil — Gearbox .... about	1.650 Kg	3.2 pts	3.8 pts
Oil — Differential .... about	1.250 Kg	2.5 pts	3.0 pts
Oil — Steering box .... about	.250 Kg	.5 pts	.6 pts

* This quantity is that needed for regular changing; the total amount of oil in the circuit (sump, filter, passages) is 5.75 Kgs (5.7 qts G.B.) (6.8 qts U.S.)

PRESCRIBED OILS AND LUBRICANTS

Refer to the directions given in the Instruction Book

SOLEX C 32 PAIA 7 CARBURETTOR

	1st barrel	2nd barrel
Venturi	23	23
Main jet	120	135
Main air metering jet	190	190
Idling jet	45	70
Idling air metering jet	100	60
Choke jet	120	-
Acceleration pump jet	45	-

Needle valve seat dia.	1.75 mm (.069")
Shim under needle valve seat	1 mm (.04")
Distance of fuel level from float chamber flange	12 mm (.47") (with a pressure of 2 mts (6' 6") H_2O upstream the needle seat)
Delivery of acceleration pump	4 to 6 cc. (for 20 strokes)
Clogging pressure measured upstream the needle seat	6 to 7 mts (20 to 23') H_2O
Weight of float	7.2 grs
Idling	500 to 600 RPM

Idling adjustment

If the engine runs unevenly at idling speed of tends to stall, the carburettor must be adjusted; this must be done when engine is hot and after making sure that spark plugs are not defective.

To adjust idling proceed as follows:

- screw in the screw 11 for a quarter turn to prevent binding of the 2nd throttle (lock in the jam nut of screw 11);
- screw in the screw 4 for about half a turn to make the engine run faster;
- unscrew the screw 5 until the engine begins to "hunt", then gradually screw it in until the engine runs smoothly;
- slowly unscrew the screw 4 until the engine speed is approximately 500-600 rpm;
- if the engine again begins to "hunt", slightly tighten screw 5; in no case must this screw be tightened to its maximum extent.

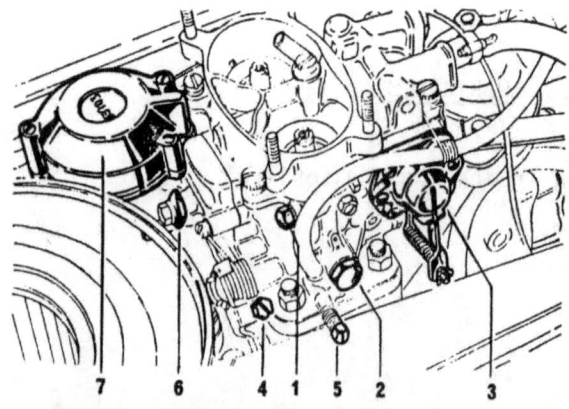
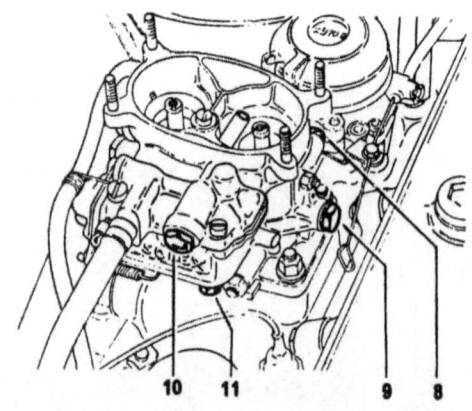

1 - Idling jet.
2 - Main jet no. 1.
3 - Acceleration pump.
4 - Adjusting screw for minimum opening of 1st throttle.
5 - Idling mixture adjusting screw.
6 - Choke control lever.
7 - Vacuum capsule.

8 - Main jet no. 2.
9 - Idling jet.
10 - Filter.
11 - Adjusting screw for minimum opening of 2nd throttle.

Adjusting the level of fuel in float chamber

To check the level of fuel in float chamber proceed as follows:

- place the car on level ground;

- run the engine at slow speed for about one minute then stop the engine;

- detach the feed pipe from carburettor and discharge the fuel from pipe complet;

- remove cover and float from chamber;

- take measurement with a gauge as shown;

- the distance from fuel level to float chamber flange should be 18 to 19 mm (.71 to .75 in.).

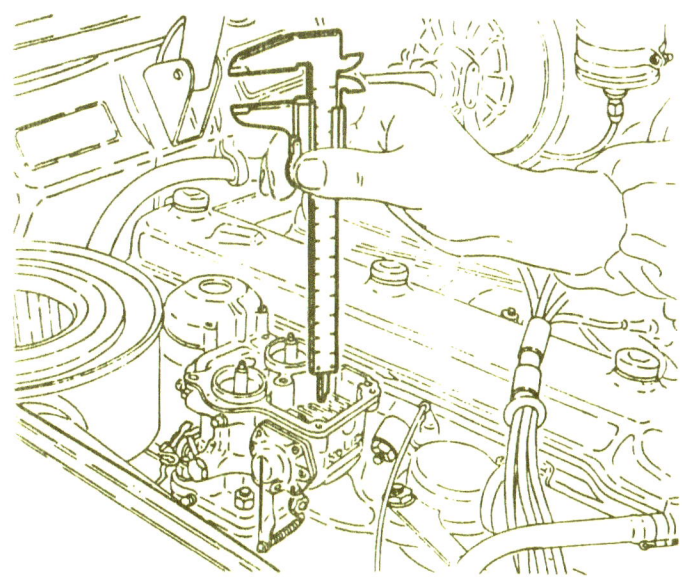

The fuel level can also be measured with the quicker method of communicating vessels as follows:

- fit the indicator in place of main jet;

- actuate the fuel pump and check that the level is 12 to 13 mm (about 1/2 in.) below the flange mating surface.

If the level is not as above specified, check the needle valve and the float.

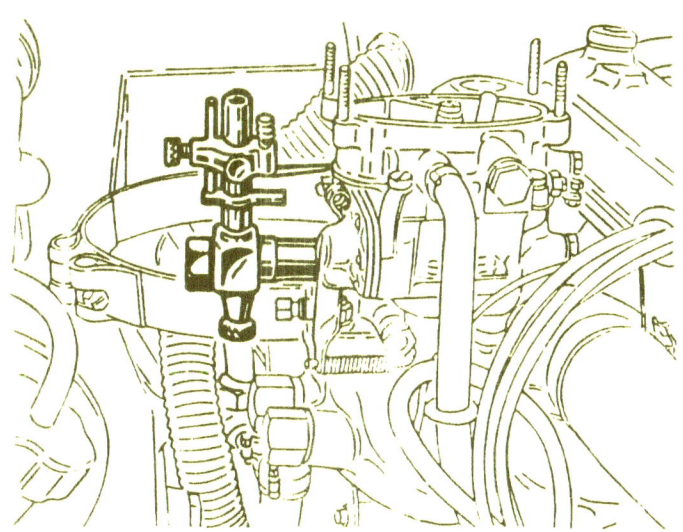

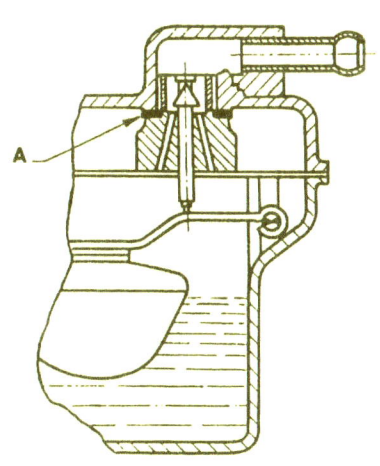

Do not touch at all the float arm: insert shims as required under the valve seat (A).
If the trouble persists check the feed pump delivery.

VALVE TIMING

Checking of valve opening and closing angles

Clearance (with cold engine) between the unlobed profile of cams and the valve cup ceiling:

intake	.475 to .500 mm (.0187 to .0197")
exhaust	.525 to .550 mm (.0206 to .0216")

Opening of intake valve:
lift of cup	.20 mm (.008")
corresponding to an angle .... before TDC of	6° ± 1°30'

Closing of intake valve:
lift of cup	.20 mm (.008")
corresponding to an angle .... after BDC of	54° ± 1°30'

Opening of exhaust valve:
lift of cup	.15 mm (.006")
corresponding to an angle .... before BDC of	54° ± 1°30'

Closing of exhaust valve:
lift of cup	.15 mm (.006")
corresponding to an angle .... after TDC of	6° ± 1°30'

Angle values of the actual diagram of valve timing system with cold engine (clockwise rotation direction of the crankshaft seen from the front side).

opening of intake valve .... before TDC	24°40'
closing of intake valve .... after BDC	72°40'
opening of exhaust valve .... before BDC	66°
closing of exhaust valve .... after TDC	18°
induction stroke	277°20'
exhaust stroke	264°

IGNITION

Firing order: 1 - 3 - 4 - 2 (no. 1 cylinder is that at the fan side)
Ignition distributor contact point's gap: S .... .35 to .40 mm (.014 to .016")

Values of advance of ignition distributor

Fixed advance F Before TDC	Maximum advance M Before TDC
2°/4°	43°/46° at 5000 rpm (3° correspond to 3.5 mm - .14" on the periphery of crankshaft pulley).

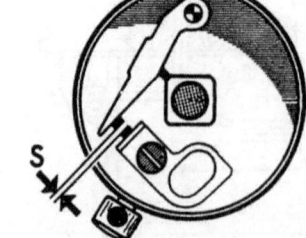

Spark plugs
Lodge H L N

Electrode gap .... .50 ÷ .60 mm (.020 ÷ .024")

ELECTRIC SYSTEM

Voltage 12 V
Battery 50 Amp/h

	BOSCH	MARELLI
Generator	EG (R) 14 V 25 A 29	
Voltage regulator	VA 14 V 25 A	
Starting motor	EF (R) 12 V 0,7 PS	
Coil	TK 12 A 19	
Ignition distributor	J F U 4	
Windshield wiper	WS 13/11 S 1 a	TGE 93 A

Bulb's wattage

Headlamps	40/45 asymmetric
Front parking lights	5 globular
Front direction indicators	21
Side direction indicators	3 tubular
Tail parking and stop lights	5/21
Tail direction indicators	21
Back-up light	21
License plate light	5 globular
Ceiling light	5 cylindrical
Instrument panel light	3 tubular
Tell-tale for lights	3 tubular
Tell-tale for direction indicator	3 tubular
Tell-tale for generator	3 tubular
Tell-tale for fuel reserve	3 tubular
Tell-tale for electric blower	3 tubular

Tightening torque specifications

ENGINE - GEARBOX UNIT

	Kgm.	lb. ft	Manner of tightening
Cylinder head nuts * — Inspection — when cold	6.2 to 6.4	44.8 to 46.3	Slacken in proper sequence, the nuts by one and one half turn and lubetorque
Cylinder head nuts * — Inspection — when hot	6.6 to 6.7	47.7 to 48.4	Warm up the engine and when hot retighten without unscrewing
Cylinder head nuts * — After repairing — when cold	6.2 to 6.4	44.8 to 46.3	Retighten with lube
Cylinder head nuts * — After repairing — when hot	6.6 to 6.7	47.7 to 48.4	Warm up the engine by actually driving the car and when hot retighten without unscrewing
Cylinder head nuts * — After repairing — when cold	6.2 to 6.4	44.8 to 46.3	After tested the car, slacken, when cold and in proper sequence, the nuts by one and one half turn and lubetorque
Spark plugs	2.5 to 3.5	18.1 to 25.3	With graphite grease, when cold
Nuts of the camshaft caps	2 to 2.25	14.5 to 16.3	in oil
Nuts of the connecting rod caps	3.4 to 3.6	24.6 to 26.1	" "
Nuts of main bearing caps	3.2 to 3.5	23.2 to 25.3	" "
Screws of flywheel on crankshaft	4.2 to 4.5	30.4 to 32.5	" "
Nut of generator pulley	3 to 3.5	21.7 to 25.3	dry
Nut of gearbox main shaft yoke	11.9 to 12	86.1 to 86.8	"
Nut of gearbox layshaft	4.5 to 5.5	32.5 to 39.7	"
Nuts of gearbox half-casing	1.8	13	"
Nut of gearbox inner swivel	3.25 to 3.65	23.6 to 26.4	"

REAR FRAME

	Kgm.	lb. ft	Manner of tightening
Screws securing ring gear to differential case	4.5 to 5	32.6 to 36.1	"
Ring nut securing yoke on final drive pinion shaft	8 to 14	58 to 101.2	"
Nuts securing bearing housings to rear axle tubes	4.8 to 5.5	34.8 to 39.7	"
Nuts securing radius rods to body	10 to 11.5	72.4 to 83	"
Nuts securing radius rods to rear axle tubes	11.5 to 13	83 to 94	"
Nut securing reaction triangle to body	4.8 to 5.5	34.8 to 39.7	"
Nut securing reaction triangle to differential carrier	11 to 15	79.6 to 108.5	"
Screws securing brake slave cylinders to axle tubes	.4 to .5	2.9 to 3.6	"
Screws securing rear brake caliper to support	2.3 to 2.8	16.7 to 20.2	"
Nuts securing wheels	6 to 8	43.4 to 57.8	"

* **Warning:** in case of any repair work involving the removal of cylinder head, the gasket must be renewed at all times.

FRONT FRAME

	Kgm.	lb. ft	Manner of tightening
Nut securing steering wheel to column	5 to 5.5	36.1 to 39.7	d r y
Screws securing Burman steering box cover	2.3 to 2.5	16.7 to 18	"
Screws securing steering box & crank bracket to body	4.8 to 5.5	34.8 to 39.7	"
Nuts of steering linkage ball joints	4.8 to 5.5	34.8 to 39.7	"
Nut securing steering arm to box	12.5 to 14	90.5 to 101.2	"
Screws securing upper attachment of shock absorber to body	2.3 to 2.8	16.7 to 20.2	"
Nut securing shock absorbers to suspension arms	7.5 to 8.5	54.3 to 61.4	"
Screws securing upper wishbone front arm to body	2.3 to 2.8	16.7 to 20.2	"
Nut securing upper wishbone front arm to rear arm	4.8 to 5.5	34.8 to 39.7	"
Nut securing upper wishbone rear arm to body	11.5 to 13	83 to 94	"
Nuts securing lower wishbone bracket to crossmember	13 to 18	94 to 130	"
Nuts securing steering arm to steering knuckle	4.8 to 5.5	34.8 to 39.7	"
Nut securing upper wishbone rear arm to steering knuckle	7.5 to 8.5	54.3 to 61.4	"
Nut securing lower ball joint to wishbone	7.5 to 8.5	54.3 to 61.4	"
Nut securing lower ball joint to steering knuckle	7.5 to 8.5	54.3 to 61.4	"
Nuts securing caliper support to steering knuckle	4.8 to 5.5	34.8 to 39.7	"
Screws securing front brake calipers to support	7.5 to 8.5	54.3 to 61.4	"
Screws securing front brake discs	7.5 to 8.5	54.3 to 61.4	"
Nuts securing wheels	6 to 8	43.4 to 57.8	"

NOTES

MAJOR INSPECTION SPECIFICATIONS

CAMSHAFTS

Diameter of journals: A	26.959 ÷ 26.980 mm (1.0614 ÷ 1.0622")
Diameter of journal bearings: B	27.000 ÷ 27.033 mm (1.0630 ÷ 1.0642")
Radial clearance between journals and bearings { factory assembly	.020 ÷ .074 mm (.0008 ÷ .0028")
wear limit	.100 mm (.004")
End play of camshaft in thrust bearing: C	.065 ÷ .182 mm (.0026 ÷ .0071")

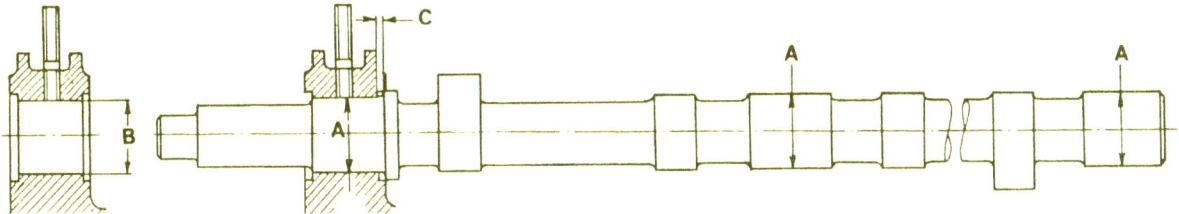

VALVES AND VALVE GUIDES

		Intake	Exhaust (sodium type)
		LIVIA H	LIVIA C
Valves	poppet dia. O	37.000 ÷ 37.150 mm (1.4567 ÷ 1.4625")	34.000 ÷ 34.150 mm (1.3386 ÷ 1.3838")
	stem dia. M	8.962 ÷ 8.987 mm (.3528 ÷ .3538")	8.935 ÷ 8.960 mm (.3518 ÷ .3527")
	Total length N	109 ÷ 109.3 mm (4.2913 ÷ 4.3131")	108.6 ÷ 108.9 mm (4.2756 ÷ 4.2874")

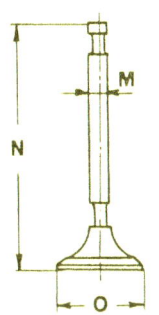

Valve guide { Outside diameter with guide removed	14.033 ÷ 14.044 mm (.5528 ÷ .5529")
Inside diameter with guide assembled in cylinder head	9.000 ÷ 9.015 mm (.3544 ÷ .3549")
Projection of intake valve guides from their recesses in cylinder head	13.8 ÷ 14 mm (.543 ÷ .551")
Projection of exhaust valve guides from their recesses in the cylinder head	16.800 ÷ 17.000 mm (.662 ÷ .669")
Clearance between guide assembled in cylinder head and valve stem { intake	.013 ÷ .043 mm (.0005 ÷ .0017")
exhaust	.040 ÷ .080 mm (.0016 ÷ .0031")
Diameter of valve guide seat in cylinder head	13.990 ÷ 14.018 mm (.5508 ÷ .5518")
Interference between seat and valve guide	.015 ÷ .054 mm (.0006 ÷ .0021")

Valve seats

		Intake	Exhaust
Outer diameter of the valve seat	standard	38.597 ÷ 38.632 mm (1.5196 to 1.5209")	35.422 ÷ 35.457 mm (1.3946 ÷ 1.3960")
	oversized	38.897 ÷ 38.932 mm (1.5314 ÷ 1.5327")	35.722 ÷ 35.757 mm (1.4054 ÷ 1.4077")
Diameter of recess in the cylinder head for valve seat	standard	38.532 ÷ 38.557 mm (1.5169 ÷ 1.5179")	35.357 ÷ 35.382 mm (1.3920 ÷ 1.3930")
	oversized	38.832 ÷ 38.857 mm (1.5288 ÷ 1.5298")	35.657 ÷ 35.682 mm (1.4038 ÷ 1.4048")

Interference between valve seat and recess in cylinder head .... .100 ÷ .040 mm (.0039 ÷ .0016")

VALVE CUPS

Diameter of cup	standard	34.973 to 34.989 mm (1.3773 to 1.3775")
	oversized	35.173 to 35.189 mm (1.3848 to 1.3853")
Diameter of cup seat in cylinder head	standard	35.000 to 35.025 mm (1.3779 to 1.3789")
	oversized	35.200 to 35.225 mm (1.3859 to 1.3868")
Clearance between seat and cup		.011 to .052 mm (.0005 to .0020")

VALVE SPRINGS

	Free length	Length under test load	Test load
Inner spring	red mark 47.3 mm (1.87") green mark 46.5 mm (1.83")	26 mm (1.02")	22.2 to 23.16 Kg 48.9 to 51.1 lbs
Outer spring	red mark 52.8 mm (2.08") green mark 51.3 mm (2.03")	27.5 mm (1.08")	35.7 to 37.1 Kg 78.6 to 81.8 lbs

CONNECTING RODS

Length between center line of big end and center line of small end of connecting rod		132.955 to 133.045 mm (5.239 to 5.242")
Inner diameter of the big end of connecting rod		48.658 to 48.671 mm (1.9172 to 1.9176")
Inner diameter of bushing in the small end of rod		20.005 to 20.015 mm (.7882 to .7886")
End play of the connecting rods on the pins of crankshaft		.200 to .300 mm (.0079 to .0118")
Thickness of connecting rod bearings	standard	1.822 to 1.829 mm (.0718 to .0720")
	1st oversize	1.949 to 1.956 mm (.0768 to .0770")
	3nd oversize	2.076 to 2.083 mm (.0817 to .0820")
Radial clearance between crankpins and bearings for big end of connecting rod		.025 to .064 mm (.0010 to .0024")
Maximum out of parallelism between center line of big end hole and center line of small end hole measured on piston pin overall length		.0317 mm (.0018")

PISTON PIN

O.D. of pin	Black color	19.994 to 19.997 mm (.78777 to .78788")
	White color	19.997 to 20.000 mm (.78788 to .78800")
Clearance between piston pin and small end hole	Black color	.008 to .021 mm (.0003 to .0008")
	White color	.005 to .018 mm (.0002 to .0007")

Piston pin hole

	Black color	White color
Borgo piston	20.000 to 20.002 mm (.7874 to .78748")	20.003 to 20.005 mm (.78752 to .7876")
Mahle piston	19.996 to 19.999 mm (.78784 to .78796")	19.999 to 20.002 mm (.78796 to .78808")
K.S. piston	20.000 to 20.0025 mm (.78800 to .78809")	20.0025 to 20.0050 mm (.78809 to .78819")

PISTONS AND CYLINDER BARRELS

Diameter of pistons to be measured to square with the hole for piston pin and at a distance of 10-12 mm (.394-.472") from the lower border of skirt.

For cylinder barrels classification purpose, use the minimum diameter recorded.

	Class A - BLUE	Class B - PINK	Class C - GREEN
Borgo piston	73.930 to 73.940 mm (2.9128 to 2.9132")	73.940 to 73.950 mm (2.9132 to 2.9136")	73.950 to 73.960 mm (2.9136 to 2.9140")
Mahle piston	73.925 to 73.935 mm (2.9126 to 2.9130")	73.935 to 73.945 mm (2.9130 to 2.9134")	73.945 to 73.955 mm (2.9134 to 2.9138")
K.S. piston	73.925 to 73.935 mm (2.9126 to 2.9130")	73.935 to 73.945 mm (2.9130 to 2.9134")	73.945 to 73.955 mm (2.9134 to 2.9138")
Cylinder barrel	73.985 to 73.994 mm (2.9150 to 2.9153")	73.995 to 74.004 mm (2.9154 to 2.9157")	74.005 to 74.014 mm (2.9158 to 2.9161")

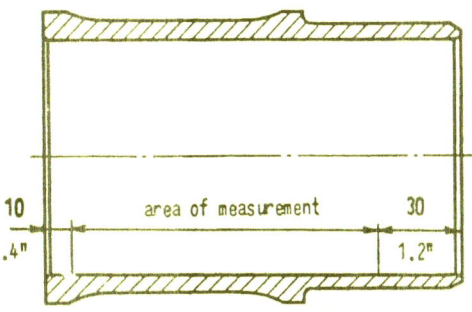

Clearance between cylinder barrel and piston — with Borgo piston		.045 to .064 mm (.0018 to .0025")
— with Mahle piston		.050 to .069 mm (.0020 to .0027")
— with K.S. piston		.050 to .069 mm (.0020 to .0027")
Wear limit		.120 mm (.0047")
Elongation and taper of barrels — new		.010 mm (.0004")
— wear limit		.050 mm (.0019")
Projection of barrels from cylinder block		.000 to .060 mm (.0000 to .0024")
Surface roughness		20 - 40 microinches RMS

COMPRESSION AND OIL CONTROL RINGS

Thickness of rings — compression (normal)		1.978 to 1.990 mm (.0779 to .0784")
— compression (chromium-plated)		1.978 to 1.990 mm (.0779 to .0784")
— oil control		3.958 to 3.970 mm (.1559 to .1564")
Gap of rings to be checked in ring gauge or in cylinder barrels		.25 to .40 mm (.010 to .015")

	Piston	Compression ring grooves	Oil control ring groove
Height of groove in piston	BORGO	2.022 to 2.047 mm (.0797 to .0806")	4.006 to 4.031 mm (.1578 to .1588")
	MAHLE	2.025 to 2.040 mm (.0798 to .0803")	4.015 to 4.030 mm (.1582 to .1587")
	K.S.	2.022 to 2.047 mm (.0797 to .0806")	4.006 to 4.031 mm (.1578 to .1588")

	Piston	Compression rings	Oil control rings
End play of ring in groove	BORGO	.032 to .069 mm (.0013 to .0027")	.036 to .073 mm (.0014 to .0028")
	MAHLE	.035 to .062 mm (.0014 to .0024")	.045 to .072 mm (.0018 to .0028")
	K.S.	.032 to .069 mm (.0013 to .0027")	.036 to .073 mm (.0014 to .0028")

CRANKSHAFT

Diameter of main journals A	Standard	59.960 to 59.973 mm (2.3606 to 2.3611")
	1st undersize	59.706 to 59.719 mm (2.3506 to 2.3511")
	2nd undersize	59.452 to 59.465 mm (2.3407 to 2.3411")
Diameter of crankpins B	Standard	44.963 to 44.975 mm (1.77154 to 1.77201")
	1st undersize	44.709 to 44.721 mm (1.76154 to 1.76200")
	2nd undersize	44.455 to 44.467 mm (1.75153 to 1.75199")
Thickness of main bearings G	Standard	1.829 to 1.835 mm (.0720 to .0722")
	1st oversize	1.956 to 1.962 mm (.0770 to .0772")
	2nd oversize	2.083 to 2.089 mm (.0820 to .0822")
Diameter of seat for main bearings in crankcase F		63.657 to 63.676 mm (2.5062 to 2.5069")
Length of central journal D	Standard	30.000 to 30.035 mm (1.1811 to 1.1824")
	1st oversize	30.127 to 30.162 mm (1.1861 to 1.1874")
	2nd oversize	30.254 to 30.289 mm (1.1911 to 1.1924")
Thickness of thrust rings for central journal E	Standard	2.311 to 2.362 mm (.0910 to .0929")
	1st oversize	2.374 to 2.425 mm (.0935 to .0954")
	2nd oversize	2.438 to 2.489 mm (.0960 to .0980")
End play of crankshaft H		.076 to .263 mm (.003 to .010")
Clearance between journals and main bearings		.014 to .058 mm (.0005 to .0022")

Note: Clearance = main bearing ID − (twice bearing thickness − journal OD).

Fillet radii	main journals and crankpins G1	1.7 to 2.1 mm (.069 to .082")
	pin on flywheel side G2	3.7 to 4.1 mm (.146 to .161")
Main journals & crankpins surface roughness		16 microinches
Maximum elongation of main journals and crankpins		.007 mm (.00027")
Maximum taper of main journals and crankpins measured on their full length		.01 mm (.00039")
Maximum error of parallelism of main journals and crankpins measured on their full length		.015 mm (.00059")
Maximum misalignment allowed between main journals		.01 mm (.00039")
Maximum misalignment between ℄ of the two pairs of crankpins and ℄ of main journals		.300 mm (.0118")

C L U T C H

Pedal free travel	23 mm (.9")
Distance between thrust ring and the reference sleeve of tool C. 6.0104 (red dot) (Refer to Tool Bulletins nos. 50 and 151)	.75 ÷ 1.25 mm (.029 ÷ .053")
Squareness of the clutch driven plate assembled on gearbox direct drive shaft	.50 mm (.019")
Wear limit of driven plate thickness	6 mm (.236")

Spring rating ....
- free length ..... 43.5 ÷ 45.5 mm (1.71 ÷ 1.79")
- length under test load 29 mm (1.14")
- test load .... 45 ÷ 49 Kg (99 ÷ 108 lbs)

G E A R B O X

Transmission ratios ....
- 1st gear   3.30 : 1
- 2nd gear   1.99 : 1
- 3rd gear   1.35 : 1
- 4th gear   1.00 : 1
- 5th gear   .79 : 1
- Reverse gear 3.01 : 1

Maximum eccentricity of main shaft .... .05 mm (.020")

End play between forks and sleeves ....
- assembly . .15 ÷ .34 mm (.006 ÷ .013")
- wear limit .85 mm (.033")

Calibration of springs for striking rod balls ....

Gear	1st - 2nd - 3rd	5th - Rev.
free length	15.2 mm (.600")	30.5 mm (1.2")
length under test load	10 mm (.390")	20 mm (.78")
test load	2.88 ÷ 3.12 Kg (6.4 ÷ 6.8 lbs)	4.32 ÷ 4.68 Kg (9.5 ÷ 10.3 lbs)

Maximum end play of the main shaft gears
- 1st speed gear   .170 ÷ .245 mm (.0067 ÷ .0096")
- 2nd & 3rd speed gear   .130 ÷ .205 mm (.0052 ÷ .0081")
- 5th speed gear & Rev.   .160 ÷ .220 mm (.0063 to .0087")

Radial clearance between gear bushings and mainshaft ....
- 1st speed gear   .125 ÷ .170 mm (.0049 ÷ .0067")
- 2nd & 3rd speed gear   .095 ÷ .140 mm (.0038 ÷ .0055")
- 5th speed gear & Rev.   .065 ÷ .107 mm (.0026 ÷ .0041")

Distance between outer planes of the engaging teeth of 3rd and 4th gears   42 ÷ 42.2 mm (1.65 ÷ 1.66")

Distance, in neutral, of the rear band (propeller shaft side) of 5th speed sleeve from the rear edge of gear engaging teeth ....   12.9 mm (.508")

REAR AXLE AND SUSPENSION

Transmission-axle overall ratios-with 41 : 8 final drive:
- 1st gear   16.933 : 1
- 2nd gear   10.189 : 1
- 3rd gear   6.944 : 1
- 4th gear   5.125 : 1
- 5th gear   4.054 : 1
- Reverse   15.426 : 1

Maximum eccentricity of axle shafts .... .10 mm (.004")
Clearance between teeth of planetary gears .... .05 mm (.002")
Play between teeth of final drive .... .05 ÷ .10 mm (.002 ÷ .004")
Reference dimension on tool C. 6.0101 for pinion-to-ring gear fitting   70 ± .0025 mm (2.7559 ± .0001")
Pre-load on pinion bearing .... 11.5 ÷ 15.5 Kgcm (10 ÷ 13.5 in. lbs)
Total pre-load on final drive bearings .... 16.5 ÷ 24.5 Kgcm (14.4 ÷ 21.3 in. lbs)

Checking of shock absorbers on test bench

Calibration data (when cold)

	GIRLING		BIANCHI - ALLINQUANT	
	Extension	Compression	Extension	Compression
High speed	121 ÷ 190 Kgs (267 ÷ 418 lbs)	27 ÷ 42 Kgs (60 ÷ 92 lbs)	135 ÷ 190 Kgs (298 ÷ 418 lbs)	50 ÷ 80 Kgs (111 ÷ 176 lbs)
Low speed	13 ÷ 32 Kgs (29 ÷ 70 lbs)	9 ÷ 18 Kgs (20 ÷ 40 lbs)	19 ÷ 55 Kgs (42 ÷ 121 lbs)	9 ÷ 22 Kgs (20 ÷ 48 lbs)

Checking of suspension springs

Free length .... 449 mm (17.7")
Length under test load ..... 252 mm (10")   } Colored marks: sky blue - sky blue
Test load .... 321 ÷ 341 Kgs (710 ÷ 740 lbs)

FRONT SUSPENSION

Adjustment of clearance in wheel bearings

When performing regular servicing or whenever the removal of wheel hubs is required, adjust the bearing clearance as follows:

1) Screw in the castellated nut and lock it to a torque of 2.5 Kgm (18 ft.lbs) while at the same time revolving the wheel hub to set the bearings properly in their seats;
2) Unscrew the nut half a turn or more;
3) Lightly tap on the stub axle end with a mallet in order to return the outboard bearing in its proper position even in the case a slight interference between bearing cone and stub axle exists;
4) Lock the nut in place to 1.5 Kgm (10.8 ft-lbs);
5) Unscrew the nut of a quarter turn;
6) If the hole in the axle is aligned with a slot in the castellated nut insert the cotter pin; if not, screw in the nut by the minimum angle needed to line up the hole and the next slot;
7) Again tap lightly on stub axle end to restore the same condition as under step 3;
8) The end play so obtained on stub axle should fall beetween .02 - .12 mm (.0008 - .0047").

Wheel bearing lubricating instructions

The quantity of lubricating grease should be about 65 grammes (2½ ozs) for each hub; do not exceed such a quantity to avoid bearing overheating, grease leakage, etc.
The grease should be well distributed inside the bearings and into side recesses.
Subsequently, at the regular schedule, remove the hub cover and pack the outboard bearing.

Ball joints

- End play of lower ball joint in its socket: 1 mm (.04").

Note - Ball joints require no regular lubrication being provided with special grease seals which retain the grease packed in by factory on assembly.

Checking of suspension springs

Free length . . . .   312.5 mm (12.31")
Length under test load . . . .   200 mm (7.8")   } Colored marks: sky blue - sky blue
Test load . . . . 911.8 - 968.2 Kgs (2100-2650 lbs)

Checking of shock absorbers on test bench

Calibration data (when cold)

	GIRLING		ALLINQUANT	
	Extension	Compression	Extension	Compression
High speed	210 to 310 Kgs (470 to 680 lbs)	27 to 52 Kgs (60 to 115 lbs)	150 to 190 Kgs (330 to 420 lbs)	55 to 80 Kgs (121 to 175 lbs)
Low speed	30 to 52 Kgs (66 to 115 lbs)	9 to 22 Kgs (20 to 48 lbs)	25 to 55 Kgs (55 to 121 lbs)	9 to 22 Kgs (20 to 48 lbs)

B R A K E S

D i s c

Whenever a brake unit is overhauled or replaced check the disc for true rotation with the disc fitted to the car. Use a dial gauge and check that runout does not exceed .15 mm (.006"). Should the reading exceed this value, then the installation of disc on stub axle must be carefully examined; if the run out persists, replace the disc. If the disc is scored, the grinding of the surfaces is allowed providing not to exceed an undersize of 1 mm (.0394"), equalized on both faces, i.e. .5 mm (.0197") each face; disc wear limit; 8.5 mm (.335") thick.

Inspection specifications after regrinding of disc surfaces:
- Max. out of parallelism with disc mounting plane: .05 mm (.0020");
- Max. out of flat: .025 mm (.0010") and max. difference in thickness: .038 mm (.0015") as measured along any radial line;
- Max. out of flat: .025 mm (.0010") and max. difference in thickness: .015 mm (.0006") as measured along any circular line;
- The surface should show no sign of scoring or porosity.

The surface roughness should be:
- 26 microinches as measured circularly;
- 36 microinches as measured radially.

Friction pads

	Front	Rear
Thickness when new	16 mm (.630")	17.5 mm (.689")
Wear limit	8 mm (.315")	10.0 mm (.394")

Calipers

On replacement of disc or caliper measure the running clearance between caliper and disc on each side; the difference should not exceed .5 mm (.0197").
To centralize the caliper about the disc, insert shims between caliper and mounting flange as required.

Hand brake

It is mechanically-operated and acts on the rear service brake pads.
The adjustment is performed by acting on the nut of control cable located between intermediate levers and calipers. After the adjustment, make sure that levers of rear calipers to which the cable is connected are all the way outward. In such a position the cable must not be tight but slightly slackened. Furthermore the brake pads must not contact the disc.

N.B. - For repair and maintenance instructions refer to: "Disc Brake System for GIULIA T.I. model" publication no. 930.

WHEEL ALIGNMENT

Checking of wheel angles and car "trim" under static load

Put the car under static load, with shock absorbers and stabilizer rod disconnected, with full tank or equivalent, with spare wheel, tool kit and the tires inflated to the prescribed pressures.
Before checking, cause the car to jolt slightly so as to settle the suspensions.

- Front seats
  - 1 weight of 45 Kgs on each seat
  - 2 weights of 25 Kgs on flooring where feet rest

- Rear seats
  - 2 weights of 45 Kgs on seat
  - 2 weights of 25 Kgs on flooring where fest rest

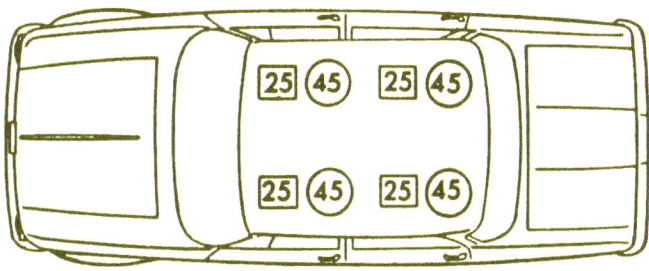

Distance of lower wishbone of front suspension from a reference level

A - B
- for round-cross-section shaft 38 ± 5 mm ($1.49 \pm .20"$)
- for elongated-cross-section shaft 34 ± 5 mm ($1.34 \pm .20"$)

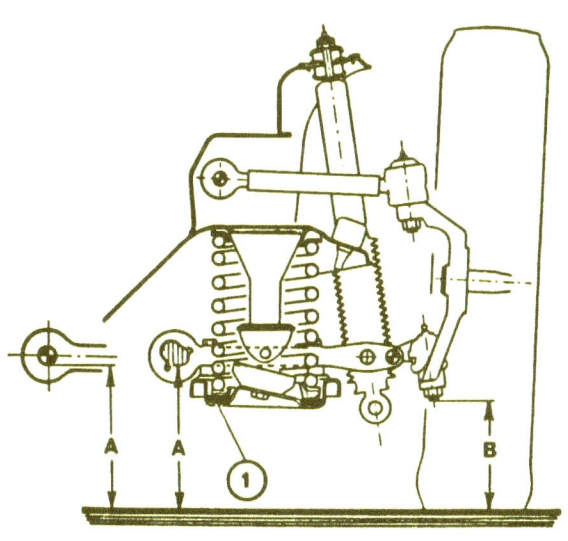

Note - Dimension **A** must be measured in correspondence of the lower line of wishbone shaft as shown.
To adjust, add shims in position 1.
Shims are available in the following thicknesses:
3.5 mm (.14")
7.0 mm (.28")
10.5 mm (.42").

Distance of rear axle from rubber buffers

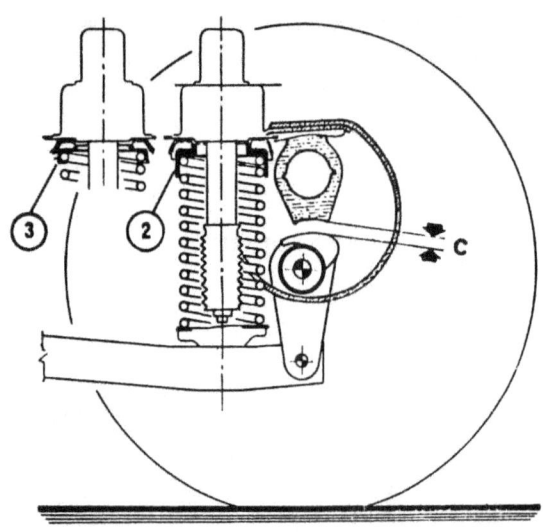

C = 10 ± 5 mm (.4 ± .2")

Note - To adjust remove the seat (3) and add shims in (2) as shown.
Shims are available in the following thicknesses:
      6.5 mm (.26")
      11.5 mm (.45")
      16.5 mm (.65")
      21.5 mm (.85").

In the conditions as specified above, check the wheel angles.

Caster angle

$\alpha = 1° \pm 30'$

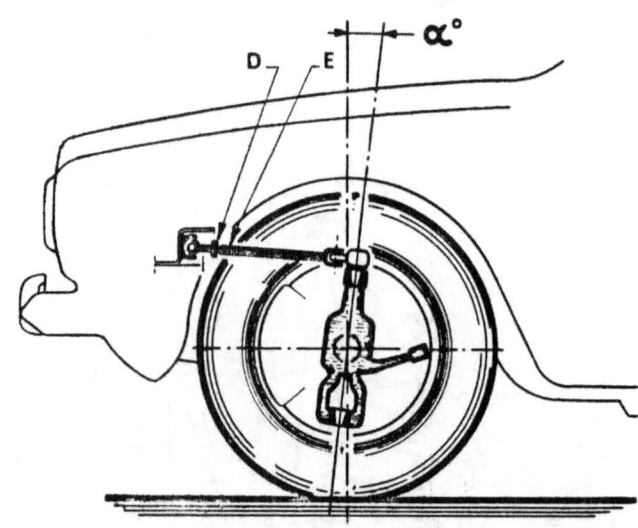

The difference in caster angle between R.H. and L.H. wheel must not exceed 0°20'.

To adjust, loosen jam nut D and rotate rod E.

Small adjustments of the caster angle allow to correct slight drift tendency of the car.

N.B. - Before checking the caster angle shake the front end of car in order to allow the rubber bushing on the front arm to settle properly.

Front wheel camber

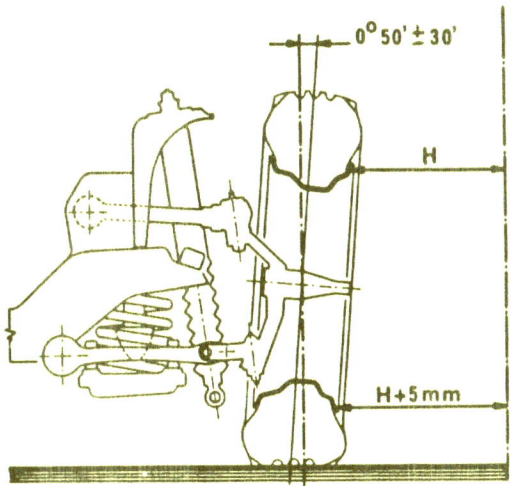

Note - Not adjustable. Make a check of chassis and suspension arms, if necessary.

Front wheel toe-in

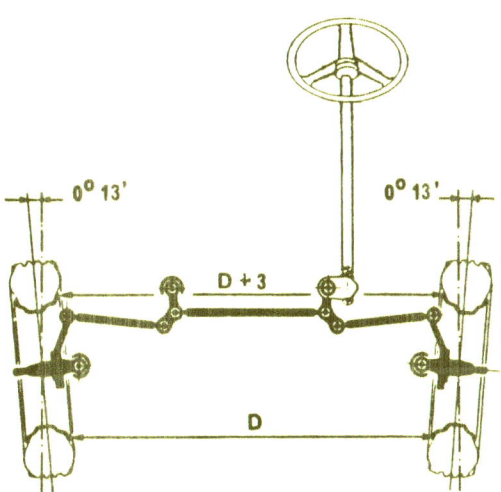

Rod length:
    side . . . . 272 to 288 mm (10.84 to 11.24")
    track . . . . 544 to 552 mm (21.41 to 21.73")

With the toe-in as specified, the length of rods as measured between ball joint centers should fall withing the limits shown. If these values cannot be restored, the cause will probably be found in distortion resulting from a collision.

MODIFICATIONS from chassis no.	645.001 (L.H.D. cars)
	763.001 (R.H.D. cars)

TIRES

CEAT Drive D 1

PRINCIPAL CHARACTERISTIC DATA

Wheel track
- front .... 1324 mm (52.1")
- rear .... 1274 mm (50.1")

Curb weight (full tank) .... 1010 Kg (2227 lbs)

REFILLINGS

Engine (pan & filter)
- to max. level (for regular changing) .... 5.800 Kg (5.75 GB qts) (6.80 US qts)
- to min. level .... 4.000 Kg (3.95 GB qts) (4.75 US qts)

The total amount of oil in the circuit (sump, filter, passages) is 6.550 Kg (6.5 GB pts) (7.8 US pts)

CARBURETION

Carburetor SOLEX C 32 PAIA 7

Choke air metering jet 500

SPARK PLUGS

Lodge 2HL

ELECTRIC SYSTEM

Battery .... 60 Ah

2-speed windscreen wiper ....
- BOSCH WS 13/11 S 1 A
- MARELLI TGE 93 BX

DRY TIGHTENING TORQUE SPECIFICATIONS

FRONT FRAME

Nut securing shock absorbers to suspension arm	8.2 to 9.2 Kgm (59.3 to 66.5 lb-ft)
Nut securing upper wishbone front arm to rear arm	4 to 4.5 Kgm (29 to 32.5 lb-ft)
Nut securing upper wishbone rear arm to body	12.5 to 14 Kgm (90.5 to 101.2 lb-ft)
Nuts securing lower arm shaft to cross-member	5.6 to 5.9 Kgm (40.5 to 42.6 lb-ft)

(To tighten these nuts use tool A.5.0161 and torque to 5.2 to 5.5 Kgm - 37.6 to 39.7 lb-ft)

Nuts securing steering arm to steering knuckle	4 to 4.5 Kgm (29 to 32.5 lb-ft)
Nuts securing splash shields to steering knuckle	.8 to 1.1 Kgm (6 to 8 lb-ft)
Nut securing lower ball joint to wishbone	8.2 to 9.2 Kgm (59.3 to 66.5 lb-ft)
Screws securing caliper to steering knuckle	7.5 to 8.5 Kgm (54.2 to 61.5 lb-ft)
Brake bleed screw	.2 to .35 Kgm (1.5 to 2.5 lb-ft)
Caliper joining bolts	2.9 to 3.4 Kgm (21 to 24.6 lb-ft)
Inlet fitting to caliper { with gasket	.8 to 1.1 Kgm (6 to 8 lb-ft)
{ without gasket	1 to 1.5 Kgm (7.2 to 10.8 lb-ft)

VALVES AND VALVE GUIDES

Sodium-cooled ATE exhaust valves

Diameter of valve poppet O	34.000 to 34.150 mm (1.3386 to 1.3838")
Diameter of valve stem M	8.935 to 8.960 mm (.3518 to .3527")
Total length N	108.5 to 108.6 mm (4.2717 to 4.2756")

VALVE SPRINGS (alternative to the existing ones)

Inner spring - free length	47 mm (1.85")
Outer spring { free length	52 mm (2.05")
{ length under test load	27.5 mm (1.08")
{ test load	35.9 to 37.3 Kg (79 to 82 lbs)

PISTON PIN HOLE

	Black color	White color
BORGO piston - new construction	20.000 to 20.002 mm (.7874 to .78748")	20.003 to 20.005 mm (.78752 to .7876")

PISTONS AND CYLINDER BARRELS

Diameter of pistons to be measured to square with the hole for piston pin and at a distance of L = 17 mm (.67") from the lower border of skirt.

	Class A - Blue	Class B - Pink	Class C - Green
BORGO piston - new construction	73.945 to 73.955 mm (2.9112 to 2.9115")	73.955 to 73.965 mm (2.9116 to 2.9119")	73.965 to 73.975 mm (2.9120 to 2.9123")

CLEARANCE BETWEEN CYLINDER BARREL AND PISTON

With new-construction BORGO piston	.030 to .049 mm (.0012 to .0019")

COMPRESSION AND OIL CONTROL RINGS

Thickness of rings (for new-construction BORGO pistons)
- compression .. 1.478 to 1.490 mm (.0582 to .0586")
- oil scraper .. 1.728 to 1.740 mm (.0680 to .0685")
- oil control .. 3.978 to 3.990 mm (.1566 to .1570")

Gap of rings to be checked in ring gauge or in cylinder barrels, for new-construction BORGO piston .... .20 to .35 mm (.08 to .13")

HEIGHT OF GROOVE IN PISTON

	Compression ring groove	Oil scraper ring groove	Oil control ring groove
BORGO - new construction	1.535 to 1.555 mm (.0605 to .0612")	1.775 to 1.795 mm (.0699 to .0706")	4.015 to 4.035 mm (.1581 to .1588")

END PLAY OF PISTON RING IN GROOVE

	Compression ring	Oil scraper ring	Oil control ring
BORGO - new construction	.045 to .077 mm (.0018 to .0030")	.035 to .067 mm (.0014 to .0026")	.025 to .057 mm (.0010 to .0022")

CLUTCH

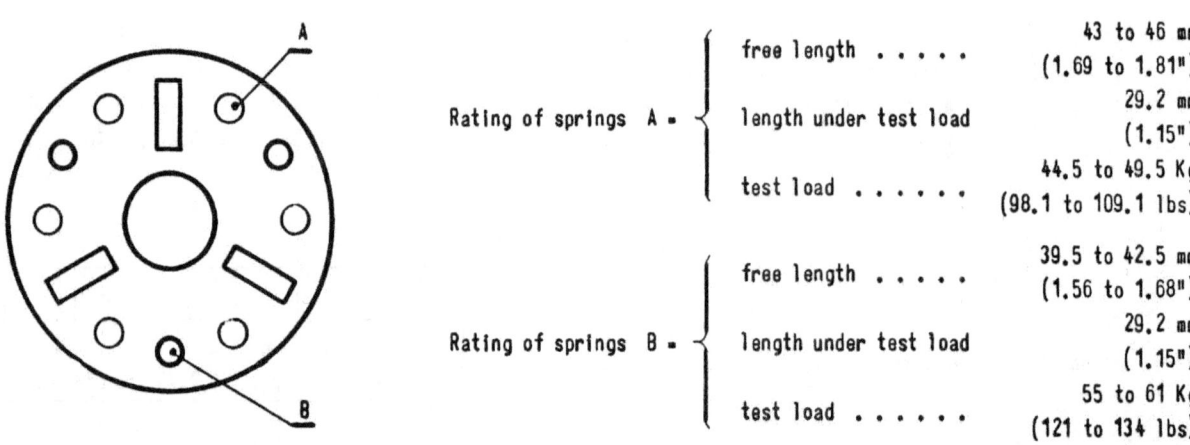

Rating of springs A =
- free length ..... 43 to 46 mm (1.69 to 1.81")
- length under test load 29.2 mm (1.15")
- test load ...... 44.5 to 49.5 Kg (98.1 to 109.1 lbs)

Rating of springs B =
- free length ..... 39.5 to 42.5 mm (1.56 to 1.68")
- length under test load 29.2 mm (1.15")
- test load ...... 55 to 61 Kg (121 to 134 lbs)

FRONT SUSPENSION

Shock absorbers

	ALLINQUANT	
	Extension	Compression
High speed	150 to 190 Kgs (330 to 520 lbs)	55 to 80 Kgs (121 to 175 lbs)
Low speed	25 to 55 Kgs (55 to 121 lbs)	9 to 22 Kgs (20 to 48 lbs)

BRAKES (ATE make)

Disc

When a brake disc is replaced it is necessary to check it for run-out after installation:

- use a dial indicator and the special tool A.2.0151 which is mounted to the caliper by means of the pad retaining pins.

Maximum permissible run out as measured at the swept surface should not exceed .22 mm (.0086").

Note - run-out readings can be misleading if bearing clearance is not as specified; therefore, check and adjust if necessary, according to factory instructions.

If the disc is scored, see I.S. 0.00.055/3; the grinding of the surfaces is allowed providing not to exceed an under size of 1 mm (.0394"), equalized on both faces, i.e. .5 mm (.0197") each face; disc wear limit: front 10 mm (.394"); rear 8.5 mm (.335") thick.

Inspection specifications after regrinding of disc surfaces:

- Max. out of parallelism with disc mounting plane: .05 mm (.0020");
- Max. out of flat: .025 mm (.0010") and max. difference in thickness: .038 mm (.0015") as measured along any radial line;
- Max. out of flat: .025 mm (.0010") and max. difference in thickness: .015 mm (.0006") as measured along any circular line;
- The surface should show no sign of scoring or porosity.

The surface roughness should be:

- 26 microinches as measured circularly;
- 36 microinches as measured radially.

Friction pads

	Front	Rear
Thickness when new	15 mm (.590")	
Wear limit	7 mm (.275")	

Calipers

On replacement of disc or caliper, measure the running clearance between caliper and disc on each side; the difference should not exceed .5 mm (.0197").

To centralize the caliper about the disc, insert shims between caliper and mounting flange as required.

Hand brake

It is mechanically operated and acts on the rear wheels through suitable shoes which spread apart against a drum machined in the disc casting.

For a brief description of repair and maintenance instructions refer to:

ATE DISC BRAKES - Publication no. 1202

Note - When reassembling the operating levers, a slight quantity of grease AGIP F.1 Gr SM or SHELL Retinax AM is to be applied to the pivot points and rubbing surfaces of levers.

DISTANCE OF LOWER WISHBONE OF FRONT SUSPENSION FROM A REFERENCE LEVEL

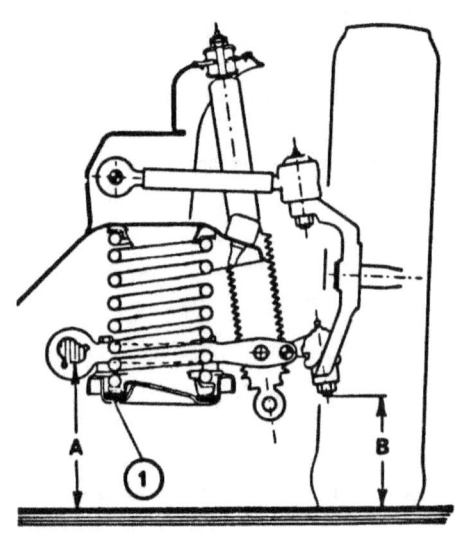

A - B = 34 ± 5 mm (1.34 ± .2")

Dimension "A" must be measured in correspondence of the lower line of wishbone shaft as shown.

To adjust, add shims in "1".

Shims are available in the following thicknesses:

3.5 mm (.14") - 7 mm (.28") - 10.5 mm (.42")

DISTANCE OF REAR AXLE FROM RUBBER BUFFERS

C = 36 ± 5 mm (1.42 ± .2")

N o t e - To adjust, remove the seat "3" and add shims in "2" as shown.

Shims are available in the following ticknesses:

6.5 mm (.26")
11.5 mm (.45")
16.5 mm (.65")
21.5 mm (.85")

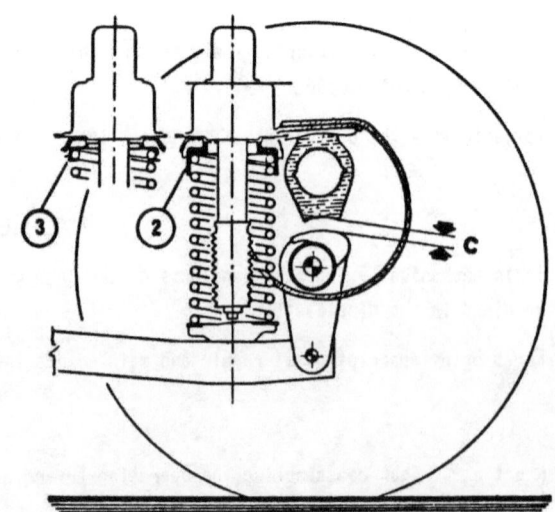

In the condition as specified check the wheel angles.

FRONT WHEEL CAMBER

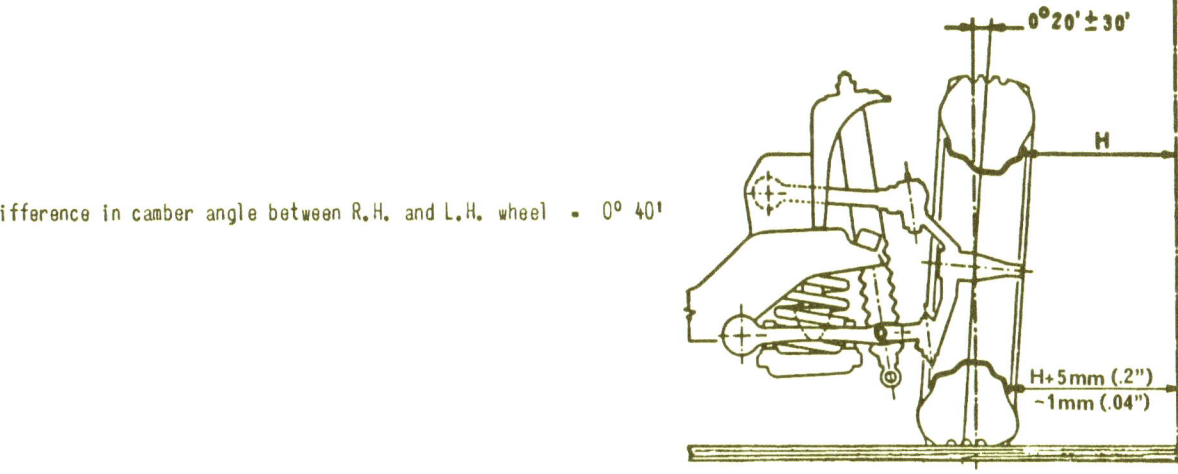

Difference in camber angle between R.H. and L.H. wheel = 0° 40'

N o t e - Not adjustable. Check the chassis and suspension arms if necessary.

FRONT WHEEL TOE-IN

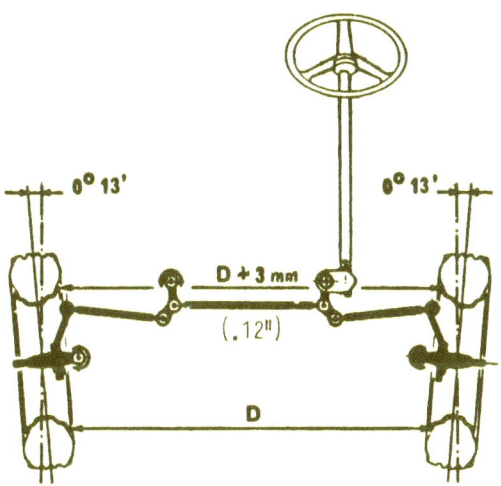

Rod length:

    side . . . . 264 to 280 mm (10.4 to 11")
    track . . . . 530 to 550 mm (20.86 to 21.65")

With the toe-in as specified, the length of rods as measured between ball joint centers should fall within the limits shown. If these values cannot be restored, the cause will probably be attributable to distortion of the body resulting from a collision.

Variants from chassis no.	1029001 (L.H.D.)
	765001 (R.H.D.)

PRINCIPAL CHARACTERISTIC DATA

Wheel track
- front (with 165 x 14 tyres) .... 1314 mm (51.7 in.)
- rear (with 165 x 14 tyres) .... 1264 mm (49.7 in.)

Overall length .... 4160 mm (164 in.)

TYRES - Inflation pressure (when cold) - Kg/cm^2

		Front	Rear
155 x 15	Ceat Drive D 1 - Pirelli cinturato S	1.6 * / 1.8 **	1.7 * / 2.1 **
	Michelin ZX	1.6 * / 1.7 **	1.7 * / 2 **
	Kleber Colombes V 10 GT	1.6 * / 1.9 **	1.7 * / 2.2 **
165 x 14	Ceat Drive D 2 - Continental - Pirelli cinturato SR (under all conditions)	1.5	1.6
	Michelin ZX (under all conditions)	1.7	1.8
	Kleber Colombes V 10	1.7 * / 1.9 **	2 * / 2.2 **

* With reduced load and touring riding
** With full load and top range of speed

REFILLINGS

Steering box
- Burman .... 0.360 kg
- ZF .... 0.120 kg

BULB'S WATTAGE

Headlamps	45/40 asymmetric
Tail parking and stop lights	5/21
Front direction indicators	21
Tail direction indicators	21
Reversing light	21
Front parking light	5 globular
Number plate light	5 globular
Ceiling light	5 cylindrical
Boot light	5 cylindrical
Side direction indicators	3 tubular
Instrument light	3 tubular
Tell-tale for direction indicators	3 tubular
Tell-tale for generator	3 tubular
Tell-tale for blower	3 tubular
Tell-tale for parking lights	3 tubular
Tell-tale for high beams	3 tubular
Tell-tale for fuel reserve	3 tubular

TIGHTENING TORQUE SPECIFICATIONS

Bolts joining gearbox output shaft yoke to prop shaft yoke	5.5 to 5.7 Kgm
Oil drain plug on sump bottom	7 to 8 Kgm
Plug on oil filter	3.5 to 4 Kgm

Rear frame

Bolts joining flanges of front shaft and sliding yoke	3.2 to 3.5 Kgm
Bolts joining differential yoke to prop. shaft yoke	3.2 to 3.5 Kgm
Nut attaching the joining flange to front shaft	9 to 11 Kgm

CLUTCH

The clutch is of the hydraulically-operated single plate dry type. The clutch pedal acts on a master cylinder supplied with the same type of fluid as the brake system.

When the clutch pedal is depressed, the fluid under pressure actuates the piston in the cylinder "4" connected to the clutch disengagement lever "5".

The pressure plate is controlled by means of diaphragm spring "6".

The clutch pedal free travel "A" should be about 30 - 32 mm. When owing to wear on the clutch disc facing, the pedal free travel is reduced to 17 - 19 mm the free travel must be restored.

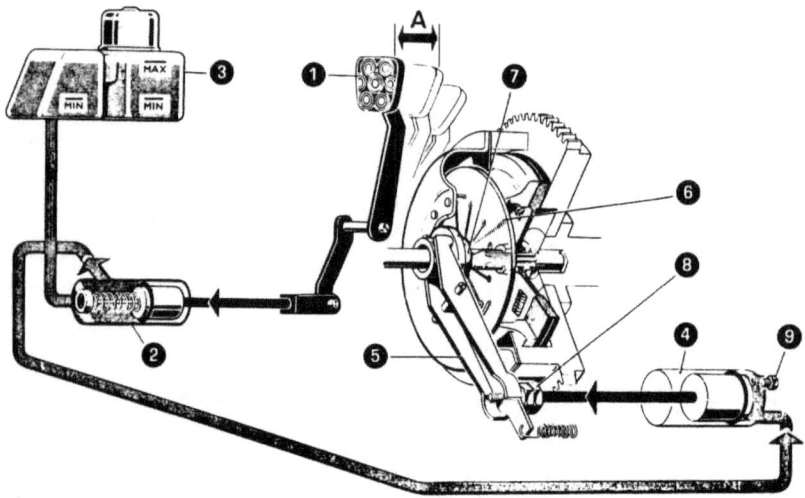

A Pedal free travel
B Disengagement lever free travel

1 Pedal
2 Master cylinder
3 Clutch & brake fluid reservoir
4 Slave cylinder
5 Disengagement lever
6 Diaphragm spring
7 Throwout bearing
8 Adjusting nuts
9 Air bleed screw

Adjustment

Measure with a rule the free travel "B" at the end of push rod of cylinder "4" depressing the clutch pedal until the throwout bearing "7" contacts the spring "6"; the travel "B" should be about 2 - 2.5 mm.

If the travel is shorter, act on the adjusting nut "8".

At the same time make sure that, by pressing the pedal as far as it will go, the push rod can move through a total travel of 13.5 - 14.2 mm. If any component of the system has been removed, thoroughly bleed the circuit. To check as specified use special tool no. C.6.0146 (see Tool Bulletin no. 135).

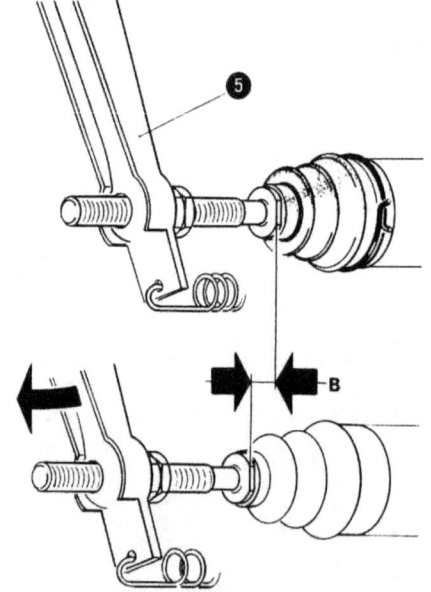

Inspection specifications

Wear limit of driven plate thickness . . . . 6.5 mm
Squareness of driven plate as mounted on gearbox output
  shaft . . . . 0.50 mm

GEARBOX

Calibration of striking rod ball springs
  free length . . . . 35.8 mm
  length under test load . . . . 17.2 mm
  test load . . . . 7.680 to 8.320 mm

BRAKE SYSTEM

The ATE brake system consists of four caliper type disc brakes operated by an assisted master cylinder. The friction pads of the front and rear brakes are directly actuated by the cylinders integral with the calipers.
The brakes are self-adjusting.
A pressure regulator controls the braking power to rear brakes. Such a regulator shall not be tampered with; specifically do not attempt to act on the adjusting nut as it is factory sealed.

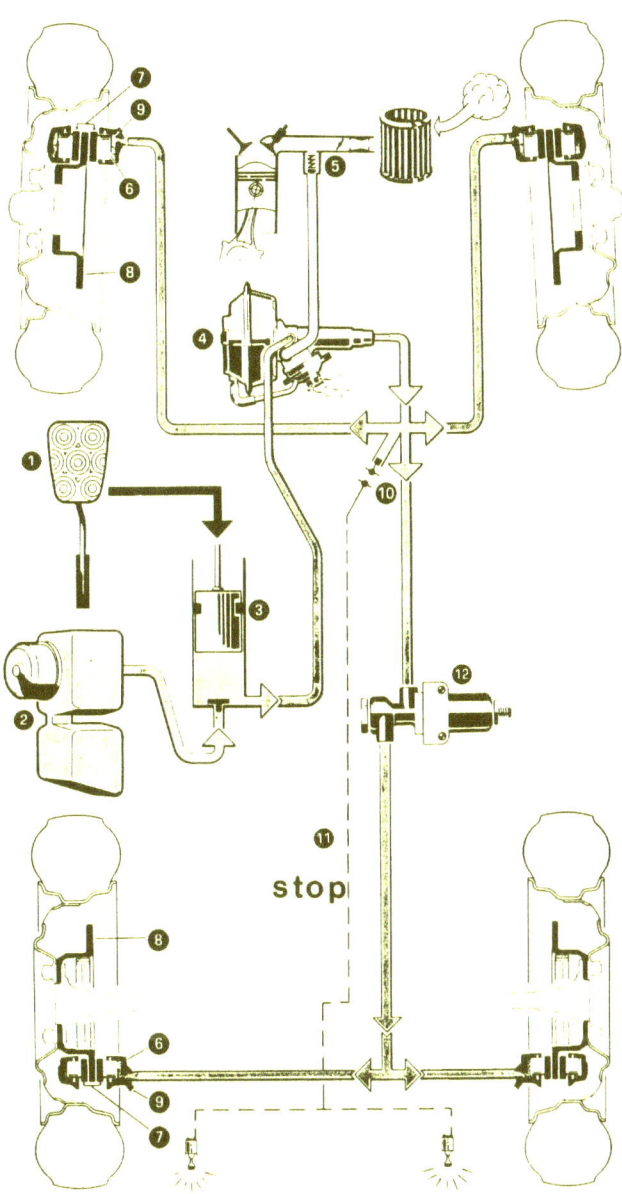

1 Brake pedal
2 Reservoir
3 Master cylinder
4 Vacuum servo
5 Vacuum connection
6 Pistons
7 Friction pads
8 Discs
9 Bleed screws
10 Stop light switch
11 Stop light cable
12 Pressure regulator

CASTER ANGLE: $\alpha = 1° \; 30' \pm 30'$

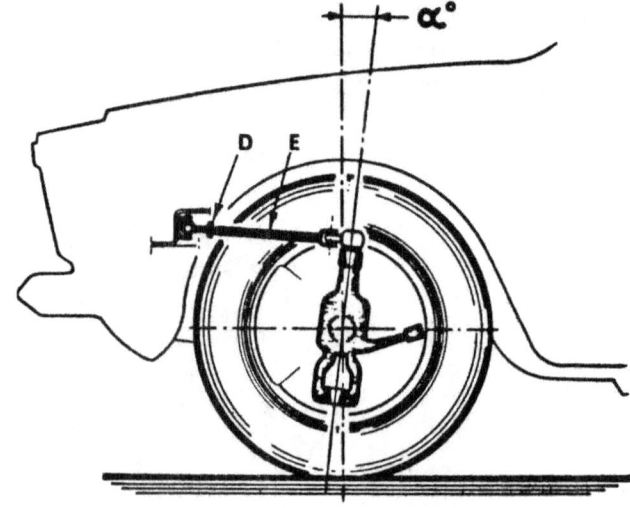

The difference in caster angle between R.H. and L.H. wheel must not exceed 0° 20'.

To adjust, loosen jam nut "D" and rotate rod "E".

Note - Small adjustments of the caster angle allow to correct slight drift tendency of the car.

N.B. - Before checking the caster angle shake the front end of car in order to allow the rubber bushing on the front slanting arm to set properly.

FRONT WHEEL CAMBER

Difference in camber angle between R.H. and L.H. wheel - 0° 40'

Note - Not adjustable. Check the chassis and suspension arms if necessary.

FRONT WHEEL TOE-IN (for L.H.D.)

Lock steering wheel in the central position i.e. with the spokes symmetrically disposed in relation to the vertical. Starting with the track rod "1" on the steering box side, place the corresponding wheel so that the toe-in is 1.5 mm. Measure the length thus obtained of the track rod and adjust the rod "2" on the other side to a length 5 mm shorter. Bring the first wheel to a 1.5 mm toe-in by adjusting the centre track rod "3".

$$A \begin{cases} \text{for 15" wheels} = 0° 13' \\ \text{for 14" wheels} = 0° 14' \end{cases}$$

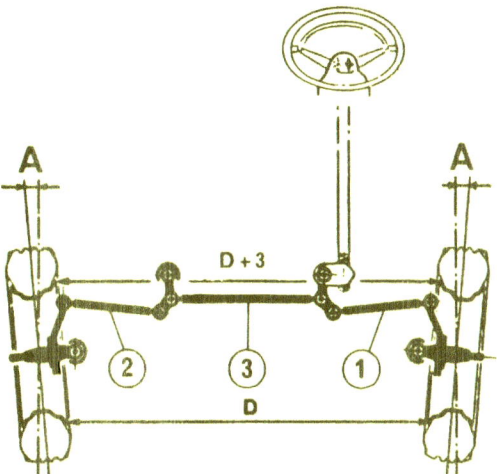

Rod length:

    side . . . . 264 to 280 mm

    track . . . . 530 to 550 mm

With the toe-in as specified, the length of rods as measured between ball joint centers should fall within the limits shown. If these values cannot be restored, the cause will probably be attributable to distortion of the body resulting from a collision.

Note - For R.H.D. the side rods maintain the same length (symmetrical adjustment).

NOTES

GIULIA 1600 cars

t. i.
spider
sprint

 alfa romeo

technical characteristics and principal inspection specifications

INDEX

TECHNICAL CHARACTERISTICS

PRINCIPAL CHARACTERISTIC DATA	Page 3
Performances	" 3
Tires	" 4
Refillings	" 4
Prescribed oils and lubricants	" 4
Carburetion	" 5
Valve timing	" 6
Ignition	" 6
Spark plugs	" 6
Electric system	" 7
Tightening torque specifications	" 8

PRINCIPAL CHECK-UP SPECIFICATIONS

Camshafts	Page 9
Valves and valve guides	" 9
Valve seats	" 9
Valve cups	" 10
Valve springs	" 10
Connecting rods	" 10
Piston pins	" 10
Pistons and cylinder barrels	" 11
Compression and oil scraper rings	" 11
Crankshaft	" 12
Clutch	" 13
Gearbox	" 13
Rear axle and suspension	" 14
Front suspension	" 15
Brakes	" 16
Wheel alignment	" 18

TECHNICAL CHARACTERISTICS

PRINCIPAL CHARACTERISTIC DATA

	T I	SPRINT	SPIDER
Number of cylinders	4	4	4
Bore	78 mm (3.072")	78 mm (3.072")	78 mm (3.072")
Stroke	82 mm (3.23")	82 mm (3.23")	82 mm (3.23")
Total cylinder capacity	1570 cc	1570 cc	1570 cc
Maximum power	92 CV (DIN) 104 HP (SAE) at 6000 r.p.m.	92 CV (DIN) 104 HP (SAE) at 6200 r.p.m.	92 CV (DIN) 104 HP (SAE) at 6200 r.p.m.
Front track	1310 mm (4'3")	1292 mm (4'2 7/8")	1292 mm (4'2 7/8")
Rear track	1270 mm (4'2")	1270 mm (4'2")	1270 mm (4'2")
Wheel base	2510 mm (8'2 7/8")	2380 mm (7'9 1/2")	2250 mm (7'4 1/2")
Minimum turning circle	10,900 mm (35'9")	11,000 mm (36'1")	11,000 mm (36'1")
Maximum length	4140 mm (13'7")	3980 mm (13'3/4")	3900 mm (12'9 5/8")
Maximum width	1560 mm (5'1 11/32")	1535 mm (5'3/8")	1580 mm (5'2 5/32")
Maximum height (empty weight)	1430 mm (4'8")	1320 mm (4'4")	1335 mm (4'4 3/4") (raised top)
Weight, empty, with tools and jack	1000 Kgs (2,204 lbs)	905 Kgs (2,000 lbs)	885 Kgs (1,870 lbs)
Number of seats	6	2 + 2	2
Tires 155 x 15	PIRELLI Cinturato S MICHELIN XA	PIRELLI Cinturato S MICHELIN XA	PIRELLI Cinturato S MICHELIN XA
Fuel consumption per 100 Km (62 miles) (Italian CUNA Standards)	10.4 lt 2.28 Imp. gals 2.74 U.S. gals	9.4 lt 1.97 Imp. gals 2.48 U.S. gals	8.8 lt 1.93 Imp. gals 2.32 U.S. gals

Performances after breaking in period - Maximum speeds.

Gear	T I Bevel drive 41 : 8		SPIDER-SPRINT Bevel drive 41 : 8	
	Km/h	mph	Km/h	mph
1st	40	25	41	26
2nd	66	41	69	43
3rd	97	60	102	63
4th	131	81	137	85
5th	165	103	172	107
Rev.	44	27	46	28

Tires
Inflation pressures (with tire cold)

TIRE	T I	
	Front wheels	Rear wheels
PIRELLI 155 x 15 Cinturato S MICHELIN 155 x 15 XA	1.6 to 1.8 Kg/cm² 22.7 to 25.6 psi	1.7 to 2.1 Kg/cm² 24.1 to 29.8 psi

- Inflate to the lower pressure for use with low load and short peaks in speed
- Inflate to the higher pressure for use with full load and maximum speeds.

TIRE		SPRINT-SPIDER			
		Front wheels		Rear wheels	
		Kg/cm²	psi	Kg/cm²	psi
PIRELLI 155 x 15 Cinturato S	Touring riding up to 160 Km/h (100 mph)	1.6	22.7	1.7	24.1
	Sport riding above 160 Km/h (100 mph)	1.7	24.1	1.8	25.6
	On track	2	28.4	2.1	29.8
MICHELIN 155 x 15 XA	Touring riding up to 160 Km/h (100 mph)	1.7	24.1	1.7	24.1
	Sport riding above 160 Km/h (100 mph)	1.9	27.0	1.9	27.0
	On track	2.1	29.8	2.1	29.8

Refillings

			IMP.	U.S.
Water (engine & radiator)		lts 7.5	1.65 gals	1.98 gals
Fuel (T I)		lts 46	10.1 gals	12.1 gals
Fuel (Sprint-Spider)		lts 53	11.7 gals	14.0 gals
Oil — Engine (pan & filter) to min. level (T I)		Kgs 3.25	3.2 qts	3.8 qts
Oil — Engine (pan & filter) to min. level (Sprint-Spider)		Kgs 3.70	3.6 qts	4.3 qts
Oil — Engine to max. level		Kgs 5.75	5.7 qts	6.8 qts
Oil — Gearbox		Kgs 1.650	3.2 pints	3.8 pints
Oil — Rear axle		Kgs 1.250	2.5 pints	3.0 pints
Oil — Steering box		Kgs 0.250	.5 pint	.6 pint

Prescribed oils and lubricants

Part	API - NLGI - SAE number	Recommended commercial equivalents
Engine	SAE 20 W 40 API MS	BP Energol Visco-Static Shell X-100 20 W 40
Gearbox	SAE 90	BP Energol Gear Oil SAE 90 Shell Dentax 90
Steering box and rear axle	SAE 90 API EP	BP Energol Gear Oil SAE 90 EP Shell Spirax 90 EP
*Front suspension arm ball joints *Front suspension arm pins Propeller shaft universal joints *Steering linkage joints	NLGI 1	BP Energrease A 1 BP Energrease A 0 Shell Retinax G Darina Grease A X
Front wheel bearings	NLGI 2/3	BP Energrease L 3 Shell Alvania Grease 3
Brake fluid reservoir	SAE 70 R 3	BP Energol brake Fluid (green) Shell Donax B 70 R 3 (red)

(*) For Sprint and Spider models only.

Carburetion

T I : Solex 32 PAIA 7 Carburetor

	1st barrel	2nd barrel
Choke tube (Venturi)	23	23
Main jet	125	130
Main air gauger	190	190
Idler jet	45	70
Idling air gauger	100	60

Acceleration pump jet = 45
Starter jet = 120
Inlet valve of acceleration pump = 40
Starter air gauger = 500
Needle seat diameter = 1.75 mm (.069")
Spacer under needle-seat = 1 mm (.039")
Distance of fuel level from bottom of float chamber = 12 mm (.47") (with a pressure of 2 mts (6'6") H_2O upstream the needle-seat)
Delivery of acceleration pump = 4 to 6 cc for every 20 pump strokes
Clogging pressure measured upstream the needle seat = 6 to 7 mts (19'8" to 23') H_2O
Weight of float = 7.2 grammes
Minimum engine RPM = 500 to 600

SPIDER - SPRINT : 32 PAIA 5 Solex Carburetor

	1st barrel	2nd barrel
Choke tube	23	23
Main jet	125	135
Main air gauger	220	200
Idler jet	45	70
Idling air gauger	100	60

Acceleration pump jet = 45
Starter jet = 120
Starter air gauger = 500
Inlet valve of acceleration pump = 40
Needle-seat diameter = 1.75 mm (.069")
Spacer under needle seat = 1 mm (.039")
Distance of fuel level from bottom of float chamber = 12 mm (.47") (with a pressure of 2 mts (6'6") H_2O upstream the needle-seat)
Delivery of acceleration pump = 4 to 6 cc every 20 pump strokes
Clogging pressure measured upward the needle seat = 6 to 7 mts (19'8" to 23') H_2O
Weight of float = 7.2 grammes
Minimum engine RPM = 500 to 600

N.B.: For the adjustment of carburetors see the instructions given in the "Instruction Books" Giulia 1600 T.I. and Giulia 1600 Sprint and Spider.

Valve Timing

T I - SPIDER - SPRINT

Checking of valve opening-and-closing angles

Clearance (with cold engine) between the unlobed profile of cam of camshaft and the cup ceiling:

- inlet .... = .475 to .500 mm (.0187 to .0197")
- exhaust .... = .525 to .550 mm (.0206 to .0216")

Opening of inlet valve:
- linear displacement of cup .... = .20 mm (.008")
- corresponding to angle value .... before T D C = 6°

Closing of inlet valve:
- linear displacement of cup .... = .20 mm (.008")
- corresponding to angle value .... after B D C = 54°

Opening of exhaust valve:
- linear displacement of cup .... = .15 mm (.006")
- corresponding to angle value .... before B D C = 54°

Closing of exhaust valve:
- linear displacement of cup .... = .15 mm (.006")
- corresponding to angle value .... after T D C = 6°

Angle values of the actual diagram of valve timing system with cold engine (clockwise rotation direction of the crankshaft seen from the front side):

- opening of inlet valve .... before T D C = 24° 40'
- closing of inlet valve .... after B D C = 72° 40'

- opening of exhaust valve .... before B D C = 66°
- closing of exhaust valve .... after T D C = 18°

- inlet stroke .... = 277° 20'
- exhaust stroke .... = 264°

Ignition

T I - SPIDER - SPRINT

Firing order = 1 - 3 - 4 - 2 (No 1 cylinder is that at the fan side)
Opening of contact points of ignition distributor = .35 to .40 mm (.014 to .016")

Values of advance of ignition distributor

Fixed advance F Before T D C	Maximum Advance M Before T D C
3° ± 2°	43° ± 3° at 5000 rpm

Spark plugs

Lodge 2HLN

Electrode gap = .55 to .65 mm (.022 to .025")

Electric system

Units	T I	Sprint - Spider
Electric system	12 Volts	
Battery	40 Amp. hours	50 Amp. hours
Generator	Bosch LJ/GEG 200/12/2700 R. 32 mr	
Voltage regulator	Bosch RS/VA 200/12 A 2	
Starting motor	Bosch AL/EEF .7/12 R 11	
Coil	Bosch TK 12 A 3	
Ignition distributor	Bosch VJU 4 BR 41 mk	
Windshield wiper	TGE 93 A Marelli	DR 2 Lucas

Power in watts of the electric system bulbs

	T I	Sprint - Spider
Inner headlights (high beams)	40 x 45	45 x 40
Outer headlights (low beams)	40 x 45	
Front parking lights	5	5
Front lights - direction indicators	20	20
Side lights - direction indicators	2.5	2.5
Rear lights - parking & stop	5 x 20	5 x 20
Rear lights - direction indicators	20	20
Reserve light	20	20
License plate light	5	5
Inspection light	10	10
Engine compartment light	5	5 (Sprint only)
Dome light inside the car	5	5 (Sprint only)
Light in luggage compartment	5	-
Lighting on instrument panel	3	3
Tell-tale for parking lights	3	3
Tell-tale for direction indicators	3	3
Tell-tale for generator	3	3
Tell-tale for choke control	-	3 (Sprint only)
Tell-tale for gasoline supply	3	3
Tell-tale for heaters	3	3
Tell-tale for headlights	-	3

Tightening torque specifications

	Kgm	ft.-lbs	Manner of tightening
Nuts of cylinder head — after repairing, when cold ...	6.2 to 6.4	44.8 to 46.3	Slacken and retighten without lubricating
Nuts of cylinder head — when hot	6.6 to 6.7	47.7 to 48.4	Lock without slackening the nut
After 500 Km (300 mi.) from replacement of gasket, when cold	6.2 to 6.4	44.8 to 46.3	Slacken a 1/4 turn and retighten
Nuts of the camshaft caps	2 to 2.25	14.5 to 16.3	in oil
Nuts of main bearing caps	4 to 4.2	29 to 30.3	in oil
Nuts of the connecting rod caps	5 to 5.3	36.2 to 38.3	in oil
Spark plugs	2.5 to 3.5	18.1 to 25.3	With graphite grease, when cold
Nuts flywheel on crankshaft	4.2 to 4.5	30.4 to 32.5	in oil
Nut of gearbox main shaft	12	86.8	dry
Nuts of gearbox layshaft	8	58	dry
Screws to secure ring gear to differential case	4.5 to 5	32.6 to 36.1	dry
Ring nut securing yoke on bevel drive pinion shaft	8 to 14	58 to 101.2	dry
Nuts to secure steering levers to knuckles	4.5 to 5.8	32.6 to 41.9	dry
Screws to secure brake shoe backplates to knuckles	4.5 to 5.8	32.6 to 41.9	dry
Screws to secure brake shoe backplates to rear axle	4.5 to 5.8	32.6 to 41.9	dry
Nuts to secure rear axle reaction trunnion body (T.I.) ...	4.2 to 4.7	30.4 to 33.9	dry

PRINCIPAL CHECK-UP SPECIFICATIONS

Camshafts

Diameter of journals	= 26.959 to 26.980 mm (1.0614 to 1.0622")
Diameter of journal bearings	= 27.000 to 27.033 mm (1.0630 to 1.0642")
Radial clearance between journals and bearings	= .020 to .074 mm (.0008 to .0029")
End play of camshaft in thrust bearing	= .065 to .182 mm (.0026 to .0071")

Valves and valve guides

		intake	exhaust	
		SANTAMBROGIO	SANTAMBROGIO	A T E
Valves	Diameter of valve poppet	41.0 to 41.15 mm (1.614 to 1.620")	37.0 to 37.15 mm (1.4567 to 1.4625")	37.0 to 37.2 mm (1.4567 to 1.4645")
	Diameter of valve stem	8.96 to 8.987 mm (.3527 to .3538")	8.935 to 8.960 mm (.3518 to .3527")	8.935 to 8.960 mm (.3518 to .3527")
	Total length	106.63 to 107.03 mm (4.1981 to 4.2137")	105.90 to 106.30 mm (4.1693 to 4.1850")	106.05 to 106.15 mm (4.1753 to 4.1791")

N.B. - The Santambrogio - ATE exhaust valves are alternate supply

Valve guide — Outside diameter with guide removed	=	14.033 to 14.044 mm (.5528 to .5529")
Valve guide — Inside diameter with guide assembled in cylinder head	=	9.000 to 9.015 mm (.3544 to .3549")
Clearance between guide assembled in cylinder head and valve stem — intake	=	.013 to .053 mm (.0005 to .0020")
Clearance between guide assembled in cylinder head and valve stem — exhaust	=	.040 to .080 mm (.0016 to .0031")
Diameter of valve guide seat on cylinder head	=	14.000 to 14.018 mm (.5512 to .5518")
Interference between seat and valve guide	=	.015 to .044 mm (.0006 to .0017")

Valve seats

		intake	exhaust
Outer diameter of the valve seat	normal	42.597 to 42.648 mm (1.6771 to 1.6790")	38.597 to 38.648 mm (1.5196 to 1.5215")
	oversized	42.897 to 42.948 mm (1.6889 to 1.6908")	38.897 to 38.948 mm (1.5314 to 1.5333")
Diameter of housing in the cylinder head for valve seat	normal	42.472 to 42.497 mm (1.6722 to 1.6731")	38.472 to 38.497 mm (1.5147 to 1.5156")
	oversized	42.772 to 42.797 mm (1.6840 to 1.6849")	38.772 to 38.797 mm (1.5265 to 1.5274")

Interference between valve seat and housing in cylinder heads = .100 to .176 mm / .0039 to .0069"

Valve cups

Diameter of cup	normal =	34.973 to 34.989 mm (1.3773 to 1.3775")
	oversized =	35.173 to 35.189 mm (1.3848 to 1.3853")
Diameter of cup seat in cylinder head	normal =	35.000 to 35.025 mm (1.3779 to 1.3789")
	oversized =	35.200 to 35.225 mm (1.3859 to 1.3868")
Clearance between seat and cup	=	.011 to .052 mm (.0005 to .0020")

Valve springs

	Free length	Length under test load	Test load
Inner spring	46.5 mm (1.83")	26 mm (1.02")	21.20 to 23.16 Kgs (46.7 to 51.1 lbs)
Outer spring	51.3 mm (2.02")	27.5 mm (1.08")	35.6 to 37.1 Kgs (78.5 to 81.8 lbs)

Connecting rods

Length between center line of big end and center line of small end of connecting rod	=	147.955 to 148.045 mm (5.8250 to 5.8285")
Inner diameter of the big end of connecting rod	=	53.695 to 53.708 mm (2.1140 to 2.1144")
Inner diameter of bushing in the small end of rod	=	22.005 to 22.015 mm (.8664 to .8667")
End play of the connecting rods on the pins of crankshaft	=	.200 to .300 mm (.0079 to .0118")
Thickness of connecting rod bearings	standard =	1.829 to 1.835 mm (.0720 to .0722")
	1st oversize =	1.956 to 1.962 mm (.0770 to .0772")
	2nd oversize =	2.083 to 2.089 mm (.0820 to .0824")
Radial clearance between crankshaft pins and bearings for big end of connecting rod	=	.025 to .063 mm (.0010 to .0024")
Maximum out of parallelism between center line of big end hole and center line of small end hole measured on a distance of 100 mm (3.94")	=	.05 mm (.0019")

	Black color	White color
Piston pin-to-small end hole clearance	.008 to .021 mm (.0003 to .0008")	.005 to .017 mm (.0002 to .0007")

Pin and hole in piston

O.D. of pin	Black color =	21.994 to 21.997 mm (.86590 to .86602")
	White color =	21.998 to 22.000 mm (.86606 to .86614")

		Black color	White color
I.D. of hole in	Borgo piston	22.000 to 22.002 mm (.86614 to .86621")	22.003 to 22.005 mm (.86626 to .86633")
	Mahle piston	21.996 to 22.002 mm (.86599 to .86621")	

		Black color	White color
Pin-to-hole clearance	Borgo piston	.003 to .008 mm (.00012 to .00030")	.003 to .007 mm (.00012 to .00027")
	Mahle piston	.001 to .008 mm (.00004 to .00030")	.004* to .004 mm (.00015* to .00015")

(*) interference fit

Pistons and cylinder barrels

Diameter of pistons to be measured to square with the hole for piston pin and at a distance of 12 mm (.472") from the lower border of skirt for Borgo piston and 11 mm (.433") for Mahle piston.

BORGO Piston

	Class A (BLUE)	Class B (PINK)	Class C (GREEN)
Normal	77.920 to 77.930 mm (3.0677 to 3.0681")	77.930 to 77.940 mm (3.0681 to 3.0685")	77.940 to 77.950 mm (3.0686 to 3.0688")

MAHLE Piston

	Class A (BLUE)	Class B (PINK)	Class C (GREEN)
Normal	77.945 to 77.955 mm (3.0687 to 3.0690")	77.955 to 77.965 mm (3.0691 to 3.0694")	77.965 to 77.975 mm (3.0694 to 3.0698")

Cylinder barrels

	Class A (BLUE)	Class B (PINK)	Class C (GREEN)
Normal	77.985 to 77.994 mm (3.0703 to 3.0706")	77.995 to 78.004 mm (3.0707 to 3.0710")	78.005 to 78.014 mm (3.0711 to 3.0714")

Clearance between cylinder barrel and piston
- with Borgo piston . . . = .055 to .074 mm (.0022 to .0029")
- with Mahle piston . . . = .030 to .049 mm (.0012 to .0019")

Projection of barrels from cylinder block . . . . = .000 to .060 mm (.0000 to .0024")

Compression and oil scraper rings

Height of grooves in piston for compression rings
- normal . . . . = 1.775 to 1.790 mm (.0699 to .0704")
- chromium-plated . . . = 1.785 to 1.800 mm (.0703 to .0708")

Height of groove in piston for oil scraper ring . . . . = 4.015 to 4.030 mm (.1581 to .1586")

Thickness of compression rings . . . . = 1.728 to 1.740 mm (.0681 to .0685")

Thickness of oil scraper ring . . . . = 3.978 to 3.990 mm (.1567 to .1571")

End play of rings in grooves
- compression rings
  - normal . . . . = .035 to .062 mm (.0014 to .0024")
  - chromium-plated . . . = .045 to .072 mm (.0018 to .0028")
- oil scraper rings . . . . = .025 to .052 mm (.0010 to .0020")

Gap of rings to be inspected in ring gauge or in cylinder barrels . . . . = .300 to .450 mm (.0012 to .0017")

Crankshaft

Diameter of main journals	Normal	= 59.960 to 59.973 mm (2.3606 to 2.3611")
	1st undersize	= 59.706 to 59.719 mm (2.3506 to 2.3511")
	2nd undersize	= 59.452 to 59.465 mm (2.3407 to 2.3411")
Diameter of connecting rod pins	Normal	= 49.987 to 50.000 mm (1.9680 to 1.9685")
	1st undersize	= 49.733 to 49.746 mm (1.9581 to 1.9585")
	2nd undersize	= 49.479 to 49.492 mm (1.9480 to 1.9485")
Thickness of main bearings	Normal	= 1.829 to 1.835 mm (.0720 to .0722")
	1st oversize	= 1.956 to 1.962 mm (.0770 to .0772")
	2nd oversize	= 2.083 to 2.089 mm (.0820 to .0822")
Diameter of seat for main bearings in crankcas	....	= 63.657 to 63.676 mm (2.5062 to 2.5069")
Lenght of central journal	Normal	= 30.000 to 30.035 mm (1.1811 to 1.1824")
	1st oversize	= 30.127 to 30.162 mm (1.1861 to 1.1874")
	2nd oversize	= 30.254 to 30.289 mm (1.1911 to 1.1924")
Thickness of thrust rings for central journal	Normal	= 2.311 to 2.362 mm (.0910 to .0929")
	1st oversize	= 2.374 to 2.425 mm (.0935 to .0954")
	2nd oversize	= 2.438 to 2.489 mm (.0960 to .0980")
End play of crankshaft		= .076 to .263 mm (.003 to .010")
Diametrical play between journals and main bearings		= .014 to .058 mm (.0005 to .0022")
Fillet radii	main journals	= 1.7 to 2.1 mm (.069 to .082")
	pins of connecting rods	= 1.7 to 2.1 mm (.069 to .082")
	pin on flywheel side	= 3.7 to 4.1 mm (.146 to .161")
Maximum elongation of main journals and connecting rod pins		= .007 mm (.00027")
Maximum taper of main journals and connecting rod pins measured on their full length		= .01 mm (.00039")
Maximum error of parallelism of main journals and connecting rod pins measured on their full length		= .015 mm (.00059")
Maximum misalignment allowed between main journals		= .01 mm (.00039")

Clutch

Pedal free travel	23 mm (.9")
Distance between the fingers of the clutch toggle arms and the reference sleeve of tool 6123.28.026	1 mm (.039")
Squareness of the clutch driven plate assembled on the direct drive shaft of gear shift	.50 mm (.020")
Driven plate inner diameter	129 to 131 mm (5.08 to 5.15")
Driven plate outer diameter	199 to 201 mm (7.84 to 7.91")
Driven plate thickness — with new facing — free	9.8 to 10.1 mm (.385 to .397")
Driven plate thickness — with new facing — engaged	9.1 to 9.4 mm (.358 to .370")
Driven plate thickness — wear limit	6 mm (.236")

Gearbox

Transmission ratios — 1st gear	3.304 : 1
Transmission ratios — 2nd gear	1.988 : 1
Transmission ratios — 3rd gear	1.355 : 1
Transmission ratios — 4th gear	1.000 : 1
Transmission ratios — 5th gear	.791 : 1
Transmission ratios — Reverse Gear	3.010 : 1
Maximum eccentricity of main shaft	.05 mm (.020")
End play between forks and sleeves — of assembly	.25 to .50 mm (.010 to .020")
End play between forks and sleeves — limit of wear	.7 mm (.027")
Calibration of springs for selector rod balls — free length	15.2 mm (.600")
Calibration of springs for selector rod balls — length under load	10 mm (.390")
Calibration of springs for selector rod balls — check load	4.67 to 5.05 Kgs (10.30 to 11.13 lbs)
Maximum end play of the main shaft gears — for 1st speed gear	.24 mm (.009")
Maximum end play of the main shaft gears — for 2nd speed gear	.21 mm (.008")
Maximum end play of the main shaft gears — for 3rd speed gear	.21 mm (.008")
Distance between outer planes of the engaging teeth of 3rd and 4th gears	42 to 42.2 mm (1.65 to 1.66")
Distance of the rear band (on propeller shaft side) of synchronizer sleeve of the 5th gear, in position of "neutral", from rear plane of engaging teeth of driven gear	12.5 mm (.492")

Rear axle and suspension

Transmission-axle overall ratios-with bevel drive 41 : 8 ....
- 1st gear = 16.933 : 1
- 2nd gear = 10.188 : 1
- 3rd gear = 6.944 : 1
- 4th gear = 5.125 : 1
- 5th gear = 4.054 : 1
- Rev... = 15.426 : 1

Maximum eccentricity of axle shaft .... = .10 mm (.0039")

Clearance between teeth of planetary gears .... = .05 mm (.002")

Clearance between teeth of bevel drive gears .... = .05 to .10 mm (.002 to .004")

Checking of shock absorbers on test bench

Calibration data (when cold)

	T I		SPRINT - SPIDER	
	Extension	Compression	Extension	Compression
High speed	135 to 165 Kgs (298 to 363 lbs)	50 to 65 Kgs (110 to 143 lbs)	137 to 171.5 Kgs (302 to 378 lbs)	45 to 59.5 Kgs (99 to 131 lbs)
Low speed	19 to 30 Kgs (42 to 66 lbs)	12 to 22 Kgs (27 to 48 lbs)	27 to 45.5 Kgs (59 to 100 lbs)	7 to 15.5 Kgs (15 to 34 lbs)

Checking of suspension springs

	T I	SPRINT	SPIDER
Free length	461 mm (18.15")	414 mm (16.30")	410 mm (16.10")
Length under static load	252 mm (9.9")	230 mm (9.0")	230 mm (9.0")
Test load	341.5 to 362.5 Kgs (753 to 799 lbs)	189.15 to 200.85 Kgs (417 to 442 lbs)	185.25 to 196.75 Kgs (408 to 433 lbs)

Front suspension

Pre-load of the bearings of wheel hub

	Kgmm	in. lbs	Weights to be placed in the proper holes of tool C.5.0109	
			Kgs	lbs
a) pre-load for assembly preparation	330	28.6	1.5	3.3
b) definitive pre-load of assembly	112	9.7	.5	1.1
c) test pre-load after functioning	62.5	5.4	.5	1.1
d) final pre-load of re-assembly	57.5	5.0	.5	1.1

Checking of suspension springs

	T I	SPIDER	SPRINT
Free length	310.5 mm (12.2")	394 mm (15.5")	394 mm (15.5")
Length under static load	200 mm (7.8")	267 mm (10.5")	267 mm (10.5")
Test load	896.20 to 952.80 Kgs (1976 to 2100 lbs)	490 to 520 Kgs (1080 to 1145 lbs)	490 to 520 Kgs (1080 to 1145 lbs)

Checking of shock absorbers on test bench

Calibration data (when cold)

	T I		SPRINT - SPIDER	
	Extension	Compression	Extension	Compression
High speed	150 to 182 Kgs (330 to 401 lbs)	55 to 70 Kgs (121 to 154 lbs)	137 to 172 Kgs (302 to 379 lbs)	45 to 59 Kgs (99 to 130 lbs)
Low speed	25 to 42 Kgs (55 to 92 lbs)	13 to 22 Kgs (28 to 48 lbs)	29 to 44 Kgs (64 to 97 lbs)	9 to 14 Kgs (20 to 30 lbs)

Brakes

Pedal travel adjustment

Before actuating the brake master cylinder, the brake pedal must be moved through a free travel corresponding to a master cylinder push rod stroke of 1-1.5 mm (.04 to .06").

Three-shoe front brakes

Brake drum specifications:
- Drum inside dia., when new = 266.7 to 266.8 mm (10.499 to 10.503")
- Max. grinding depth beyond new drum inside dia. = 1 mm (.04")
- Max. eccentricity = .045 mm (.0018")
- Max. elongation = .045 mm (.0018")
- Max. taper = .03 mm (.0012")
- Surface roughness = 40 to 60 microinches

Maximum diameter of lathing of brake shoes = 265.94 mm (10.470")

Calibration of brake shoe springs:
- free length = 137.35 mm (5.4")
- length under load = 151.1 mm (5.9")
- test load = 50 to 60 Kgs (110 to 132 lbs)

Values of the chamfer to be made on linings:
- A = 7 to 9 mm (.28 to .35")
- B = .5 mm (.02")

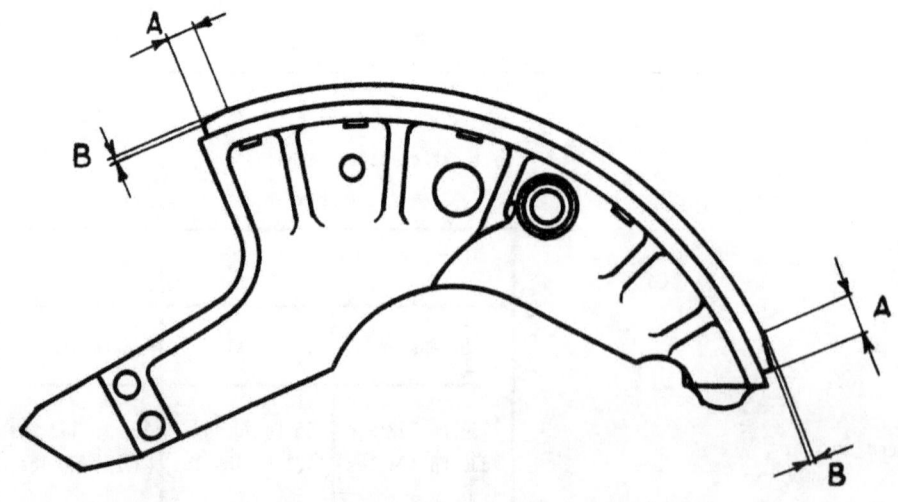

Two-shoe rear brakes

Brake drum specifications	Drum inside dia., when new	254 to 254.1 mm (10.000 to 10.004")
	Max. grinding depth beyond new drum inside dia.	1 mm (.04")
	Max. eccentricity	.045 mm (.0018")
	Max. elongation	.045 mm (.0018")
	Max. taper	.03 mm (.0012")
	Surface roughness	40 to 60 microinches

Max. diameter of lathing of brake shoes = 252.984 to 253.340 mm (9.960 to 9.974")

Calibration of brake shoe springs	free length	121.4 mm (4.78")
	length under load	134 mm (5.3")
	test load	18 Kgs (39.7 lbs)

Values of the chamfer to be made on linings	A =	6 to 7 mm (.24 to .27")
	B =	1.5 to 2 mm (.06 to .08")

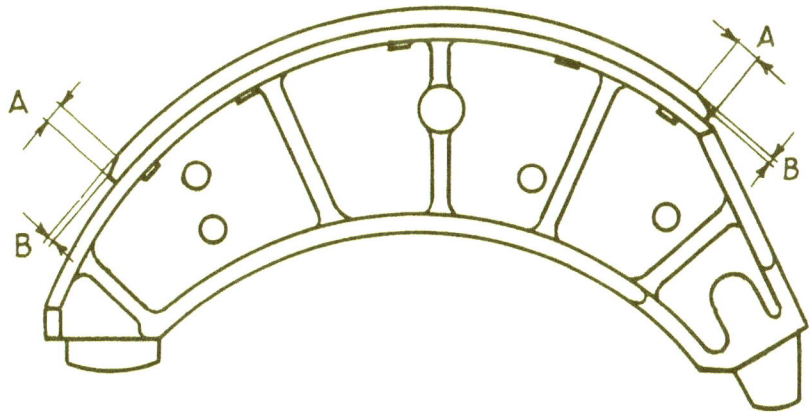

Wheel alignment

Conditions of load for checking the wheel alignment (with fuel tank full, spare wheel, complete equipment of tools)

SPRINT - SPIDER .... { 2 weights of 50 Kgs on front seats
{ 2 weights of 20 Kgs on flooring where feet rest

T I .... { front seats { 1 weight of 50 Kgs on each seat
{ 2 weights of 20 Kgs on flooring where feet rest
{ rear seats { 2 weights of 50 Kgs on seat
{ 2 weights of 20 Kgs on flooring where feet rest

50 Kgs = 110 lbs   20 Kgs = 44 lbs

Distance of front suspension lower arms from a reference level

T. I.

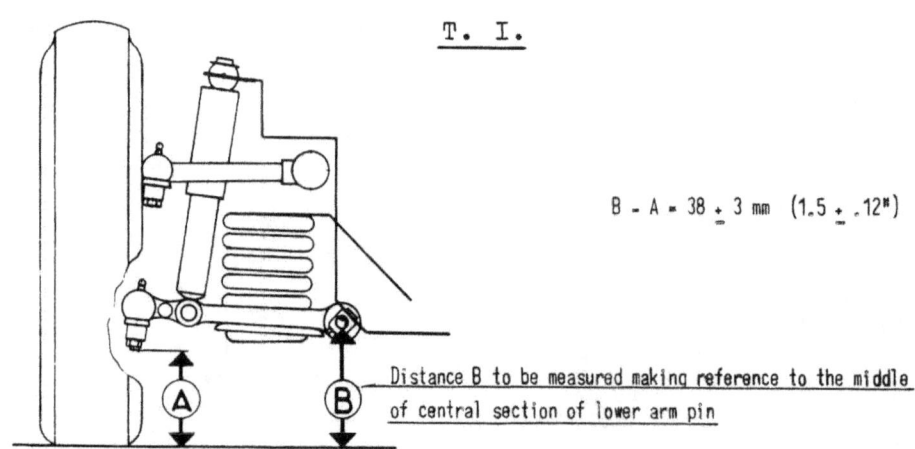

B - A = 38 ± 3 mm (1.5 ± .12")

Distance B to be measured making reference to the middle of central section of lower arm pin

SPRINT - SPIDER

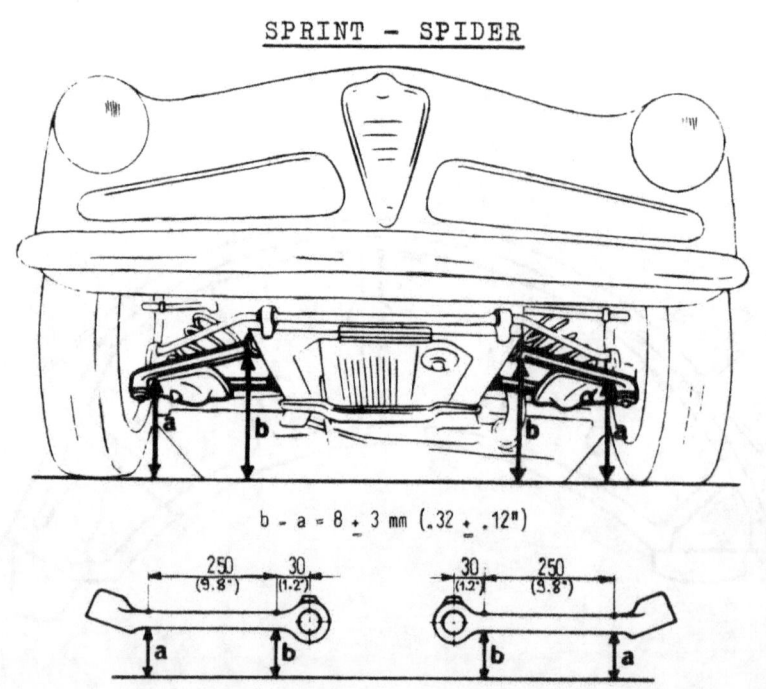

b - a = 8 ± 3 mm (.32 ± .12")

Clearance of rear axle from limit buffers

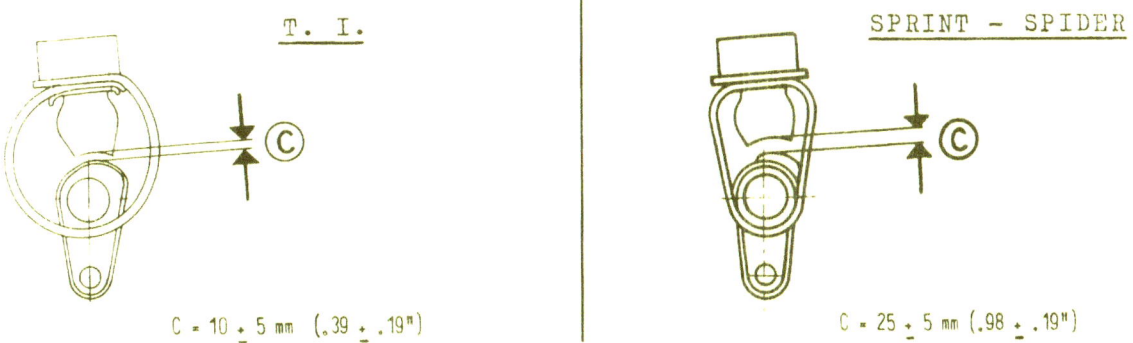

T. I.
C = 10 ± 5 mm (.39 ± .19")

SPRINT - SPIDER
C = 25 ± 5 mm (.98 ± .19")

King pin caster angle

T.I. .... 1°
SPRINT-SPIDER .... 40'   } Allowance .... ± 30'

Difference in caster angle between R.H. and L.H. king pins should never exceed 0°20'.

Adjustment of caster angle on T. I. model

The t.i. model is provided with a caster angle adjuster.
To perform this adjustment, loosen the lock nut and rotate the tie-rod properly.

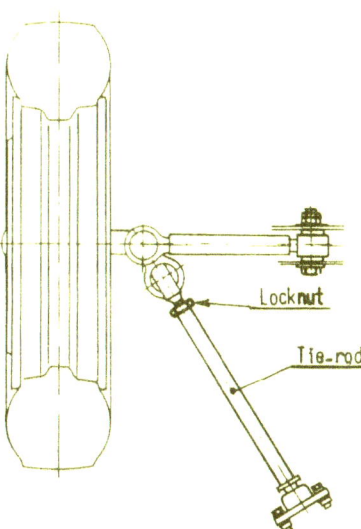

Locknut
Tie-rod

Inspection and adjustment must be performed on cars in the specified loading conditions and with shock absorbers detached from one end.

N.B. - Before checking the caster angle shake the front end of car in order to allow the silentblock on the front tie rod to bed down properly.

Front wheel camber

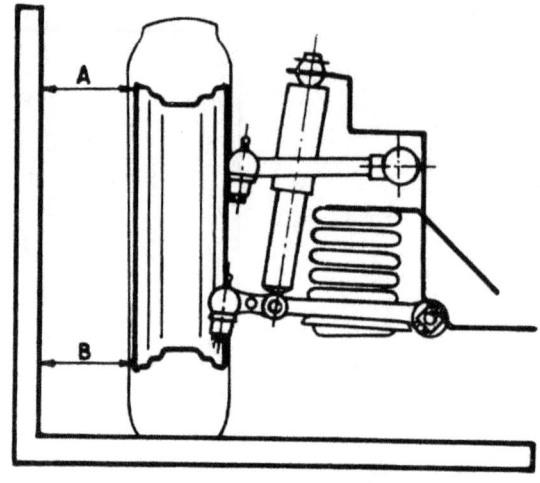

With the car loaded as prescribed the camber should be:

    TI . . . .   B = A + 5 (.19")
    SPRINT-SPIDER . . . . .   A = B

Front wheel toe-in

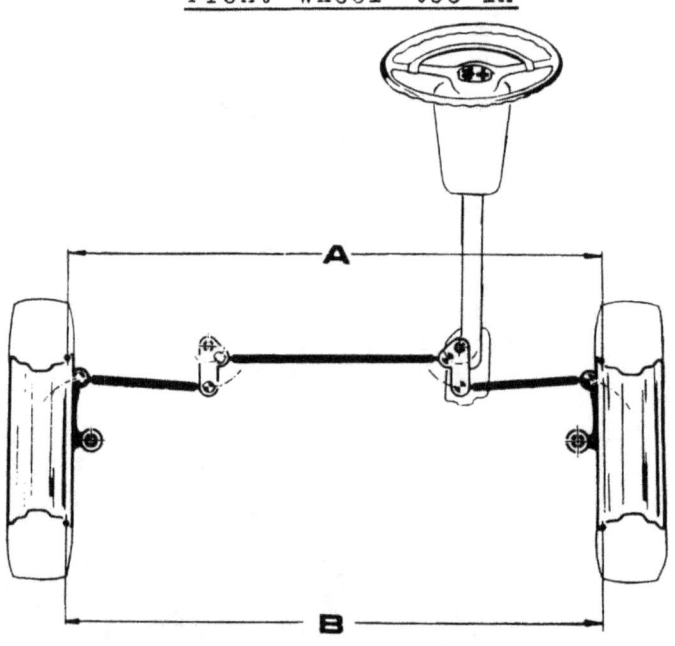

Between the inner edges of rims:

    A = B + 3 (.12")

Length of rods measured between the centers of joints:

TI . . . .
- lateral rods = 283 to 293 mm (11.2 to 11.5")
- track rod = 530 to 550 mm (20.9 to 21.6")

SPRINT-SPIDER . . . .
- lateral rods = 265 to 285 mm (10.5 to 11.2")
- track rod = 470 to 490 mm (18.5 to 19.3")

SPIDER 1600

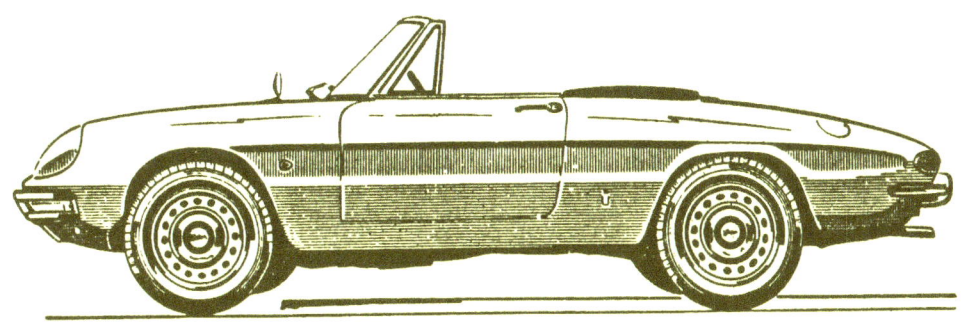

technical characteristics and principal inspection specifications

CONTENTS

TECHNICAL CHARACTERISTICS

PRINCIPAL CHARACTERISTIC DATA .... Page 3

- Performance .... » 3
- Tires .... » 4
- Refillings .... » 4
- Prescribed oils and lubricants .... » 4
- Carburetion .... » 5
- Idling adjustment .... » 5
- Float level adjustment .... » 6
- Valve timing .... » 7
- Electric system .... » 8
- Electric system bulb's wattage .... » 8
- Tightening torque specifications .... » 9

MAJOR INSPECTION SPECIFICATIONS

- Camshafts .... » 10
- Valves and valve guides .... » 10
- Valve seats .... » 10
- Valve cups .... » 11
- Valve springs .... » 11
- Connecting rods .... » 11
- Piston pin .... » 11
- Piston pin hole .... » 11
- Pistons and piston rings .... » 12
- Cylinder barrels .... » 12
- Crankshaft .... » 13
- Clutch .... » 14
- Gearbox .... » 14
- Rear axle and suspension .... » 15
- Front suspension .... » 16
- Brakes .... » 17

WHEEL ALIGNMENT

- Checking of wheel angles and car «trim» under static load .... » 18

TECHNICAL CHARACTERISTICS

PRINCIPAL CHARACTERISTIC DATA

Number of cylinders	4
Bore	78 mm (3.07")
Stroke	82 mm (3.23")
Total cylinder capacity	1570 cc
Max. power at 6,000 rpm	DIN 109 HP / SAE 125 HP
Front track	1310 mm 51.6"
Rear track	1270 mm 50.0"
Wheel base	2250 mm 88.6"
Min. turning circle	10500 mm 413.4"
Overall length	4250 mm 167.3"
Overall with	1630 mm 64.2"
Overall height (unladen)	1290 mm 50.8"
Dry weight	940 kg 2,072 lbs
Number of seats	2
Tires 155 × 15	PIRELLI cinturato S / MICHELIN XA
Fuel consumption per 100 Km. (CUNA standard)	10.5 lt (32.0 mpg G.B.) (27.0 mpg U.S.)

(For best engine performance, the use of premium-grade fuel is advised)

With 41 : 9 final drive

	Max. Speeds					
Gear	Running in				After running in	
	up to 1000 Km (600 mi.)		1000 to 3000 Km (600 to 1900 mi)			
	Km/h	mph	Km/h	mph	Km/h	mph
1st	25	16	35	20	44	27
2nd	45	28	55	35	74	46
3rd	65	40	80	50	108	67
4th	90	55	110	70	146	91
5th	115	70	140	85	over 185	115
Rev.	–	–	–	–	48	30

Oil pressures with hot engine
- min. pressure at idling speed : .5 - 1 Kg/cm² (7 - 14 psi)
- min. pressure at top speed : 3.5 Kg/cm² (50 psi)
- max. pressure at top speed : 4.5 - 5 Kg/cm² (65 - 70 psi)

WARNING: Check that generator warning light goes off as soon the engine exceeds 1.100 rpm.

TIRES

Inflation pressures (with tire cold)

	Front wheels		Rear wheels	
	Kg/cm^2	psi	Kg/cm^2	psi
PIRELLI 155 × 15 Cinturato S.	1.7*	24.1	1.8*	25.6
	1.8**	25.6	2.1**	29.8
MICHELIN 155 × 15 XA	1.7*	24.1	1.7*	24.1
	1.9**	27	1.9**	27

* Inflate to the lower pressure for use with low load and short peaks in speed.
** Inflate to the higher pressure for use with full load and max. speeds (highways).

REFILLINGS

		G.B.	U.S.
Water (engine & radiator)	7.5 lts	1.65 gals	1.98 gals
Fuel (reserve 7 lts/ 1.5 gals GB/ 1.8 gals US)	46 lts	10.1 gals	12.1 gals
Oil — Engine (pan & filter) to max level *	5.00 Kgs	4.95 qts	5.95 qts
Oil — Engine to min. level	3.25 Kgs	3.2 qts	3.8 pts
Oil — Gearbox	1.65 Kgs	3.2 pts	3.8 pts
Oil — Differential	1.25 Kgs	2.5 pts	3.0 pts
Oil — Steering box	.25 Kg	.5 pt	.6 pt

(*) This quantity is that needed for regular changing; the total amount of oil in the circuit (sump, filter, passages) is 5.75 Kgs. (5.7 qts G.B.) (6.8 qts U.S.).

PRESCRIBED OILS AND LUBRICANTS

Parts to be lubricated	API-SAE-NLGI Number	Recommended commercial equivalent	
		AGIP	SHELL
Engine *	SAE 20 W 40 API MS	F.1 Supermotoroil Multigrade 20 W/40	X 100 Multigrade 20 W/40
Gearbox	SAE 90	F.1 Rotra SAE 90	Dentax 90
Steering box and differential	SAE 90 EP	F.1 Rotra Hypoid SAE 90	Spirax 90 EP
Propeller shaft universal joints and sliding sleeve	NLGI 1	F.1 Grease 15	Retinax G
Front wheel bearings	NLGI 2/3	F.1 Grease 33 FD	Retinax A X
Brake fluid	Castrol Girling Brake Fluid Amber		

(*) For steady temperatures below 0°C (32°F) we advise the use of: AGIP F.1 Supermotoroil Multigrade 10 W/40 / SHELL Super Motor Oil

SAE - Society of Automotive Engineers
API - American Petroleum Institute
NLGI - National Lubricating Grease Institute

In countries where recommended lubricants are not available it is possible to replace them with products of other leading Companies provided that in accordance with the prescribed specifications.

CARBURETION

2 Carburettors Weber 40 DCOE 27

Venturi	30 mm (1 3/16")
Main jet	120
Main air metering jet	180
Idling jet	50 F 11
Idling air metering jet	120
Choke jet	65 F 5
Acceleration pump jet	35
Travel of acceleration pump control rod	14 mm (.55")
Delivery of acceleration pump every 20 strokes (for each barrel)	5 ± 1 cc.
Needle valve seat dia.	150
Float weight	26 grs
Distance of fuel level from float chamber flange (with a pressure of 2 mts (6'6") H₂O upstream the needle valve	29 + .5 mm (1.12 to 1.16")

IDLING ADJUSTMENT

- **F** Adjusting screw for minimum opening of throttle.

- **M** Idling mixture adjusting screw.

- **S** Screw for synchronizing throttles of the two carburettors.

- **T** Joint for control linkage (to pedal).

PREPARATORY STEPS

- Check the ignition timing and inspect the electric system (spark plugs, distributor, coil, etc.) for proper operation.
- Remove the air filter element and clean it thoroughly.
- Check the flexible mounts between carburettors and intake manifold for tightness.

ALIGNING THE THROTTLE VALVES

- Detach the control linkage T from carburettors.
- Slacken the screws F and S almost fully.
- Operate the throttles a few times to make sure there is no binding.
- Fully depress the throttle control lever of rear carburettor so that the throttles are fully closed; then screw in the screw S until contact is made.

IDLING

- Back up the screw M of half a turn.
- Tighten the screw F to contact, then screw it in one more turn to ensure feeding of engine.
- Connect the acceleration control linkage T to carburettors.
- Start the engine and warm it up.
- If necessary, back up the screw F very slowly until the engine runs at about 600 to 700 rpms.

FLOAT LEVEL ADJUSTMENT
WEBER 40 DCOE 27 Carburettor

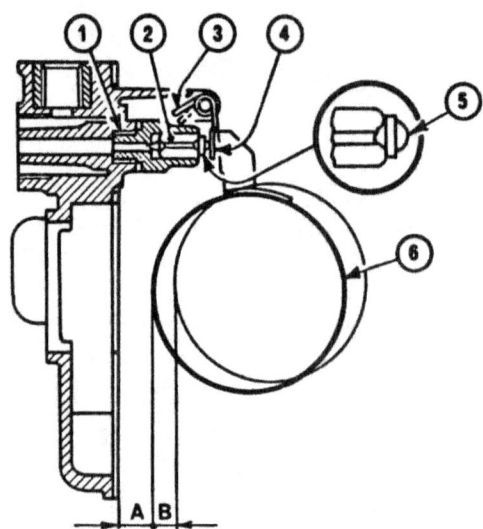

Check the level of fluid in float chamber as follows :

- Make sure the float weight is as specified (26 grs - .9 oz), that there are no leaks or indentations and that float can rotate freely about the pivot pin.

- The float weight must not be altered; consequently haphazard repairs (tinning, etc.) are detrimental to proper float operation.

- Check that needle valve (1) is well screwed into its seating and that the spring-loaded ball (5) part of the needle (2) is not jammed.

- Hold the carburettor cover in a vertical position as shown in the figure so that the float (6) does not depress the ball (5).

- With the cover vertical and the float tongue (4) in light contact with the ball, the two floats should be at a distance A = 8.5 mm (.33") from the cover mating surface with the gasket fitted and well stuck to the cover.

- When the level has been set, check that the travel (B) of the float is 6.5 mm (.26"); if necessary, adjust the position of float pivot tail (3).

- The adjustment described above will correspond to a fuel level of 29 + .5 mm (1.14 + .02") from the upper face of the float chamber (with a pressure of 2 mts - 6'6" H2O upstream the needle valve).

- If distance A is not as specified, slightly bend the float tongue (4) until the correct distance is obtained; inspect the working surface of the float tongue for any sign of nicks which may restrict the free movement of needle (2).

- Then fit the carburettor cover and check that the float can move freely without rubbing against the walls of the float chamber.

CAUTION - The float level should be checked whenever the float or the needle valve has been changed. In the latter case it is also advisable to replace the gasket and make certain the new valve is securely screwed into its seating.

VALVE TIMING

Checking of valve opening and closing angles

Clearance (with cold engine) between the unlobed profile of cams and the valve cup ceiling:

lift of cup	.475 to .500 mm (.0187 to .0197")
exhaust	.525 to .550 mm (.0206 to .0216")

Opening of intake valve:
   lift of cup . . . . .20 mm (.008")
   corresponding to an angle   before TDC of 18° 30' ± 1° 30'

Closing of intake valve:
   lift of cup . . . . .20 mm (.008")
   corresponding to an angle   after BDC of 42° 30' ± 1° 30'

Opening of exhaust valve:
   lift of cup . . . . .15 mm (.006")
   corresponding to an angle   before BDC of 42° 30' ± 1° 30'

Closing of exhaust valve:
   lift of cup . . . . .15 mm (.006")
   corresponding to an angle   after TDC of 18° 30' ± 1° 30'

ANGLE VALUES OF THE ACTUAL DIAGRAM OF VALVE TIMING SYSTEM WITH COLD ENGINE

(clockwise rotation direction of the crank shaft seen from the front side):

opening of intake valve	before TDC	36° 50'
closing of intake valve	after BDC	60° 50'
opening of exhaust valve	before BDC	54° 10'
closing of exhaust valve	after TDC	30° 10'
Induction stroke		277° 40'
exhaust stroke		264° 20'

IGNITION

Firing order: 1 - 3 - 4 - 2 (no. 1 cylinder is that at the fan side)

Opening of contact points of ignition distributor

S = .35 to .40 mm (.014 to .016")

The distributor is correctly fitted when the oiler is toward the engine.

VALUES OF ADVANCE OF IGNITION DISTRIBUTOR

Fixed advance F Before TDC	Maximum advance M Before TDC
3° ± 1°	43° +0° −3° at 5000 rpm

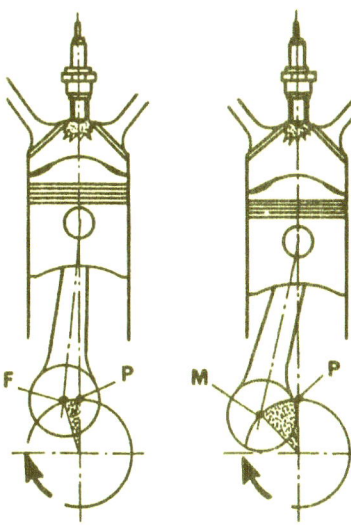

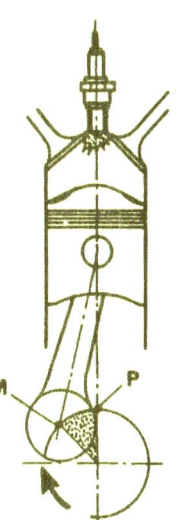

P = T.D.C.

F = Fixed advance

M = Maximum advance

SPARK PLUGS

Lodge 2HL

ELECTRIC SYSTEM

Voltage 12 V
Battery 60 Ah

	BOSCH
Generator	EG (R) 14 V 25 A 29
Voltage regulator	VA 14 V 25 A
Starting motor	EF (R) 12 V 0,7 PS
Coil	TK 12 A 19
Ignition distributor	J F 4
Windshield wiper	WS 13/11 T3 a

BULB'S WATTAGE

Headlamps	45/40	asymmetric
Tail parking and stop lights	5/20	
Front direction indicators		
Tail direction indicators	20	
Back-up light		
Front parking lights		
Side direction indicators	5	globular
License plate light		
Engine compartment light	5	cylindrical
Courtesy light (in the rearview mirror)		
Instrument panel light		
Tell-tale for generator		
Tell-tale for fuel reserve	3	tubular
Tell-tale for blower		
Cigar lighter lamp		
Tell-tale for parking lights		
Tell-tale for direction indicator	1.2	tubular
Tell-tale for headlamp high beam		

TIGHTENING TORQUE SPECIFICATIONS

ENGINE/GEARBOX UNIT

	Kgm	lb. ft	Manner of tightening
Nuts of cylinder head — after repairing, when cold	6.2 to 6.4	44.8 to 46.3	Slacken and re-tighten without lubricating
Nuts of cylinder head — when hot	6.6 to 6.7	47.7 to 48.4	Lock without slackening the nut
Spark plugs	2.5 to 3.5	18.1 to 25.3	With graphite grease, when cold
Nuts of the camshaft caps	2 to 2.25	14.5 to 16.3	in oil
Nuts of the connecting rod caps	5 to 5.3	36.2 to 38.3	in oil
Nuts of main bearing caps	4.7 to 5	33.9 to 36.1	in oil
Screws of flywheel on crankshaft	4.2 to 4.5	30.4 to 32.5	in oil
Nut of generator pulley	3 to 3.5	21.7 to 25.3	dry
Nut of gearbox main shaft yoke	12	86.8	dry
Nut of gearbox layshaft	5	36.1	dry
Nuts of gearbox half-casings	1.8	13	dry
Bolts joining gearbox output shaft yoke to prop. shaft yoke	4.5 to 5.5	32.6 to 39.7	dry

REAR FRAME

	Kgm	lb. ft	Manner of tightening
Screws securing ring gear to differential case	4.5 to 5	32.6 to 36.1	dry
Ring nut securing yoke on final drive pinion shaft	8 to 14	58 to 101.2	dry
Nuts securing bearing housing to rear axle banjo	4.8 to 5.5	34.8 to 39.7	dry
Nuts securing radius rods to body	10 to 11.5	72.4 to 83	dry
Nuts securing radius rods to rear axle banjo	11.5 to 13	83 to 94	dry
Nuts securing reaction triangle to body	4.8 to 5.5	34.8 to 39.7	dry
Nut securing reaction triangle to rear axle	11 to 15	79.6 to 108.5	dry
Screws securing brake slave cylinders to axle banjo (Dunlop brakes)	.4 to .5	2.9 to 3.6	dry
Screws securing rear brake caliper to support (Dunlop brakes)	2.3 to 2.8	16.7 to 20.2	dry
Nuts securing wheels	6 to 8	43.4 to 57.8	dry
Bolts joining differential yoke to prop. shaft yoke	3.5 to 4	25.3 to 28.9	dry

FRONT FRAME

	Kgm	lb. ft	Manner of tightening
Nut securing steering wheel to column	5 to 5.5	36.1 to 39.7	dry
Screws securing Burman steering box cover	2.3 to 2.5	16.7 to 18	dry
Screws securing steering box & bellcrank bracket to body	4.8 to 5.5	34.8 to 39.7	dry
Nuts of steering linkage ball joints	4.8 to 5.5	34.8 to 39.7	dry
Nut securing steering arm to box	12.5 to 14	90.5 to 101.2	dry
Screws securing upper attachment of shock absorber to body	2.3 to 2.8	16.7 to 20.2	dry
Nut securing shock absorber to suspension arms	7.5 to 8.5	54.3 to 61.4	dry
Screws securing upper wishbone front arm to body	2.3 to 2.8	16.7 to 20.2	dry
Nut securing upper wishbone front arm to rear arm	4.8 to 5.5	34.8 to 39.7	dry
Nut securing upper wishbone rear arm to body	11.5 to 13	83 to 94	dry
Nut securing lower wishbone bracket to cross-member	13 to 18	94 to 130	dry
Nuts securing steering arm to steering knuckle	4.8 to 5.5	34.8 to 39.7	dry
Nut securing upper wishbone rear arm to steering knuckle	7.5 to 8.5	54.3 to 61.4	dry
Nut securing lower ball joint to wishbone	7.5 to 8.5	54.3 to 61.4	dry
Nut securing lower ball joint to steering knuckle	7.5 to 8.5	54.3 to 61.4	dry
Nuts securing caliper support to steering knuckle (Dunlop)	4.8 to 5.5	34.8 to 39.7	dry
Screws securing front brake calipers to support (Dunlop)	7.5 to 8.5	54.3 to 61.4	dry
Screws securing front brake discs (Dunlop)	7.5 to 8.5	54.3 to 61.4	dry
Nuts securing wheels	6 to 8	43.4 to 57.8	dry

MAJOR INSPECTION SPECIFICATIONS

Camshafts

Diameter of journals	A = 26.959 to 26.980 mm (1.0614 to 1.0622")
Diameter of journal bearings	B = 27.000 to 27.033 mm (1.0630 to 1.0642")
Radial clearance between journals and bearings . .	= .020 to .074 mm (.0008 to .0029")
End play of camshaft in thrust bearing	C = .065 to .182 mm (.0026 to .0071")

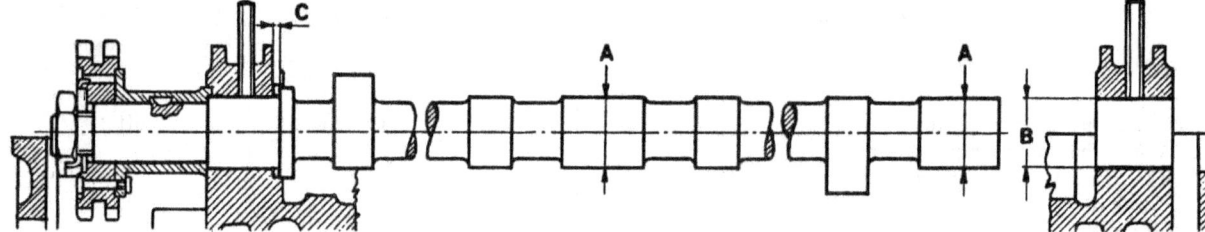

VALVES AND VALVE GUIDES

		INTAKE		EXHAUST (sodium cooled)	
		LIVIA H	ATE	GARRONE	ATE	LIVIA C
Valves	Diameter of valve poppet O	41.000 to 41.150 mm (1.614 to 1.620")	41.000 to 41.200 mm (1.614 to 1.620")	41.000 to 41.150 mm (1.614 to 1.620")	37.000 to 37.200 mm (1.4567 to 1.4645")	37.000 to 37.150 mm (1.4567 to 1.4625")
	Diameter of valve stem M	8.962 to 8.987 mm (.3528 to .3538")	8.962 to 8.987 mm (.3528 to .3538")	8.962 to 8.987 mm (.3528 to .3538")	8.935 to 8.960 mm (.3518 to .3527")	
	Total length L	106.900 to 107.150 mm (4.2087 to 4.2186")	106.800 mm (4.2047")	107.000 mm (4.2126")	106.050 to 106.150 mm (4.1753 to 4.1791")	106.300 mm (4.1850")

N.B. : ATE - LIVIA - GARRONE intake valves and ATE - LIVIA exhaust valves are alternate supply.

Valve guide { Outside diameter with guide removed	E = 14.033 to 14.044 mm (.5528 to .5529")
Inside diameter with guide assembled in cylinder head.	D = 9.000 to 9.015 mm (.3544 to 3549")
Clearance between guide assembled in cylinder head and valve stem . . . . . { intake	= .013 to .053 mm (.0005 to .0020")
{ exhaust	= .040 to .080 mm (.0016 to .0031")
Projection of valve guides from their recesses in the cylinder head	= 16.800 to 17.000 mm (.662 to .669")

VALVE SEATS

Diameter of valve guide seat on cylinder head	= 13.990 to 14.018 mm (.5508 to .5518")
Interference between seat and valve guide	= .015 to .054 mm (.0006 to .0021")

		INTAKE	EXHAUST
Outer diameter of the valve seat . . H	standard	42.597 to 42.632 mm (1.6771 to 1.6784")	38.597 to 38.632 mm (1.5196 to 1.5209")
	oversized	42.897 to 42.932 mm (1.6889 to 1.6902")	38.897 to 38.932 mm (1.5314 to 1.5327")
Diameter of recess in the cylinder head G for valve seat	standard	42.532 to 42.557 mm (1.6744 to 1.6754")	38.532 to 38.557 mm (1.5169 to 1.5179")
	oversized	42.832 to 42.857 mm (1.6862 to 1.6872")	38.832 to 38.857 mm (1.5288 to 1.5298")

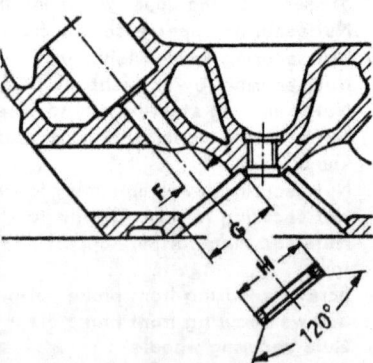

Interference between valve seat and recess in cylinder head . . . . .100 to .040 mm (.0039 to .0016")

VALVE CUPS

Diameter of cup **A** = standard = 34.973 to 34.989 mm (1.3773 to 1.3775")
oversized = 35.173 to 35.189 mm (1.3848 to 1.3853")

Diameter of cup seat in cylinder **B** = standard = 35.000 to 35.025 mm (1.3779 to 1.3789")
head. oversized = 35.200 to 35.225 mm (1.3859 to 1.3868")

Clearance between seat and cup = .011 to .052 mm (.0005 to .0020")

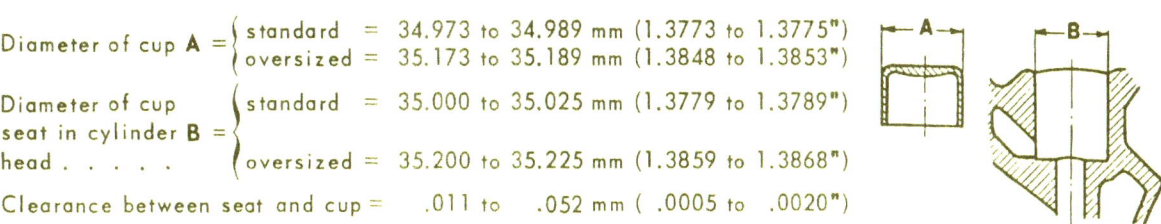

VALVE SPRINGS

	Free length	Length under test load	Test load
Inner spring I	red mark 47.3 mm (1.87") green mark 46.5 mm (1.83")	l_1 26 mm (1.02")	22.2 to 23.1 Kg 48.9 to 51.1 lbs.
Outer spring S	red mark 52.8 mm (2.08") green mark 51.3 mm (2.03")	L_1 27.5 mm (1.08")	35.7 to 37.1 Kg 78.6 to 81.8 lbs

Note: The red-marked valve springs should be fitted with the color marked coil downward.

CONNECTING RODS

Length between center line of big end and center line of small end of connecting rod . . . . **D** = 147.955 to 148.045 mm (5.8250 to 5.8285")
Inner diameter of the big end of connecting rod . . . **E** = 53.695 to 53.708 mm (2.1140 to 2.1144")
Inner diameter of bushing in the small end of rod . . **C** = 22.005 to 22.015 mm (.8664 to .8667")
Thickness of connecting rod bearings **F** standard . . = 1.829 to 1.835 mm (.0720 to .0722")
1st oversize = 1.956 to 1.962 mm (.0770 to .0772")
2nd oversize = 2.083 to 2.089 mm (.0820 to .0824")
Radial clearance between crankpins and bearings for big end of connecting rod . . . . = .025 to .063 mm (.0010 to .0024")
Maximum out of parallelism between center line of big end hole and center line of small end hole . . . . . = (.074 mm (.0029")

PISTON PIN

O.D. of pin I
Black color = 21.994 to 21.997 mm (.86590 to .86602")
White color = 21.998 to 22.000 mm (.86606 to .86614")

Clearance between small end bushing and piston pin
Black color = .008 to .021 mm (. 0003 to . 0008")
White color = .005 to .017 mm (. 0002 to . 0007")

PISTON PIN HOLE

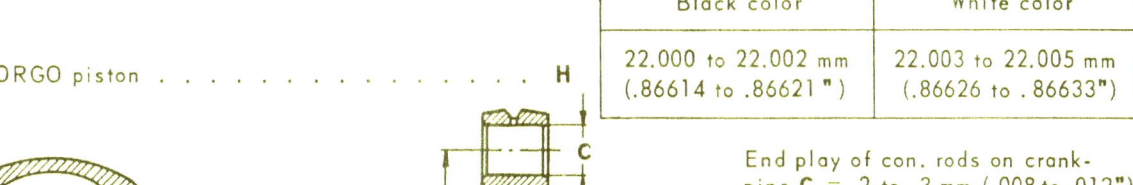

	Black color	White color
BORGO piston . . . . **H**	22.000 to 22.002 mm (.86614 to .86621")	22.003 to 22.005 mm (.86626 to .86633")

End play of con. rods on crankpins **G** = .2 to .3 mm (.008 to .012")

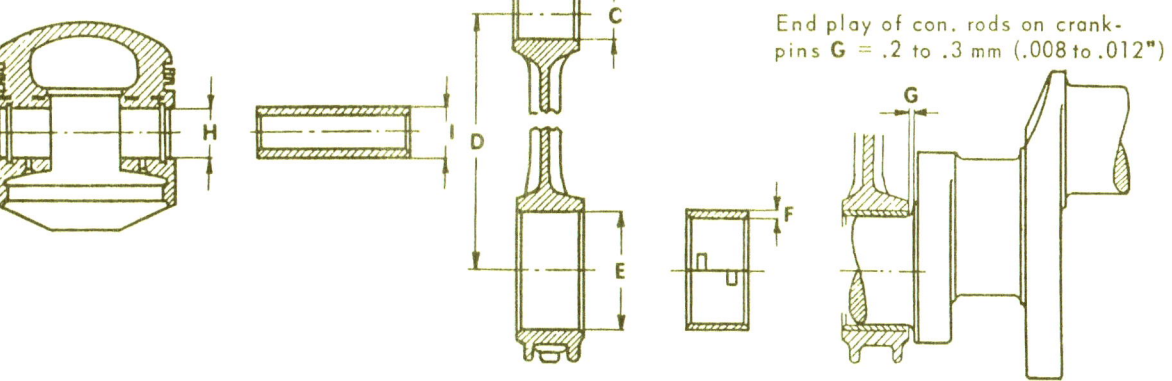

PISTONS AND PISTON RINGS

Diameter of pistons to be measured to square with the hole for piston pin and at a distance of L = 12 mm (.472") from the lower border of skirt.

	CLASS A (BLUE)	CLASS B (PINK)	CLASS C (GREEN)
BORGO piston diameter	77.920 to 77.930 mm (3.0677 to 3.0681")	77.931 to 77.940 mm (3.0682 to 3.0685")	77.941 to 77.950 mm (3.0686 to 3.0688")

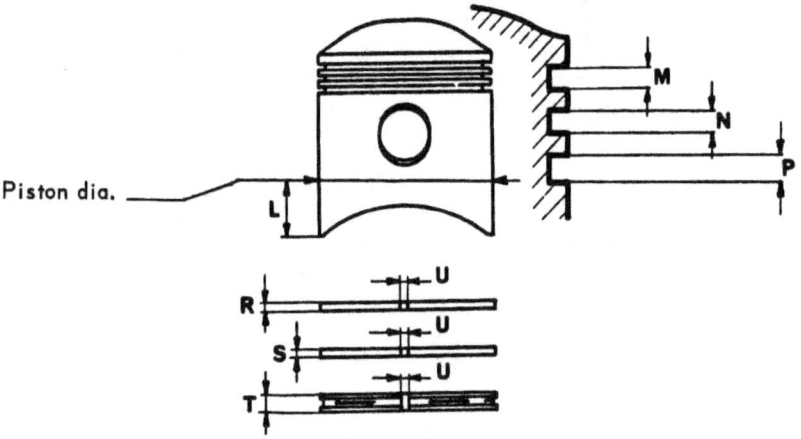

Height of grooves in piston for compression rings	normal	N = 1.775 to 1.790 mm (.0699 to .0704")
	chromium-plated	M = 1.535 to 1.550 mm (.0605 to .0612")
Height of groove in piston for oil scraper ring		P = 4.015 to 4.030 mm (.1581 to .1586")
Thickness of compression rings	normal	S = 1.728 to 1.740 mm (.0681 to .0685")
	chromium-plated	R = 1.478 to 1.490 mm (.0582 to .0586")
Thickness of oil scraper ring		T = 3.978 to 3.990 mm (.1567 to .1571")
End play of rings in grooves	compression rings normal	– .035 to .062 mm (.0014 to .0024")
	chromium-plated	– .045 to .072 mm (.0018 to .0028")
	oil scraper rings	– .025 to .052 mm (.0010 to .0020")
Gap of rings to be inspected in ring gauge or in cylinder barrels		U = .300 to .450 mm (.0012 to .0017")

CYLINDER BARRELS	CLASS A (BLUE)	CLASS B (PINK)	CLASS C (GREEN)
Cylinder barrel bore	77.985 to 77.994 mm (3.0703 to 3.0706")	77.995 to 78.004 mm (3.0707 to 3.0710")	78.005 to 78.014 mm (3.0711 to 3.0714")

Clearance between cylinder barrel and piston . . . . . .055 to .074 mm (.0022 to .0029")

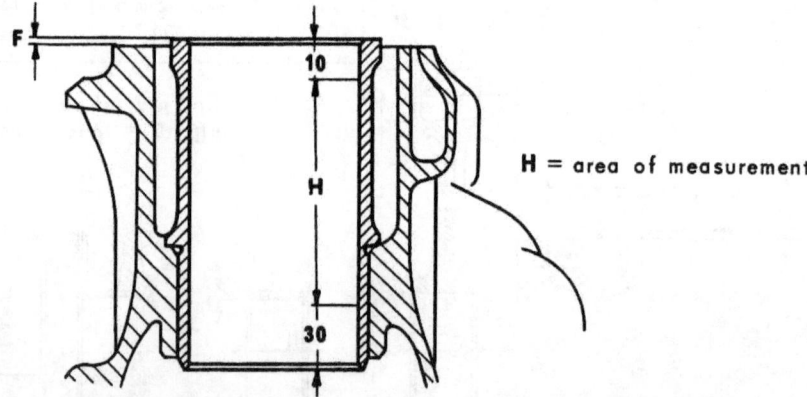

H = area of measurement

Projection of barrels from cylinder block . . . . F = .000 to .060 mm (.0000 to .0024)
Surface roughness of barrel bore . . . . 20 to 40 microinches RMS

CRANKSHAFT

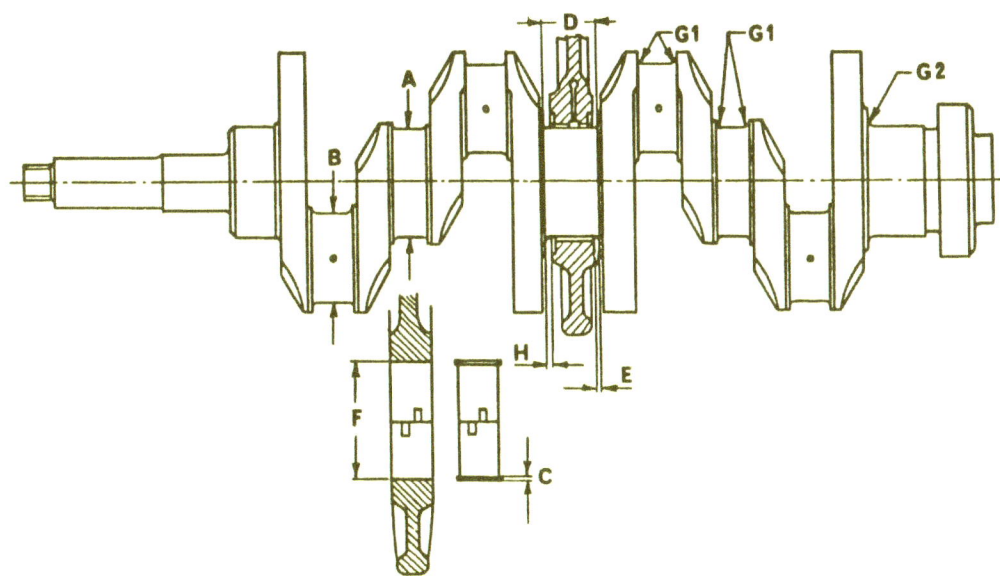

Diameter of main journals ...... A	standard =	59.960 to 59.973 mm	(2.3606 to 2.3611")
	1st undersize =	59.706 to 59.719 mm	(2.3506 to 2.3511")
	2nd undersize =	59.452 to 59.465 mm	(2.3407 to 2.3411")
Diameter of crankpins .... B	standard =	49.987 to 50.000 mm	(1.9680 to 1.9685")
	1st undersize =	49.733 to 49.746 mm	(1.9581 to 1.9585")
	2nd undersize =	49.479 to 49.492 mm	(1.9480 to 1.9485")
Thickness of main bearings C	standard =	1.829 to 1.835 mm	(.0720 to .0722")
	1st oversize =	1.956 to 1.962 mm	(.0770 to .0772")
	2nd oversize =	2.083 to 2.089 mm	(.0820 to .0822")
Diameter of seat main bearings in crankcase ..... F =		63.657 to 63.676 mm	(2.5062 to 2.5069")
Length of central journal .... D	standard =	30.000 to 30.035 mm	(1.1811 to 1.1824")
	1st oversize =	30.127 to 30.162 mm	(1.1861 to 1.1874")
	2nd oversize =	30.254 to 30.289 mm	(1.1911 to 1.1924")
Thickness of thrust rings for central E journal	standard =	2.311 to 2.362 mm	(.0910 to .0929")
	1st oversize =	2.374 to 2.425 mm	(.0935 to .0954")
	2nd oversize =	2.438 to 2.489 mm	(.0960 to .0980")
End play of crankshaft .... H =		.076 to .263 mm	(.003 to .010")
Radial clearance between journals and main bearings . . =		.014 to .058 mm	(.0005 to .0022")

Note - Radial clearance = main bearing ID - (twice bearing thickness + journal OD).

Fillet radii	main journals & crankpins	G_1 = 1.7 to 2.1 mm (.07 to .08")
	journal on flywheel side	G_2 = 3.7 to 4.1 mm (.15 to .16")

Main journals & crankpins surface roughness .... 63 microinches RMS

Maximum elongation of main journals and crankpins .... .007 mm (.00027")

Maximum taper of main journals and crankpins measured on their full length. . . .01 mm (.00039")

Maximum error of parallelism of main journals and crankpins measured of their full length .... .015 mm (.00059")

Maximum misalignment allowed between main journals .... .01 mm (.00039")

Maximum misalignment allowed between ¢ of the two pairs of crakpins and ¢ of main journals .... .300 mm (.0118")

CLUTCH

Pedal free travel	23 mm (.9")
Distance between thrust ring and the reference sleeve of tool C. 6.0104 (red-painted dot) See IS 1.05.080	.75 to 1.25 mm (.03 to .05")
Squareness of the clutch driven plate assembled on gearbox direct drive shaft.	.50 mm (.019")
Wear limit of driven plate thickness	6 mm (.236")
Spring rating: free length	43 to 46 mm (1.69 to 1.81")
length under test load	29.2 mm (1.15")
test load	44.5 to 49.5 Kgs (98.1 to 109 lbs)

GEARBOX

Transmission ratios	1st gear	3.304 : 1
	2nd gear	1.988 : 1
	3rd gear	1.355 : 1
	4th gear	1.000 : 1
	5th gear	.791 : 1
	Rev.	3.010 : 1
Maximum eccentricity of main shaft		.050 mm (.020")
End play between forks and sleeves	assembly	.150 to .340 mm (.006 to .013")
	wear limit	.850 mm (.033")

		Gear	1st - 2nd - 3rd	5th - Rev.
Calibration of springs for striking rod balls		free length	15.2 mm (.60")	30.5 mm (1.2")
		length under test load	10 mm (.39")	20 mm (.78")
		test load	2.88 to 3.12 Kg (6.4 to 6.8 lbs)	4.32 to 4.68 Kg (9.5 to 10.3 lbs)
Maximum end play of mainshaft gears	1st speed gear		.170 to .245 mm (.0067 to .0096")	
	2nd & 3rd speed gears		.130 to .205 mm (.0052 to .0081")	
	5th speed gear & Rev.		.160 to .220 mm (.0063 to .0087")	
Radial clearance between gear bushings and mainshaft	1st speed gear		.125 to .170 mm (.0049 to .0067")	
	2nd & 3rd speed gears		.095 to .140 mm (.0038 to .0055")	
	5th speed gear		.065 to .107 mm (.0026 to .0041")	

Distance between outer planes of the engaging teeth of 3rd and 4th gears	42.000 to 42.200 mm (1.65 to 1.66")
Distance, in neutral, of the rear band (propeller shaft side) of 5th speed sleeve from the rear edge of gear engaging teeth . .	12.900 mm (.508")

REAR AXLE AND SUSPENSION

Transmission-axle overall ratios-with 41 : 9 final drive
- 1st gear . . . . 15.049 : 1
- 2nd gear . . . . 9.055 : 1
- 3rd gear . . . . 6.172 : 1
- 4th gear . . . . 4.555 : 1
- 5th gear . . . . 3.603 : 1
- Reverse . . . . 13.710 : 1

Maximum eccentricity of axle shafts	.10 mm (.004")
Clearance between teeth of planetary gears	.05 mm (.002")
Play between teeth of final drive	.05 to .10 mm (.002 to .004")
Max factory end play between reaction trunnion and attachment to body	1 mm (.04")
Reference dimension on tool C. 6.0101 for pinion-to-ring gear fitting	70 ± .0025 mm (2.7559 ± .0001")
Pre-load on pinion bearing	11.5 to 15.5 Kgcm (10 to 13.5 in. lbs)
Total pre-load on final drive bearings	16.5 to 24.5 Kgcm (14.4 to 21.3 in. lbs)

CHECKING OF SHOCK ABSORBERS ON TEST BENCH - Calibration data (when cold)

	BIANCHI - ALLINQUANT	
	Extension	Compression
High speed	135 - 190 Kgs (298 - 418 lbs)	50 - 80 Kgs (111-176 lbs)
Low speed	19 - 55 Kgs (42 - 121 lbs)	9 - 22 Kgs (20 - 48 lbs)

CHECKING OF SUSPENSION SPRINGS

Free length	429 mm (16.9")
Length under test load	252 mm (10")
Test load	257 to 273 Kg (565 to 600 lbs)
Colored marks	White-white / Blue-white

FRONT SUSPENSION

ADJUSTMENT OF CLEARANCE IN WHEEL BEARINGS

When performing regular servicing or whenever the removal of wheel hubs is required, adjust the bearing clearance as follows:

1) Screw in the castellated nut and lock it to a torque of 2.5 Kgm (18 lb.ft.) while at the same time revolving the wheel hub to set the bearings properly in their seats;
2) Unscrew the nut half a turn or more;
3) Lightly tap on the stub axle end with a mallet in order to return the outboard bearing in its proper position even in the case a slight interference between bearing cone and stub axle exists;
4) Lock the nut in place to 1.5 Kgm (10.8 lb.ft.);
5) Unscrew the nut of a quarter turn;
6) If the hole in the axle is aligned with a slot in the castellated nut insert the cotter pin; if not, screw in the nut by the minimum angle needed to line up the hole and the next slot;
7) Again tap lightly on stub axle end to restore the same condition as under step 3;
8) The end play so obtained on stub axle should fall between .02 - .12 mm (.0008 - .0047").

WHEEL BEARING LUBRICATING INSTRUCTIONS

The quantity of lubricating grease should be about 65 grammes (2½ ozs) for each hub; do not exceed such a quantity to avoid bearing overheating, grease leakage, etc.
The grease should be well distributed inside the bearings and into side recesses.
Subsequently, at the regular schedule, remove the hub cover and pack the outboard bearing.

BALL JOINTS

- End play of lower ball joint in its socket . . . . 1 mm (.04")

Note - Ball joints require no regular lubrication being provided with special grease seals which retain the grease packed in by factory on assembly. Only if strictly needed (joint sqeaking) grease with Shell Retinax A or AGIP F.1 Grease 30 (See I.S. 1.05.097/1).

CHECKING OF SUSPENSION SPRINGS

Free length . . . . 317 mm (12.5")
Length under test load . . . . 200 mm (7.8")
Test load . . . . 820.6 to 871.4 Kg (1810 to 1920 lbs)
Colored marks . . . . Blue-white
Blue-blue

CHECKING OF SHOCK ABSORBERS ON TEST BENCH

	GIRLING		BIANCHI - ALLINQUANT	
	Extension	Compression	Extension	Compression
High speed	210 to 310 Kgs (470 to 680 lbs)	27 to 52 Kgs (60 to 115 lbs)	150 to 190 Kgs (330 to 420 lbs)	55 to 80 Kgs (121 to 175 lbs)
Low speed	30 to 52 Kgs (66 to 115 lbs)	9 to 22 Kgs (20 to 48 lbs)	25 to 55 Kgs (55 to 121 lbs)	9 to 22 Kgs (20 to 48 lbs)

BRAKES
Dunlop

Whenever a brake unit is overhauled or replaced check the disc for true rotation with the disc fitted to the car.

Use a dial gauge and check that runout does not exceed .15mm. (.006"). Should the reading exceed this value, then the installation of disc on stub axle must be carefully examined; if the run out persists, replace the disc.

If the disc is scored, the grinding of the surfaces is allowed providing not to exceed an undersize of 1 mm (.0394"), equalized on both faces, i.e. .5 mm (.0197") each face; disc wear limit : 8.5 mm (.335") thick.

Inspection specifications after regrinding of disc surfaces :

- Max. out of parallelism with disc mounting plane : .05 mm (.0020");
- Max. out of flat : .025 mm (.0010") and max. difference in thickness : .038 mm (.0015") as measured along any radial line;
- Max. out of flat : .025 mm (.0010") and max. difference in thickness : .015 mm (.0006") as measured along any circular line;
- The surface should show no sign of scoring or porosity.

The surface roughness should be :

- 26 microinches as measured circularly;
- 36 microinches as measured radially

FRICTION PADS

	Front	Rear
Thickness when new	16 mm (.630")	17.5 mm (.689")
Wear limit	8 mm (.315")	10.0 mm (.394")

CALIPERS

On replacement of disc or caliper measure the running clearance between caliper and disc on each side; the difference should not exceed .5 mm (.0197").
To centralize the caliper about the disc, insert shims between caliper and mounting flange as required.

HAND BRAKE

It is mechanically-operated and acts on the rear service brake pads.

The adjustment is performed by acting on the nut of control cable located between intermediate levers and calipers. After the adjustment, make sure that levers of rear calipers to which the cable is connected are all the way outward. In such a position the cable must not be tight but slightly slackened. Furthermore the brake pads must not contact the disc.

WHEEL ALIGNMENT

Checking of wheel angles and car «trim» under static load

Put the car under static load, with shock absorbers and stabilizer rod connected, with full tank or equivalent, with spare wheel, tool kit and the tires inflated as specified.

Before checking, slightly jolt the car so as to settle the suspensions.

Static load
- 2 weights of 45 Kgs (100 lbs) on front seats
- 2 weights of 25 Kgs (55 lbs) on flooring where feet rest

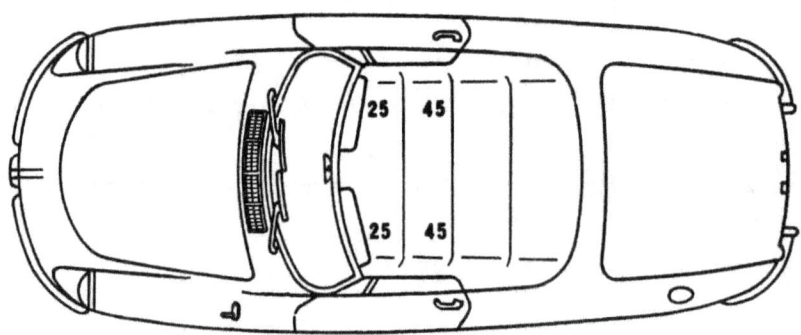

DISTANCE OF LOWER WISHBONE OF FRONT SUSPENSION FROM A REFERENCE LEVEL

A − B = 28 ± 3 mm (1.10 ± .12")

Note - Dimension A must be measured in correspondence of the lower line of wishbone shaft as shown.
To adjust add shims in (1).

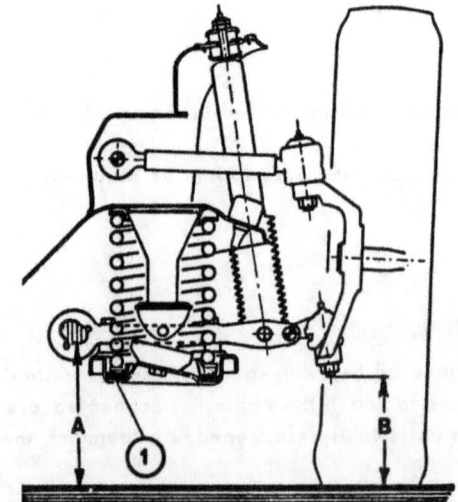

DISTANCE OF REAR AXLE FROM RUBBER BUFFERS

$$C = 33 \pm 5 \text{ mm} (1.30 \pm .20")$$

Note - To adjust, remove the seat 3 and add shims in 2 as shown.

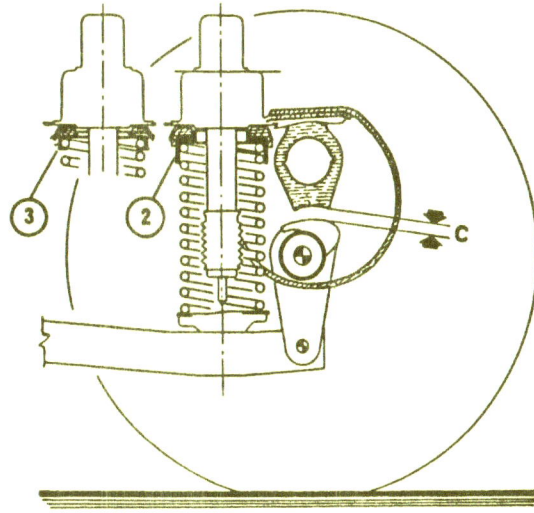

- In the conditions as specified check the wheel angles.

CASTER ANGLE

$$\alpha = 1° \pm 30'$$

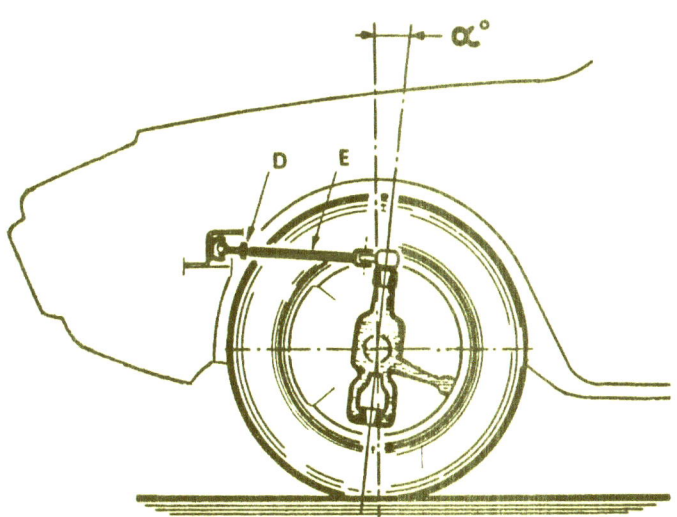

The difference in caster angle between R.H. and L.H. wheel must not exceed 0° 20'.

To adjust, loosen jam nut D and rotate rod E.

Note - Small adjustments of the caster angle allow to correct slight drift tendency of the car.

The caster angle should be checked under static load and alignment conditions as specified and with shock absorbers disconnected at an end.

N.B. - Before checking the caster angle shake the front end of car in order to allow the rubber bushing on the front slanting arm to set properly.

FRONT WHEEL CAMBER

Difference in camber angle between R.H. and L.H. wheel = 0° 40'

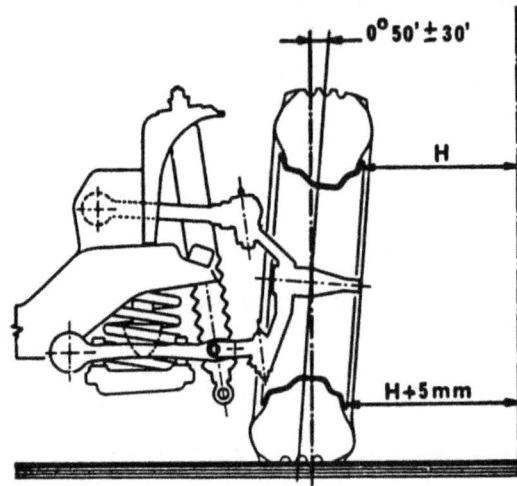

Note - Not adjustable. Check the chassis, if necessary.

FRONT WHEEL TOE-IN

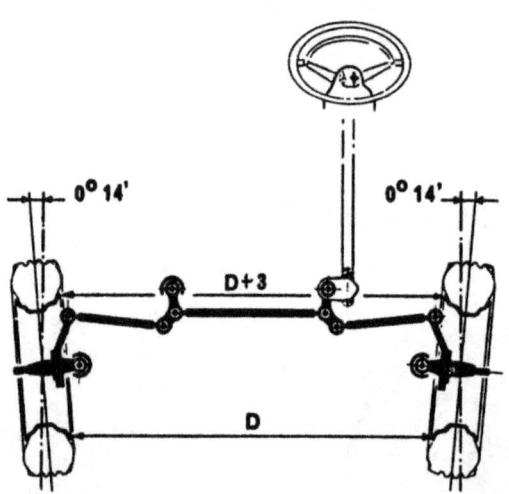

Rod length:

    side . . . . 272 to 288 mm (10.7 to 11.3")

    track . . . . 530 to 550 mm (20.86 to 21.66")

With the toe-in as specified, the length of rods as measured between ball joint centers should fall within the limits shown. If these values cannot be restored, the cause will probably be attributable to distortion of the body resulting from a collision.

Giulia sprint GT Veloce

**technical characteristics
and
principal inspection specifications**

CONTENTS

TECHNICAL CHARACTERISTICS

PRINCIPAL CHARACTERISTIC DATA .... Page 3
    Performance .... " 3
    Tires .... " 4
    Refillings .... " 4
    Prescribed oils and lubrificants .... " 4
    Carburetion .... " 5
    Idling adjustment .... " 5
    Float level adjustment .... " 6
    Valve timing .... " 7
    Electric system .... " 8
    Electric system bulb's wattage .... " 8
    Tightening torque specifications .... " 9

MAJOR INSPECTION SPECIFICATIONS

Camshafts .... Page 10
Valves and valve guides .... " 10
Valve seats .... " 10
Valve cups .... " 11
Valve springs .... " 11
Connecting rods .... " 11
Piston pin .... " 11
Piston pin hole .... " 11
Piston and piston rings .... " 12
Cylinder barrels .... " 12
Crankshaft .... " 13
Clutch .... " 14
Gearbox .... " 14
Rear axle and suspension .... " 15
Front suspension .... " 16
Brakes .... " 17

WHEEL ALIGNMENT
    Checking of wheel angles and car trim under static load .... " 18

TECHNICAL CHARACTERISTICS

PRINCIPAL CHARACTERISTIC DATA

Number of cylinders	4
Bore	78 mm (3.07")
Stroke	82 mm (3.23")
Total cylinder capacity	1570 cc.
Max. power at 6,000 rpm — DIN	109 HP
Max. power at 6,000 rpm — SAE	125 HP
Front track	1310 mm (51.6")
Rear track	1270 mm (50.0")
Wheelbase	2350 mm (92.7")
Min. turning circle	10700 mm (420.1")
Overall length	4080 mm (161")
Overall width	1580 mm (62.2")
Overall height (unladen)	1315 mm (51.8")
Dry weight with tools and jack	950 Kg (2100 lbs)
Number of seats	2 + 2
Tires 155 x 15	PIRELLI cinturato S / MICHELIN X A
Fuel consumption per 100 Km (CUNA standard)	10.5 lt (32 mpg G.B. - 27 mpg U.S.)

(For best engine performance, the use of premium-grade fuel is advised)

With 41 : 9 final drive

Gear	Max. Speeds					
	Running in				After running in	
	up to 1000 Km (600 mi.)		1000 to 3000 Km (600 to 1900 mi)			
	Km/h	mph	Km/h	mph	Km/h	mph
1st	25	16	35	20	44	27
2nd	45	28	55	35	74	46
3rd	65	40	80	50	108	67
4th	90	55	110	70	146	91
5th	115	70	140	85	over 185	115
Rev.	-	-	-	-	48	30

Oil pressures with hot engine:
- min. pressure at idling speed: .5-1 Kg/cm^2 (7-14 psi)
- min. pressure at top speed: 3.5 Kg/cm^2 (50 psi)
- max. pressure at top speed: 4.5-5 Kg/cm^2 (65-70 psi)

W A R N I N G : Check that generator warning light goes off as soon as the engine exceeds 1,100 rpm.

Tires
Inflation pressures (with tire cold)

	Front wheels		Rear wheels	
	Kg/cm²	psi	Kg/cm²	psi
PIRELLI 155 x 15 Cinturato S	1.7 *	24.1	1.8 *	25.6
	1.8 **	25.6	2.1 **	29.8
MICHELIN 155 x 15 X A	1.7 *	24.1	1.7 *	24.1
	1.9 **	27	1.9 **	27

* Inflate to the lower pressure for use with low load and short peaks in speed.
** Inflate to the higher pressure for use with full load and max. speeds (highways).

Refillings

		G. B.	U. S.
Water (engine & radiator)	7.5 lts	1.65 gals	1.98 gals
Fuel (reserve 6 to 7 lts (1.3 - 1.5 gals G.B.) (1.6 - 1.8 gals U.S.)	46 lts	10.1 gals	12.1 gals
Oil — Engine (pan & filter) to max. level *	5.00 Kgs	4.95 qts	5.95 qts
Oil — Engine (pan & filter) to min. level	3.25 Kgs	3.2 qts	3.8 qts
Oil — Gearbox	1.65 Kgs	3.2 pts	3.8 pts
Oil — Differential	1.25 Kgs	2.5 pts	3.0 pts
Oil — Steering box	.25 Kgs	.5 pts	.6 pts

* This quantity is that needed for regular changing; the total amount of oil in the circuit (sump, filter, passages) is 5.75 Kgs (5.7 qts G.B.) (6.8 qts U.S.).

Prescribed oils and lubricants

	API - SAE - NLGI Number	Recommended commercial equivalent	
		A G I P	S H E L L
Engine (*)	SAE 20 W/40 API MS	F.1 Supermotoroil Multigrade 20 W/40	X 100 Multigrade 20 W/40
Gearbox (for correct use of lubricant refer to footnote 1)	SAE 90 SAE 90 EP	F.1 Rotra SAE 90 F.1 Rotra Hypoid SAE 90	Dentax 90 Spirax 90 EP
Steering box and differential	SAE 90 EP	F.1 Rotra Hypoid SAE 90	Spirax 90 EP
Propeller shaft universal joints and sliding yoke	NLGI 1	F.1 Grease 15	Retinax G
Front wheel bearings	NLGI 2/3	F.1 Grease 33 FD	Retinax AX
Brake fluid	Castrol Girling Brake Fluid Amber		

(*) For steady temperatures below 0°C (32°F) we advise the use of .... AGIP F.1 Supermotoroil Multigrade 10 W/40
SHELL Super Motor Oil

Note 1 - AGIP F.1 Rotra Hypoid or SHELL Spirax should be used <u>exclusively in gearboxes as directed on the red transfer applied on them.</u>

SAE - Society of Automotive Engineers
API - American Petroleum Institute
NLGI - National Lubricating Grease Institute

In countries where the recommended lubricants are not available it is possible to replace them with products of other leading Companies provided that in accordance with the prescribed specifications.

Carburetion
2 Carburettors WEBER 40 DCOE 27

Venturi	30 mm (1 3/16")
Main jet	120
Main air metering jet	180
Idling jet	50 F11
Idling air metering jet	120
Choke jet	65 F5
Acceleration pump jet	35
Travel of acceleration pump control rod	14 mm (.55")
Delivery of acceleration pump every 20 strokes (for each barrel)	5 ± 1 cc.
Needle valve seat dia.	1.50 mm (.06")
Float weight	26 grs
Distance of fuel level from float chamber flange (with a pressure of 2 mts (6'6") H2O upstream the needle valve)	29 + .5 mm (1.12 to 1.16")

Idling adjustment

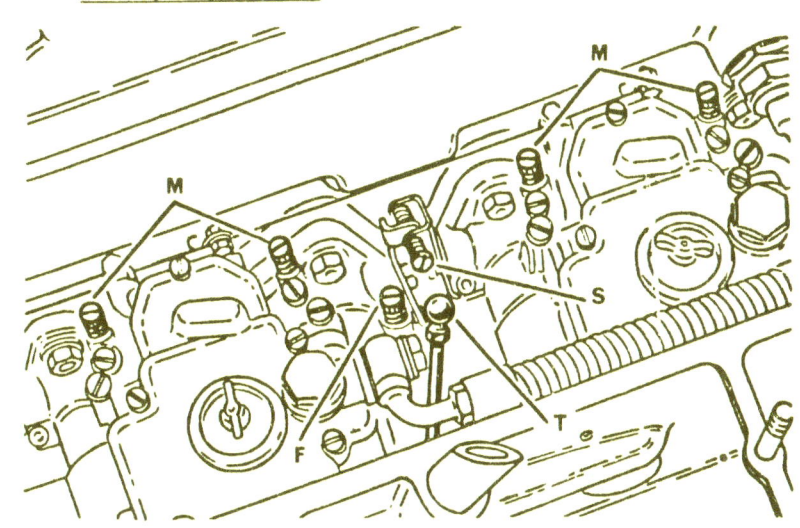

F Adjusting screw for minimum opening of throttle.

M Idling mixture adjusting screw.

S Screw for synchronizing throttles of the two carburettors.

T Joint for control linkage (to pedal).

PREPARATORY STEPS

- Check the ignition timing and inspect the electric system (spark plugs, distributor, coil, etc.) for proper operation.
- Remove the air filter element and clean it thoroughly.
- Check the flexible mounts between carburettors and intake manifold for tightness.

ALIGNING THE THROTTLE VALVES

- Detach the control linkage "T" from carburettors.
- Slacken the screws "F" and "S" almost fully.
- Operate the throttles a few times to make sure there is no binding.
- Fully depress the throttle control lever of rear carburettor so that the throttles are fully closed; then screw in the screw "S" until contact is made.

IDLING

- Back up the screw "M" of half a turn.
- Tighten the screw "F" to contact, then screw it in one more turn to ensure feeding of engine.
- Connect the accelerator control linkage "T" to carburettors.
- Start the engine and warm it up.
- If necessary, back up the screw "F" very slowly until the engine runs at about 600 to 700 rpms.

Float level adjustment

WEBER 40 DCOE 27 carburettor

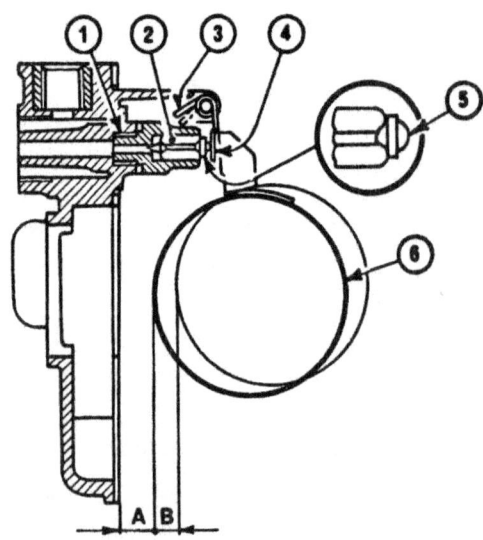

Check the level of fluid in float chamber as follows:

- Make sure the float weight is as specified (26 grs - .9 oz), that there are no leaks or indentations and that float can rotate freely about the pivot pin.

- The float weight must not be altered; consequently haphazard repairs (tinning, etc.) are detrimental to proper float operation.

- Check that needle valve (1) is well screwed into its seating and that the spring-loaded ball (5) part of the needle (2) is not jammed.

- Hold the carburettor cover in a verical position as shown in the figure so that the float (6) does not depress the ball (5).

- With the cover vertical and the float tongue (4) in light contact with the ball, the two floats should be at a distance A = 8.5 mm (.33") from the cover mating surface with the gasket fitted and well stuck to the cover.

- When the level has been set, check that the travel (B) of the float is 6.5 mm (.26"); if necessary, adjust the position of float pivot tail (3).

- The adjustment described above will correspond to a fuel level of 29 - .5 mm (1.12 to 1.16") from the upper face of the float chamber (with a pressure of 2 mts - 6'6" H$_2$O upstream the needle valve).

- If distance (A) is not as specified, slightly bend the float tongue (4) until the correct distance is obtained; inspect the working surface of the float tongue for any sign of nicks wich may restrict the free movement of needle (2).

- Then fit the carburettor cover and check that the float can move freely without rubbing against the walls of the float chamber.

C A U T I O N - The float level should be checked whenever the float or the needle valve has been changed. In the latter case it is also advisable to replace the gasket and make certain the new valve is securely screwed into its seating.

Checking of valve opening and closing angles

Clearance (with cold engine) between the unlobed profile of cams and the valve cup ceiling:
- intake .... .475 to .500 mm (.0187 to .0197")
- exhaust .... .525 to .550 mm (.0206 to .0216")

Opening of intake valve:
- lift of cup .... .20 mm (.008")
- corresponding to an angle .... before TDC of 18°30' ± 1°30'

Closing of intake valve:
- lift of cup .... .20 mm (.008")
- corresponding to an angle .... after BDC of 42°30' ± 1°30'

Opening of exhaust valve:
- lift of cup .... .15 mm (.006")
- corresponding to an angle .... before BDC of 42°30' ± 1°30'

Closing of exhaust valve:
- lift of cup .... .15 mm (.006")
- corresponding to an angle .... after TDC of 18°30' ± 1°30'

Angle values of the actual diagram of valve timing system with cold engine
(clockwise rotation direction of the crankshaft seen from the front side):

- opening of intake valve (before TDC) .... 36° 50'
- closing of intake valve (after BDC) .... 60° 50'
- opening of exhaust valve (before BDC) .... 54° 10'
- closing of exhaust valve (after TDC) .... 30° 10'
- induction stroke .... 277° 40'
- exhaust stroke .... 264° 20'

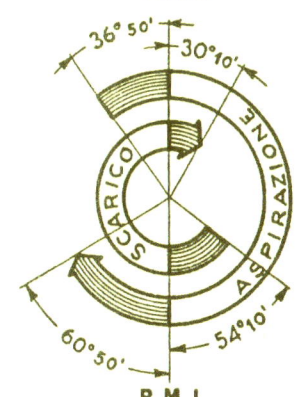

Ignition

Firing order: 1 - 3 - 4 - 2 (no. 1 cylinder is that at the fan side)

Values of advance of ignition distributor

Opening of contact points of ignition distributor .... S = .30 to .40 mm (.014 to .016")
The distributor is correctly fitted when the oiler is toward the engine.

Fixed advance F Before T D C	Maximum Advance M Before T D C
3° ± 1°	43° +0°/−3° at 5000 rpm

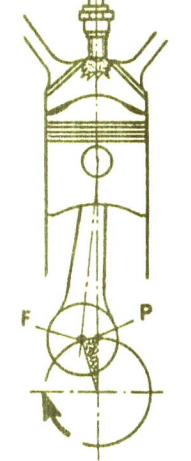
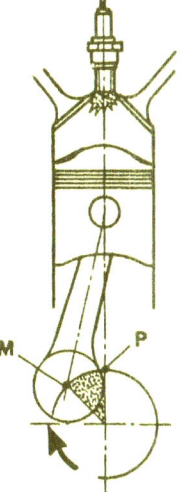

P - T.D.C.
F - Fixed advance
M - Maximum advance

Spark plugs

Lodge 2HL

Electric system

Voltage	12 Volts
Battery	60 Amp.h

	BOSCH
Generator	EG (R) 14 V 25 A 29
Voltage regulator	VA 14 V 25 A
Starting motor	EF (R) 12 V 0.7 PS
Coil	TK 12 A 19
Ignition distributor	JF 4
Windshield wiper	WS 13/11 T3a

Bulb's wattage

Headlights (high and low beams)	45/40 asymmetric
Tail lights - parking & stop	5/20
Front lights - direction indicators	
Tail lights - direction indicators	20
Back-up light	
Front parking lights	5 globular
Side lights - direction indicators	3 tubular
License plate light	5 globular
Engine compartment light	
Dome light inside the car and map reading lamp (under the dashboard)	5 cylindrical
Instrument panel light	
Tell-tale for generator	
Tell-tale for fuel reserve	
Tell-tale for blower	
Cigar lighter lamp	3 tubular
Tell-tale for parking lights	
Tell-tale for direction indicators	
Tell-tale for high beams	

Tightening torque specifications

ENGINE - GEARBOX UNIT	Kgm.	lb. ft	Manner of tightening
Nuts of cylinder head { after repairing, when cold	6.2 to 6.4	44.8 to 46.3	Slacken and retighten without lube
when hot	6.6 to 6.7	47.7 to 48.4	Lock without slackening the nut
Spark plugs	2.5 to 3.5	18.1 to 25.3	With graphite grease, when cold
Nuts of the camshaft caps	2 to 2.25	14.5 to 16.3	in oil
Nuts of the connecting rod caps	5 to 5.3	36.2 to 38.3	" "
Nuts of main bearing caps	4.7 to 5	33.9 to 36.1	" "
Screws of flywheel on crankshaft	4.2 to 4.5	30.4 to 32.5	" "
Nut of generator pulley	3 to 3.5	21.7 to 25.3	d r y
Nut of gearbox main shaft yoke	12	86.8	"
Nut of gearbox layshaft	5	36.1	"
Nut of gearbox half-casing	1.8	13	"
Bolts joining gearbox output shaft yoke to prop. shaft yoke	4.5 to 5.5	32.6 to 39.7	"
REAR FRAME			
Screws securing ring gear to differential case	4.5 to 5	32.6 to 36.1	d r y
Ring nut securing yoke on final drive pinion shaft	8 to 14	58 to 101.2	"
Nuts securing bearing housings to rear axle banjo	4.8 to 5.5	34.8 to 39.7	"
Nuts securing radiud rods to body	10 to 11.5	72.4 to 83	"
Nuts securing radius rods to rear axle banjo	11.5 to 13	83 to 94	"
Nut securing reaction triangle to body	4.8 to 5.5	34.8 to 39.7	"
Nut securing reaction triangle to rear axle	11 to 15	79.6 to 108.5	"
Screws securing brake slave cylinders to axle banjo	.4 to .5	2.9 to 3.6	"
Screws securing rear brake caliper to support	2.3 to 2.8	16.7 to 20.2	"
Nuts securing wheels	6 to 8	43.4 to 57.8	"
Bolts joining differential yoke to prop. shaft yoke	3.5 to 4	25.3 to 28.9	"
FRONT FRAME			
Nut securing steering wheel to column	5 to 5.5	36.1 to 39.7	d r y
Screws securing Burman steering box cover	2.3 to 2.5	16.7 to 18	"
Screws securing steering box & bellcrank bracket to body	4.8 to 5.5	34.8 to 39.7	"
Nuts of steering linkage ball joints	4.8 to 5.5	34.8 to 39.7	"
Nut securing steering arm to box	12.5 to 14	90.5 to 101.2	"
Screws securing upper attachment of shock absorber to body	2.3 to 2.8	16.7 to 20.2	"
Nut securing shock absorber to suspension arms	7.5 to 8.5	54.3 to 61.4	"
Screws securing upper wishbone front arm to body	2.3 to 2.8	16.7 to 20.2	"
Nut securing upper wishbone front arm to rear arm	4.8 to 5.5	34.8 to 39.7	"
Nut securing upper wishbone rear arm to body	11.5 to 13	83 to 94	"
Nuts securing lower wishbone bracket to cross-member	13 to 18	94 to 130	"
Nuts securing steering arm to steering knuckle	4.8 to 5.5	34.8 to 39.7	"
Nut securing upper wishbone rear arm to steering knuckle	7.5 to 8.5	54.3 to 61.4	"
Nut securing lower ball joint to wishbone	7.5 to 8.5	54.3 to 61.4	"
Nut securing lower ball joint to steering knuckle	7.5 to 8.5	54.3 to 61.4	"
Nuts securing caliper support to steering knuckle	4.8 to 5.5	34.8 to 39.7	"
Screws securing front brake calipers to support	7.5 to 8.5	54.3 to 61.4	"
Screws securing front brake discs	7.5 to 8.5	54.3 to 61.4	"
Nuts securing wheels	6 to 8	43.4 to 57.8	"

MAJOR INSPECTION SPECIFICATIONS

Camshafts

Diameter of journals	A =	26.959 to 26.980 mm (1.0614 to 1.0622")
Diameter of journal bearings	B =	27.000 to 27.033 mm (1.0630 to 1.0642")
Clearance between journals and bearings	B-A =	.020 to .074 mm (.0008 to .0028")
End play of camshaft in thrust bearing	C =	.065 to .182 mm (.0026 to .0071")

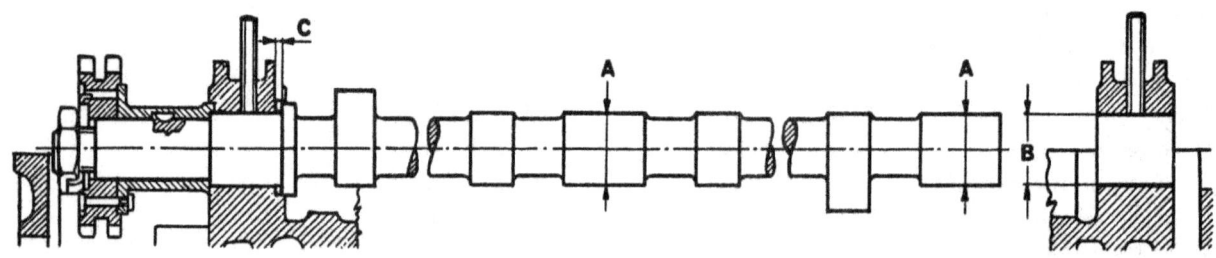

Valves and valve guides

	INTAKE			EXHAUST	(sodium cooled)
	LIVIA H	ATE	GARRONE	ATE	LIVIA C
Diameter of valve poppet ... O	41.000 to 41.150 mm (1.614 to 1.620")	41.000 to 41.200 mm (1.614 to 1.622")	41.000 to 41.150 mm (1.614 to 1.620")	37.000 to 37.200 mm (1.4567 to 1.4645")	37.000 to 37.150 mm (1.4567 to 1.4625")
Diameter of valve stem ... M		8.962 to 8.987 mm (.3528 to .3538")			8.935 to 8.960 mm (.3518 to .3527")
Total length .. L	106.900 to 107.150 mm (4.2087 to 4.2186")	106.800 mm (4.2047")	107.000 mm (4.2126")	106.050 to 106.150 mm (4.1753 to 4.1791")	106.300 mm (4.1850")

N.B.: ATE - LIVIA - GARRONE intake valves and ATE - LIVIA exhaust valves are alternate supply.

Valve guide Outside diameter with guide removed	E =	14.033 to 14.044 mm (.5525 to .5529")
Inside diameter with guide assembled in cylinder head	F =	9.000 to 9.015 mm (.3544 to .3549")
Projection of valve guides from their recesses in the cylinder head		16.800 to 17.000 mm (.662 to .669")
Clearance between guide assembled in cylinder head and valve stem	intake	.013 to .053 mm (.0005 to .0020")
	exhaust	.040 to .080 mm (.0016 to .0031")

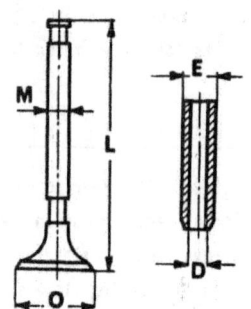

Valve seats

Diameter of valve guide seat in cylinder head F = 13.990 to 14.018 mm (.5508 to .5519")
Interference between seat and valve guide E-F = .015 to .054 mm (.0006 to .0021")

		Intake	Exhaust
Outer diameter of the valve seat insert ... H	standard	42.597 to 42.632 mm (1.6771 to 1.6784")	38.597 to 38.632 mm (1.5196 to 1.5209")
	oversized	42.897 to 42.932 mm (1.6889 to 1.6902")	38.897 to 38.932 mm (1.5314 to 1.5327")
Diameter of recess in the cylinder head for valve seat insert ... G	standard	42.532 to 42.557 mm (1.6744 to 1.6754")	38.532 to 38.557 mm (1.5169 to 1.5179")
	oversized	42.832 to 42.857 mm (1.6862 to 1.6872")	38.832 to 38.857 mm (1.5288 to 1.5298")

Interference between valve seat insert and recess in cylinder head .... H-G = .100 to .040 mm (.0039 to .0010")

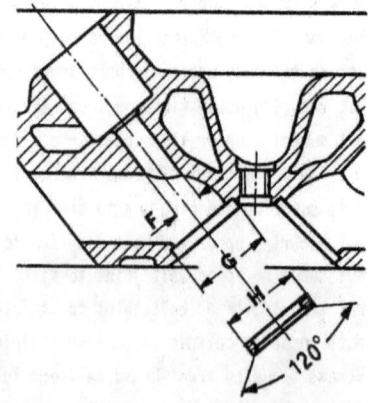

Valve cups

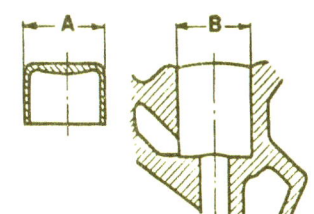

Diameter of cup .... A	{ standard .	34.973 to 34.989 mm (1.3769 to 1.3775")
	oversized .	35.173 to 35.189 mm (1.3848 to 1.3854")
Diameter of cup seat in cylinder head .... B	{ standard .	35.000 to 35.025 mm (1.3780 to 1.3789")
	oversized .	35.200 to 35.225 mm (1.3859 to 1.3868")
Clearance between seat and cup		.011 to .052 mm (.0005 to .0020")

Valve springs

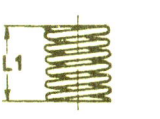 

	Free length	Length under test load	Test load
Inner spring .. l	red mark 47.3 mm (1.87")	l = 26 mm (1.02")	22.2 to 23.1 Kg. 48.9 to 51.1 lbs
	green mark 46.5 mm (1.83")		
Outer spring .. L	red mark 52.8 mm (2.08")	L1 = 27.5 mm (1.08")	35.7 to 37.1 Kg. 78.6 to 81.8 lbs
	green mark 51.3 mm (2.02")		

<u>Note</u> - The valve springs should be fitted with the color-marked coil downward.

Connecting rods

Length between center line of big end and center line of small end of connecting rod D 147.955 to 148.045 mm (5.8250 to 5.8285")
Inner diameter of the big end of connecting rod .... E 53.695 to 53.708 mm (2.1140 to 2.1144")
Inner diameter of bushing in the small end of rod .... C 22.005 to 22.015 mm (.8664 to .8667")
Thickness of connecting rod bearings F { standard .... 1.829 to 1.835 mm (.0720 to .0722")
1st oversize .... 1.956 to 1.962 mm (.0770 to .0772")
2nd oversize .... 2.083 to 2.089 mm (.0820 to .0824")
Radial clearance between crankpins and bearings for big end of connecting rod .... .025 to .063 mm (.0010 to .0024")
Maximum out of parallelism between ℄ of big end hole and ℄ of small end hole ..... .074 mm (.0029")

Piston pins

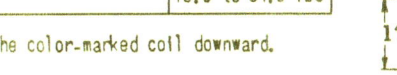

	Black	White
O.D. of pin	21.994 to 21.997 mm (.86590 to .86602")	21.998 to 22.000 mm (.86606 to .86614")
Clearance between con. rod small end bore and piston pin	.008 to .021 mm (.0003 to .0008")	.005 to .017 mm (.0002 to .0006")

Piston pin hole

	Black	White
BORGO piston .... H	22.000 to 22.002 mm (.86614 to .86621")	22.003 to 22.005 mm (.86626 to .86633")

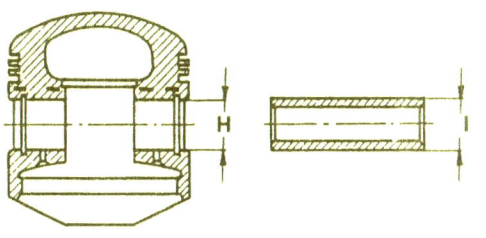

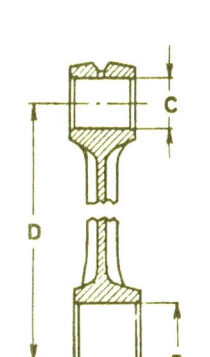

End play of the connecting rods on the crankpins G .200 to .300 mm (.0079 to .0118")

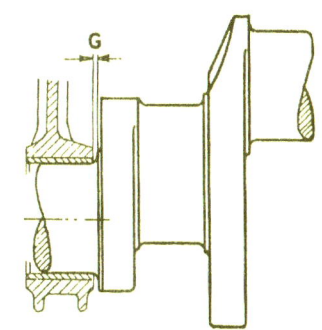

Pistons and piston rings

Diameter of pistons to be measured to square with the hole for piston pin and at a sistance of L = 12 mm (.472") from the lower border of skirt.

	CLASS A (BLUE)	CLASS B (PINK)	CLASS C (GREEN)
BORGO piston diameter	77.920 to 77.930 mm (3.0677 to 3.0681")	77.931 to 77.940 mm (3.0682 to 3.0685")	77.941 to 77.950 mm (3.0686 to 3.0688")

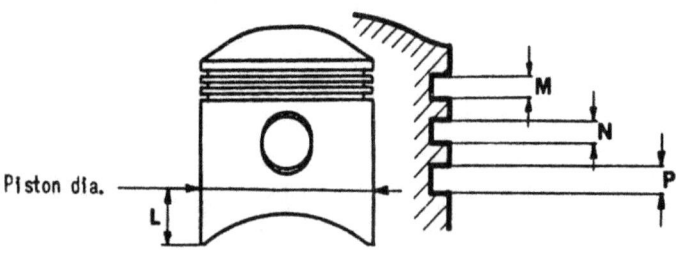
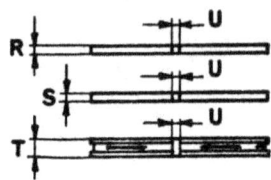

Height of grooves in piston for compression rings { chromium-plated ... M	1.535 to 1.550 mm (.0605 to .0612")
normal ... N	1.775 to 1.790 mm (.0699 to .0704")
Height of groove in piston for oil scraper ring ... P	4.015 to 4.030 mm (.1581 to .1586")
Thickness of compression rings { chromium-plated ... R	1.478 to 1.490 mm (.0582 to .0586")
normal ... S	1.728 to 1.740 mm (.0681 to .0685")
Thickness of oil scraper ring ... T	3.978 to 3.990 mm (.1567 to .1571")
End play of rings in grooves { compression rings { chromium-plated ...	.045 to .072 mm (.0018 to .0028")
normal ...	.035 to .062 mm (.0014 to .0024")
oil scraper rings ...	.025 to .052 mm (.0010 to .0020")
Gap of rings to be inspected in ring gauge or in cylinder barrels ... U	.300 to .450 mm (.0012 to .0017")

Cylinder barrels

	CLASS A (BLUE)	CLASS B (PINK)	CLASS C (GREEN)
Cylinder barrel bore	77.985 to 77.994 mm (3.0703 to 3.0706")	77.995 to 78.004 mm (3.0707 to 3.0710")	78.005 to 78.014 mm (3.0711 to 3.0714")

Clearance between cylinder barrel and piston .... .055 to .074 mm (.0022 to .0029")

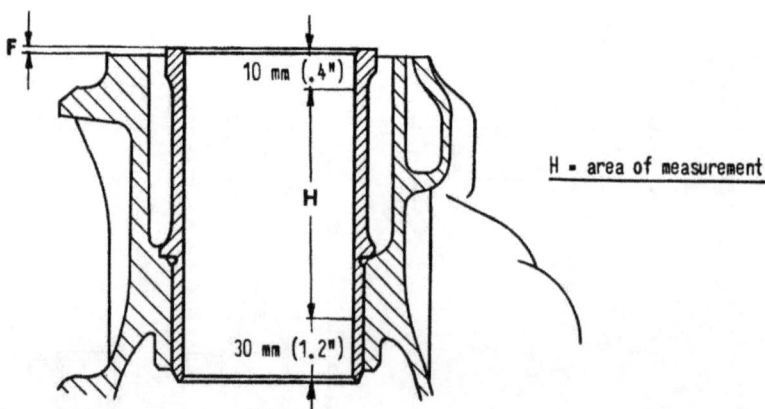

H = area of measurement

Projection of barrels from cylinder block .... F   .000 to .060 mm (.0000 to .0024")
Surface roughness of barrel bore ....   20 to 40 microinches RMS

Crankshaft

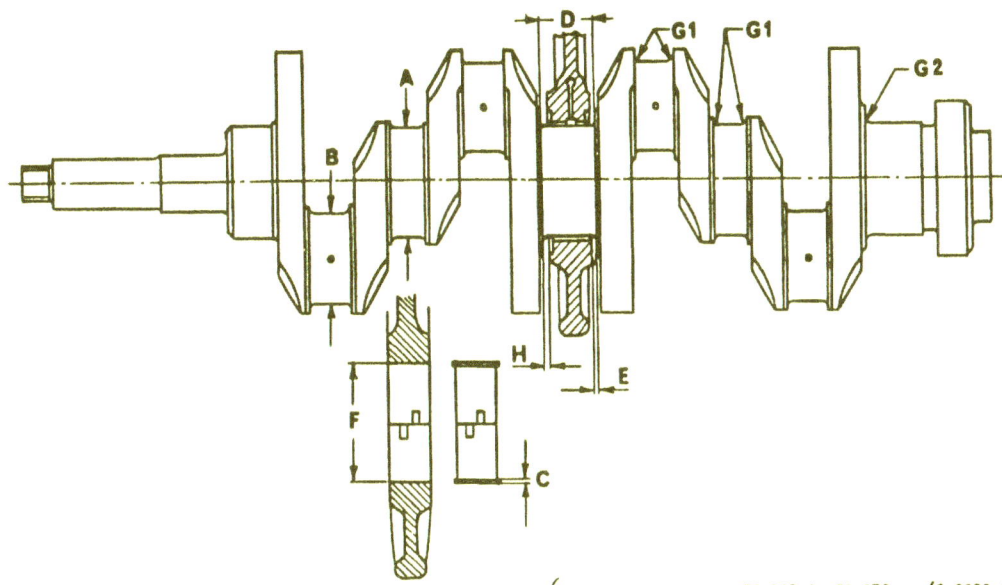

Diameter of main journals ... A	standard ...	59.960 to 59.973 mm	(2.3606 to 2.3611")
	1st undersize .	59.706 to 59.719 mm	(2.3506 to 2.3511")
	2nd undersize .	59.452 to 59.465 mm	(2.3407 to 2.3411")
Diameter of crankpins ... B	standard ...	49.987 to 50.000 mm	(1.9680 to 1.9685")
	1st undersize .	49.733 to 49.746 mm	(1.9581 to 1.9585")
	2nd undersize .	49.479 to 49.492 mm	(1.9480 to 1.9485")
Thickness of main bearings ... C	standard ...	1.829 to 1.835 mm	(.0720 to .0722")
	1st oversize .	1.956 to 1.962 mm	(.0770 to .0772")
	2nd oversize .	2.083 to 2.089 mm	(.0820 to .0822")
Diameter of seat for main bearings in crankcase ... F		63.657 to 63.676 mm	(2.5062 to 2.5069")
Length of central journal ... D	standard ...	30.000 to 30.035 mm	(1.1811 to 1.1824")
	1st oversize .	30.127 to 30.162 mm	(1.1861 to 1.1874")
	2nd oversize .	30.254 to 30.289 mm	(1.1911 to 1.1924")
Thickness of thrust rings for central journal ... E	standard ...	2.311 to 2.362 mm	(.0910 to .0929")
	1st oversize .	2.374 to 2.425 mm	(.0935 to .0954")
	2nd oversize .	2.438 to 2.489 mm	(.0960 to .0980")
End play of crankshaft ... H		.076 to .263 mm	(.003 to .010")
Radial clearance between journals and main bearings		.014 to .058 mm	(.0005 to .0022")

Note - Radial clearance = main bearing ID - (twice bearing thickness + journal OD).

Fillet radii	main journals & crankpins ... G1	1.7 to 2.1 mm	(.07 to .08")
	pin on flywheel side ... G2	3.7 to 4.1 mm	(.15 to .16")
Main journals & crankpins surface roughness		63 microinches RMS	
Maximum elongation of main journals and crankpins		.007 mm	(.00027")
Maximum taper of main journals and crankpins measured on their full length		.01 mm	(.00039")
Maximum error of parallelism of main journals and crankpins measured on their full length		.015 mm	(.00059")
Maximum misalignment allowed between main journals		.01 mm	(.00039")
Maximum misalignment allowed between ₵ of the two pairs of crankpins and ₵ of main journals		.300 mm	(.0118")

Clutch

Pedal free travel	23 mm (.9")
Distance between thrust ring and the reference sleeve of tool C.6.0104 (See I.S. 1.05.080)	.75 to 1.25 mm (.030 to .053")
Squareness of the clutch driven plate assembled on gearbox direct drive shaft	.50 mm (.019")
Spring rating — free length	46 to 49 mm (1.82 to 1.93")
Spring rating — length under test load	28.3 (1.13")
Spring rating — test load	55 to 61 Kgs (122 to 134 lbs)
Wear limit of driven plate thickness	6 mm (.24")

Gearbox

Transmission ratios — 1st gear	3.304 : 1
Transmission ratios — 2nd gear	1.988 : 1
Transmission ratios — 3rd gear	1.355 : 1
Transmission ratios — 4th gear	1.000 : 1
Transmission ratios — 5th gear	.791 : 1
Transmission ratios — Rev.	3.010 : 1
Maximum eccentricity of main shaft	.050 mm (.020")
End play between forks and sleeves — assembly	.150 to .340 mm (.006 to .013")
End play between forks and sleeves — wear limit	.850 mm (.033")

Gear	1st - 2nd - 3rd	5th - Rev.
Calibration of springs for striking rod balls — free length	15.2 mm (.60")	30.5 mm (1.2")
Calibration of springs for striking rod balls — length under test load	10 mm (.39")	20 mm (.78")
Calibration of springs for striking rod balls — test load	2.88 to 3.12 Kg (6.4 to 6.8 lbs)	4.32 to 4.68 Kg (9.5 to 10.3 lbs)

Maximum end play of mainshaft gears — 1st speed gear	.170 to .245 mm (.0067 to .0096")
Maximum end play of mainshaft gears — 2nd & 3rd speed gears	.130 to .205 mm (.0052 to .0081")
Maximum end play of mainshaft gears — 5th speed gear & Rev.	.160 to .220 mm (.0063 to .0087")
Radial clearance between gear bushings and mainshaft — 1st speed gear	.125 to .170 mm (.0049 to .0067")
Radial clearance between gear bushings and mainshaft — 2nd & 3rd speed gears	.095 to .140 mm (.0038 to .0055")
Radial clearance between gear bushings and mainshaft — 5th speed gear	.065 to .107 mm (.0026 to .0041")
Distance between outer planes of the engaging teeth of 3rd and 4th gears	42.000 to 42.200 mm (1.65 to 1.66")
Distance, in neutral, of the rear band (propeller shaft side) of 5th speed sleeve from the <u>rear</u> edge of gear engaging teeth	12.9 mm (.508")

Rear axle and suspension

Transmission-axle overall ratios-with 41 : 9 final drive	1st gear .	15.049 : 1
	2nd gear .	9.055 : 1
	3rd gear .	6.172 : 1
	4th gear .	4.555 : 1
	5th gear .	3.603 : 1
	Rev. . . .	13.710 : 1

Maximum eccentricity of axle shafts	.10 mm (.004")
Play between teeth of planetary gears	.05 mm (.002")
Play between teeth of final drive	.05 to .10 mm (.002 to .004")
Reference dimension on tool C.6.0101 for pinion-to-ring gear fitting	70 ± .0025 mm (2.7559 ± .0001")
Max. factory end play between reaction trunnion and attachment to body	1 mm (.04")
Pre-load on pinion bearing	11.5 to 15.5 Kgcm (10 to 13.5 in. lbs)
Total preload on final drive bearings	16.5 to 24.5 Kgcm (14.4 to 21.3 in. lbs)

CHECKING OF SHOCK ABSORBERS ON TEST BENCH - Calibration data (when cold)

	BIANCHI - ALLINQUANT	
	Extension	Compression
High speed	135 to 190 Kgs (298 to 418 lbs)	50 to 80 Kgs (111 to 176 lbs)
Low speed	19 to 55 Kgs (42 to 121 lbs)	9 to 22 Kgs (20 to 48 lbs)

CHECKING OF SUSPENSION SPRINGS

Free length	437 mm (17.2")
Length under test load	252 mm (10")
Test load	268.7 to 285.3 Kgs (592 to 628 lbs)
Colored marks	Blue-Blue / Blue-White

Front suspension

ADJUSTMENT OF CLEARANCE IN WHEEL BEARINGS

When performing regular servicing or whenever the removal of wheel hubs is required, adjust the bearing clearance as follows:

1) Screw in the castellated nut and lock it to a torque of 2.5 Kgm (18 ft-lbs) while at the same time revolving the wheel hub to set the bearings properly in their seats;

2) Unscrew the nut half a turn or more;

3) Lightly tap on the stub axle end with a mallet in order to return the outboard bearing in its proper position even in the case a slight interference between bearing cone and stub axle exists;

4) Lock the nut in place to 1.5 Kgm (10.8 ft-lbs);

5) Unscrew the nut of a quarter turn;

6) If the hole in the axle is aligned with a slot in the castellated nut insert the cotter pin; if not, screw in the nut by the minimum angle needed to line up the hole and the next slot;

7) Again tap lightly on stub axle end to restore the same condition as under step 3;

8) The end play so obtained on stub axle should fall between .02 - .12 mm (.0008 - .0047").

WHEEL BEARING LUBRICATING INSTRUCTIONS

The quantity of lubricating grease should be about 65 grammes (2½ ozs) for each hub; do not exceed such a quantity to avoid bearing overheating, grease leakage, etc.
The grease should be well distributed inside the bearings and into side recesses.
Subsequently, at the regular schedule, remove the hub cover and pack the outboard bearing.

BALL JOINTS

End play of lower ball joint in its socket . . . . 1 mm (.04")

N o t e - Ball joints require no regular lubrication being provided with special grease seals which retain the grease packed in by factory on assembly - Only if strictly needed (joints squealing) grease with SHELL Retinax A or AGIP F.1 Grease 30 (See I.S. 1.05.097/1).

CHECKING OF SUSPENSION SPRINGS

Free length . . . . 303 mm (11.9")
Length under test load . . . . 200 mm (7.8")
Test load . . . . 778 to 828 Kg (1720 to 1825 lbs)
Colored marks . . . . { White-White / Sky blue

CHECKING OF SHOCK ABSORBERS ON TEST BENCH

Calibration data (when cold)

	GIRLING		BIANCHI - ALLINQUANT	
	Extension	Compression	Extension	Compression
High speed	210 to 310 Kgs (463 to 683 lbs)	27 to 52 Kgs (60 to 114 lbs)	150 to 190 Kgs (331 to 418 lbs)	55 to 80 Kgs (121 to 176 lbs)
Low speed	30 to 52 Kgs (66 to 114 lbs)	9 to 22 Kgs (20 to 48 lbs)	25 to 55 Kgs (56 to 121 lbs)	9 to 22 Kgs (20 to 48 lbs)

Brakes (Dunlop make)

Whenever a brake unit is overhauled or replaced check the disc for true rotation with the disc fitted to the car.

Use a dial gauge and check that runout does not exeed .15 mm (.006"). Should the reading exceed this value, then the installation of disc on stub axle must be carefully examined; if the run out persists, replace the disc.

If the disc is scored, the grinding of the surfaces is allowed providing not to exceed an undersize of 1 mm (.0394"), equalized on both faces, i.e. .5 mm (.0197") each face; disc wear limit: 8.5 mm (.335") thick.

Inspection specifications after regrinding of disc surfaces:

- Max. out of parallelism with disc mounting plane: .05 mm (.0020");
- Max. out of flat: .025 mm (.0010") and max. difference in thickness: .038 mm (.0015") as measured along any radial line;
- Max. out of flat: .025 mm (.0010") and max. difference in thickness: .015 mm (.0006") as measured along any circular line;
- The surface should show no sign of scoring or porosity.

The surface roughness should be:

- 26 microinches as measured circularly;
- 36 microinches as measured radially.

FRICTION PADS

	Front	Rear
Thickness when new	16 mm (.630")	17.5 mm (.689")
Wear limit	8 mm (.315")	10.0 mm (.394")

CALIPERS

On replacement of disc or caliper measure the running clearance between caliper and disc on each side; the difference should not exceed .5 mm (.0197").

To centralize the caliper about the disc, insert shims between caliper and mounting flange as required.

HAND BRAKE

It is mechanically-operated and acts on the rear service brake pads.

The adjustment is performed by acting on the nut of control cable located between intermediate levers and calipers. After the adjustment, make sure that levers of rear calipers to which the cable is connected are all the way outward. In such a position the cable must not be tight but slightly slackened. Furthermore the brake pads must not contact the disc.

Brakes (ATE make)

Refer to the Publication " A T E   D I S C   B R A K E S " no. 1202.

N o t e - The car features a "LOCKHEED" type vacuum servo.

WHEEL ALIGNMENT AND CAR "TRIM"

Put the car under static load, with shock absorbers and stabilizer rod connected, with full tank or equivalent with spare wheel, tool kit and the tires inflated as specified.

Before checking, slightly jolt the car so as to settle the suspensions.

Static load
- 2 weights of 45 Kgs (100 lbs) on front seats
- 2 weights of 25 Kgs (55 lbs) on flooring where feet rest

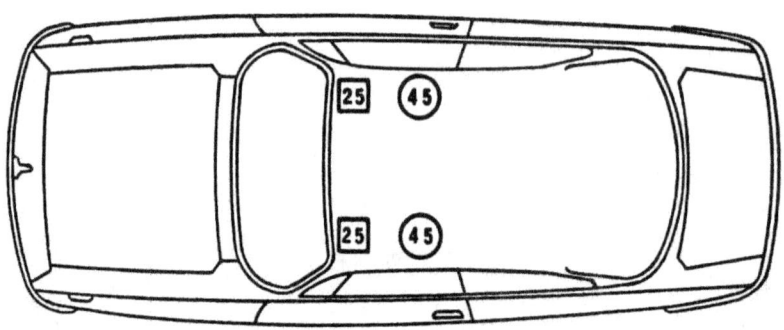

DISTANCE OF LOWER WISHBONE OF FRONT SUSPENSION FROM A REFERENCE LEVEL

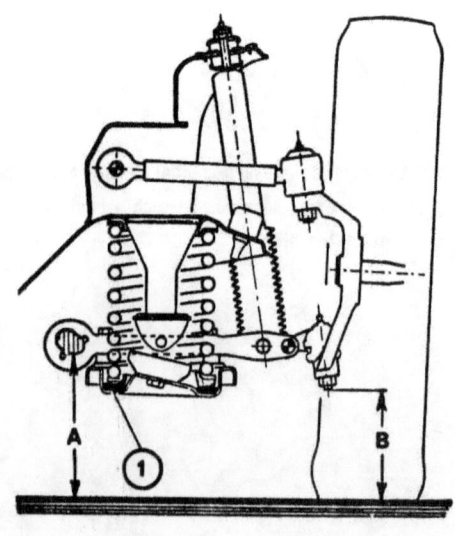

A-B = 34 ± 3 mm (1.34 ± .12")

N o t e - for suspensions having the upper limiting bumper outside the spring A-B should be: 14 ± 3 mm (.55 ± .12")

Dimension A must be measured in correspondence of the lower line of wishbone shaft as shown.

To adjust add shims in (1).

Shims are available in the following thicknesses:

3.5 mm (.14") - 7 mm (.28") - 10.5 mm (.42")

DISTANCE OF REAR AXLE FROM RUBBER BUFFERS

$$C = 15 \pm 5 \text{ mm} (.59 \pm 2")$$

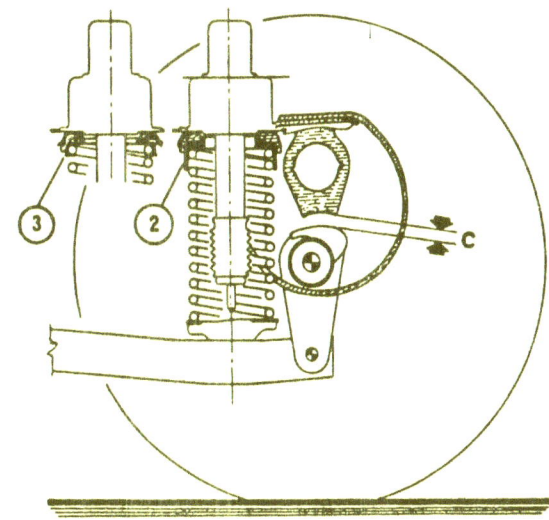

Note - To adjust, remove the seat 3 and add shims in 2 as shown.

Shims are available in the following ticknesses:

6.5 mm (.26")
11.5 mm (.45")
16.5 mm (.65")
21.5 mm (.85")

In the conditions as specified check the wheel angles.

CASTER ANGLE: $\alpha = 1° \pm 30'$

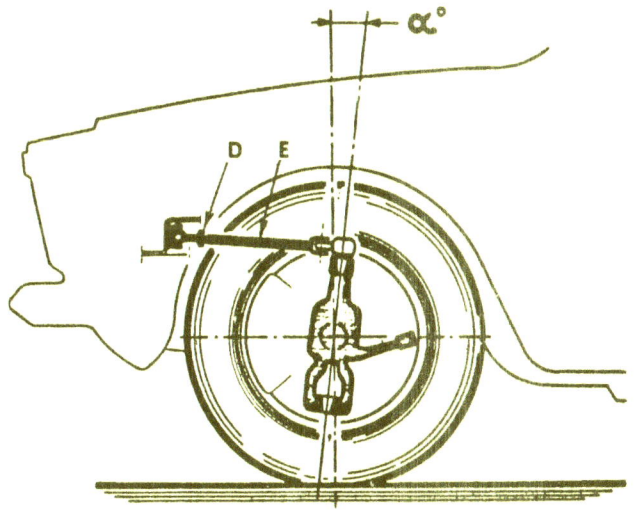

The difference in caster angle between R.H. and L.H. wheel must not exceed 0°20'.

To adjust, loosen jam nut "D" and rotate rod "E".

Note - Small adjustments of the caster angle allow to correct slight drift tendency of the car.

The caster angle should be checked under static load and alignment conditions as specified and with shock absorbers disconnected at an end.

N.B. - Before checking the caster angle shake the front end of car in order to allow the rubber bushing on the front slanting arm to set properly.

FRONT WHEEL CAMBER

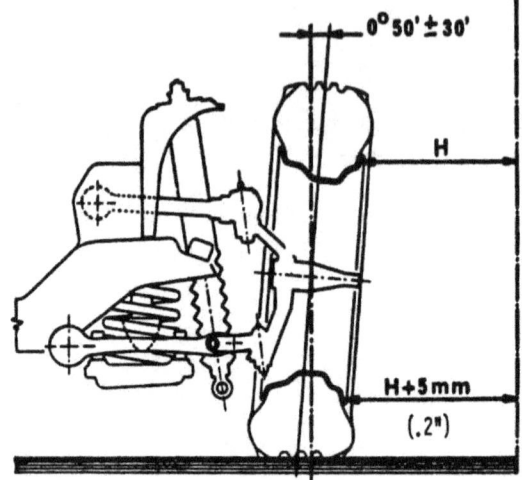

Difference in camber angle between R.H. and L.H. wheel = 0° 40'

N o t e - Not adjustable. Check the chassis, if necessary.

FRONT WHEEL TOE-IN

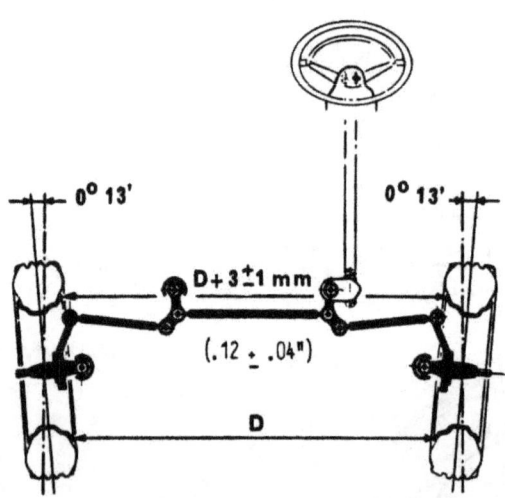

Rod length:

side .... 272 to 288 mm (10.7 to 11.3")

track .... 530 to 550 mm (20.86 to 21.66")

With the toe-in as specified, the length of rods as measured between ball joint centers should fall within the limits shown. If these values cannot be restored, the cause will probably be attributable to distortion of the body resulting from a collision.

giulia super

**technical characteristics
and
principal inspection specifications**

C O N T E N T S

T E C H N I C A L   C H A R A C T E R I S T I C S

PRINCIPAL CHARACTERISTIC DATA	Page	2
Performances	"	2
Tires	"	3
Refillings	"	3
Oils and lubricants	"	3
Carburetion	"	4
Valve timing	"	5
Ignition	"	5
Spark plugs	"	5
Electric system	"	6
Tightening torque specifications	"	7

M A J O R   I N S P E C T I O N   S P E C I F I C A T I O N S

Camshafts	"	9
Valves and valve guides	"	9
Valve seats	"	9
Valve cups	"	10
Valve springs	"	10
Connecting rods	"	10
Piston pin	"	10
Piston pin hole	"	10
Pistons and cylinder barrels	"	11
Compression and oil scraper rings	"	11
Crankshaft	"	12
Clutch	"	13
Gearbox	"	13
Rear axle and suspension	"	14
Front suspension	"	15
Brakes	"	16
Wheel alignment	"	17

Variants from chassis no. { 862001 (L.H.D.) / 722501 (R.H.D.) } . . . . . . " 20

Variants from chassis no. { 880001 (L.H.D.) / 724001 (R.H.D.) } . . . . . . " 28

TECHNICAL CHARACTERISTICS

PRINCIPAL CHARACTERISTIC DATA

Number of cylinders	4
Bore	78 mm
Stroke	82 mm
Total cylinder capacity	1570 cc
Maximum power at 5500 rpm	DIN 98 CV / SAE 112 CV
Front track	1310 mm
Rear track	1270 mm
Wheel base	2510 mm
Minimum turning circle	10,900 mm
Overall length	4140 mm
Overall width	1560 mm
Overall height (unladen)	1430 mm
Dry weight	1000 Kg
Number of seats	5
Tires 155 x 15	PIRELLI Cinturato S / MICHELIN X
Fuel consumption per 100 Km (62 miles) (Italian CUNA Standards)	10.4 lt (27.1 mpg)
Water pump & generator drive belt	n° 60675

With 41 : 9 final drive

	Max. Speeds					
	Running in				After running in	
Gear	up to 1000 Km (600 mi)		1000 to 3000 Km (600 to 1900 mi)			
	Km/h	mph	Km/h	mph	Km/h	mph
1st	27	17	34	21	42	26
2nd	46	29	56	35	69	43
3rd	67	42	82	51	102	63
4th	91	57	111	69	138	85
5th	115	71	141	83	over 175	110
Rev.	-	-	-	-	46	28

Oil pressures with hot engine:
- min. pressure at idling speed .... .5 - 1 Kg/cm² (7 - 14 psi)
- min. pressure at top speed .... 3.5 Kg/cm² (50 psi)
- max. pressure at top speed .... 4.5 - 5 Kg/cm² (65 - 70 psi)

W a r n i n g : Check that generator warning light goes off as soon as the engine exceeds idling speed.

Tires

Inflation pressures (with tire cold)

Front wheels - 1.6 to 1.8 Kg/cm^2 (22.7 to 25.6 psi)

Rear wheels - 1.7 to 2.1 Kg/cm^2 (24.1 to 29.8 psi)

- Inflate to the lower pressure for use with low load and short bursts of speed.
- Inflate to the higher pressure for use with full load and maximum speeds.

Refillings

Water (engine & radiator)	7.5 lts	1.65 gals
Fuel (reserve 6 to 7 lt / 1.3 - 1.5 gals)	46 lts	10.1 gals
Oil — Engine (sump & filter) to min. level	3.25 Kgs	3.2 qts
Oil — Engine (sump & filter) to max. level*	5.00 Kgs	4.95 qts
Oil — Gearbox	1.650 Kgs	3.2 pints
Oil — Differential	1.250 Kgs	2.5 pints
Oil — Steering box	.250 Kg	.5 pint

* This quantity is that needed for regular changing; the total amount of oil in the circuit (sump, filter, passages) is 5.75 Kg (5.7 qts).

Oils and lubricants

Refer to the directions given in the Instruction Book

CARBURETION

2 Weber 40 DCOE 24 Carburettors

Venturi	27
Main jet (3 mm dia. ball)	110
Main air metering jet	180
Idling jet (150 axial hole)	50
Idling air metering jet	120
Choke jet	65 F 5
Choke air metering jet	200
Acceleration pump jet	35
Acceleration pump inlet valve	50
Acceleration pump stroke	14 mm
Delivery of acceleration pump (every 20 pump strokes for each barrel)	4 to 6 cc
Needle valve (spring preload 50 grs)	150
Weight of float	26 grs
Distance of fuel level from float chamber flange (with a pressure of 2 mts H2O upstream the needle valve)	28.5 to 29.5 mm
Idling speed	600 to 700 rpm

2 Solex C 40 PHH/2 Carburettors

Venturi	28
Main jet	125
Main air metering jet	125
Idling jet	55
Idling air metering jet	80
Choke jet	100
Choke air metering jet	300
Acceleration pump jet	35
Delivery of acceleration pump (per 20 pump strokes for each barrel)	3.5 to 4.5 cc
Needle valve	1.75
Spacer under needle valve	1 mm
Weight of float	12.5 gr
Distance of fuel level (with a pressure of 2 mts H2O upstream the needle valve)	21 mm

N o t e - WEBER and SOLEX carburettors are alternative supply.

VALVE TIMING

Checking of valve opening and closing angles

Clearance (with cold engine) between the unlobed profile of cam of camshaft and the cup ceiling
- intake .... .475 to .500 mm
- exhaust .... .525 to .550 mm

Opening of intake valve
- lift of cup .... .20 mm
- corresponding to an angle .... before T D C of 18° 30' ± 1° 30'

Closing of intake valve
- lift of cup .... .20 mm
- corresponding to an angle .... after B D C of 42° 30' ± 1° 30'

Opening of exhaust valve
- lift of cup .... .15 mm
- corresponding to an angle .... before B D C of 42° 30' ± 1° 30'

Closing of exhaust valve
- lift of cup .... .15 mm
- corresponding to an angle .... after T D C of 18° 30' ± 1° 30'

Angle values of the actual diagram of valve timing system with cold engine
(clockwise rotation direction of the crankshaft seen from the front side)

Opening of intake valve	before T D C	36° 50'
Closing of intake valve	after B D C	60° 50'
Opening of exhaust valve	before B D C	54° 10'
Closing of exhaust valve	after T D C	30° 10'
Induction stroke		277° 40'
Exhaust stroke		264° 20'

IGNITION

Firing order: 1 - 3 - 4 - 2 (No. 1 cylinder is that at the fan side)

Opening of contact points of ignition distributor .... .35 to 40 mm

The distributor is correctly fitted when the oiler is toward the engine.

Values of advance of ignition distributor

Fixed advance F Before T D C	Maximum advance M Before T D C
3° ± 1°	43° $^{+0°}_{-3°}$ at 5300 rpm

SPARK PLUGS

Lodge 2HL

ELECTRIC SYSTEM

Voltage .... 12 V
Battery .... 60 Ah

	BOSCH	MARELLI
Generator	EG (R) 14 V 25 A 29	DN 62 E/P
Voltage regulator	VA 14 V 25 A	SD 368 A 300/12
Starting motor	EF (R) 12 V .7 PS	MT 54 B
Coil	TK 12 A 19	BZR 200 D
Ignition distributor	VJ 4 BR 35 mk	S 103 A
Windshield wiper	WS 13/11 S 1 a	TGE 93 A

Bulb's wattage

Inner headlights (high beams) .... 40/45 asymmetric
Outer headlights (low beams) .... 40/45 asymmetric
Front parking lights .... 5 globular
Front lights - direction indicators 20
Side lights - direction indicators .... 3 tubular
Tail lights - parking & stop 5/20
Tail lights - direction indicators 20
Back-up light 20
License plate light .... 5 globular
Cigar lighter lamp .... 3 tubular
Engine compartment light .... 5 globular
Dome light inside the car .... 5 cylindrical
Light in luggage compartment .... 5 cylindrical
Lighting on instrument panel .... 3 tubular
Tell-tale for parking lights .... 3 tubular
Tell-tale for direction indicators .... 3 tubular
Tell-tale for generator .... 3 tubular
Tell-tale for high beams .... 3 tubular
Tell-tale for fuel reserve .... 3 tubular
Tell-tale for blower .... 3 tubular

TIGHTENING TORQUE SPECIFICATIONS

ENGINE - GEARBOX UNIT

	Kgm.	Manner of tightening
*Cylinder head nuts — Inspection — when cold	6.2 to 6.4	Slacken in proper sequence, the nuts by one and one half turn and lubetorque
*Cylinder head nuts — Inspection — when hot	6.6 to 6.7	Warm up the engine and when hot retighten without unscrewing
*Cylinder head nuts — After repairing — when cold	6.2 to 6.4	Retighten with lube
*Cylinder head nuts — After repairing — when hot	6.6 to 6.7	Warm up the engine by actually driving the car and when hot retighten without unscrewing
*Cylinder head nuts — After repairing — when cold	6.2 to 6.4	After tested the car, slacken, when cold and in proper sequence, the nuts by one and one half turn and lubetorque
Spark plugs	2.5 to 3.5	With graphite grease, when cold
Nuts of the camshaft caps	2 to 2.25	in oil
Nuts of the connecting rod caps	5 to 5.3	" "
Nuts of main bearing caps	4.7 to 5	" "
Screws of flywheel on crankshaft	4.2 to 4.5	" "
Nut of generator pulley	3 to 3.5	dry
Oil sump drain plug	7 to 8	"
Nut of gearbox main shaft yoke	11 to 12	"
Nut of gearbox layshaft	4.5 to 5.5	"
Nuts of gearbox half-casing	1.8	"
Nut of gearbox inner swivel	3.25 to 3.65	"
Bolts joing gearbox output shaft yoke to prop. shaft yoke	5.5 to 5.7	"
Plug on oil filter	3.5 to 4	"

REAR FRAME

Screws securing ring gear to differential case	4.5 to 5	"
Ring nut securing yoke on final drive pinion shaft	8 to 14	"
Nuts securing bearing housings to rear axle banjo	4.8 to 5.5	"
Nuts securing radius rods to body	10 to 11.5	"
Nuts securing radius rods to rear axle banjo	11.5 to 13	"
Nut securing reaction triangle to body	4.8 to 5.5	"
Nut securing reaction triangle to differential housing	11 to 15	"
Screws securing brake slave cylinders to axle banjo	.4 to .5	"
Screws securing rear brake caliper to support	2.3 to 2.8	"
Nuts securing wheels	6 to 8	"
Bolts joining differential yoke to prop. shaft yoke	4.5 to 5.5	"

* **Warning**: In case of any repair work involving the removal of cylinder head, the gasket must be renewed at all times.

FRONT FRAME

	Kgm.	Manner of tightening
Nut securing wheel to column	5 to 5.5	dry
Screws securing Burman steering box cover	2.3 to 2.5	"
Screws securing steering box & relay arm bracket to body	4.8 to 5.5	"
Nuts of steering linkage ball joints	4.8 to 5.5	"
Nut securing steering arm to box	12.5 to 14	"
Screws securing upper attachment of shock absorber to body	2.3 to 2.8	"
Nut securing shock absorber to suspension arms	7.5 to 8.5	"
Screws securing upper wishbone front arm to body	2.3 to 2.8	"
Nut securing upper wishbone front arm to rear arm	4.8 to 5.5	"
Nut securing upper wishbone rear arm to body	11.5 to 13	"
Nuts securing lower wishbone shaft to cross-member	13 to 18	"
Nuts securing steering arm to steering knuckle	4.8 to 5.5	"
Nut securing upper wishbone rear arm to steering knuckle	7.5 to 8.5	"
Nut securing lower ball joint to wishbone	7.5 to 8.5	"
Nut securing lower ball joint to steering knuckle	7.5 to 8.5	"
Nuts securing caliper support to steering knuckle	4.8 to 5.5	"
Screws securing front brake calipers to support	7.5 to 8.5	"
Screws securing front brake discs	7.5 to 8.5	"

MAJOR INSPECTION SPECIFICATIONS

Camshafts

Diameter of journals . . . . 26.959 to 26.980 mm

Diameter of journals bearings . . . . 27.000 to 27.033 mm

Radial clearance between journals and bearings . . . . .020 to .074 mm

End play of camshaft in thrust bearing . . . . .065 to .182 mm

Valves and valve guides

	Intake	Exhaust	
	LIVIA H	LIVIA C	ATE
Diameter of valve poppet	41.000 to 41.150 mm	37.000 to 37.150 mm	37.000 to 37.200 mm
Diameter of valve stem	8.962 to 8.987 mm	8.935 to 8.960 mm	8.935 to 8.960 mm
Total length	106.903 to 107.157 mm	106.173 to 106.427 mm	106.05 to 106.15 mm

Valve guide { Outside diameter with guide removed . . . . 14.033 to 14.044 mm
Inside diameter with guide assembled in cylinder head . . . . 9.000 to 9.015 mm

Clearance between guide assembled in cylinder head and valve stem { intake . . . . .013 to .053 mm
exhaust . . . . .040 to .080 mm

Diameter of valve guide seat on cylinder head . . . . 13.990 to 14.018 mm

Interference between seat and valve guide . . . . .015 to .054 mm

Projection of valve guides from their recesses in the cylinder head . . . . 16.800 to 17.000 mm

Valve seats

	Intake	Exhaust
Outer diameter of the valve seat { standard	42.597 to 42.632 mm	38.597 to 38.632 mm
oversized	42.897 to 42.932 mm	38.897 to 38.932 mm
Diameter of recess in the cylinder head for valve seat { standard	42.532 to 42.557 mm	38.532 to 38.557 mm
oversized	42.832 to 42.857 mm	38.832 to 38.857 mm

Interference between valve seat and recess in cylinder head . . . . .100 to .040 mm

Seat angle . . . . 120°

Valve cups

Diameter of cup	standard	34.973 to 34.989 mm
	oversized	35.173 to 35.189 mm
Diameter of cup seat in cylinder head	standard	35.000 to 35.025 mm
	oversized	35.200 to 35.225 mm
Clearance between seat and cup		.011 to .052 mm

Valve springs

	Free length		Length under test load	Test load
Inner spring	red mark green mark	47.3 mm 46.5 mm	26 mm	22.2 to 23.1 Kg
Outer spring	red mark green mark	52.8 mm 51.3 mm	27.5 mm	35.7 to 37.1 Kg

N o t e - The valve springs should be fitted with the marked coil downward.

Connecting rods

Length between center line of big end and center line of small end of connecting rod		147.955 to 148.045 mm
Inner diameter of the big end of connecting rod		53.695 to 53.708 mm
Inner diameter of bushing in the small end of rod		22.005 to 22.015 mm
End play of the connecting rods on the crankpins		.200 to .300 mm
Thickness of connecting rod bearings	standard	1.829 to 1.835 mm
	1st oversize	1.956 to 1.962 mm
	2nd oversize	2.083 to 2.089 mm
Radial clearance between crankpins and bearings for big end of connecting rod		.025 to .063 mm
Maximum out of parallelism between center line of big end hole and center line of small end hole		.074 mm

Piston pin

O.D. of pin	Black color	21.994 to 21.997 mm
	White color	21.997 to 22.000 mm

Piston pin hole

	Black color	White color
BORGO piston	22.000 to 22.002 mm	22.003 to 22.005 mm

Pistons and cylinder barrels

Diameter of pistons to be measured to square with the hole for piston pin and at a distance of 12 mm from the lower border of skirt.

For cylinder classification purpose, use the minimum diameter recorded.

	Class A - BLUE	Class B - PINK	Class C - GREEN
BORGO piston	77.920 to 77.930 mm	77.9341 to 77.940 mm	77.941 to 77.950 mm
Cylinder barrel	77.985 to 77.994 mm	77.995 to 78.004 mm	78.005 to 78.014 mm

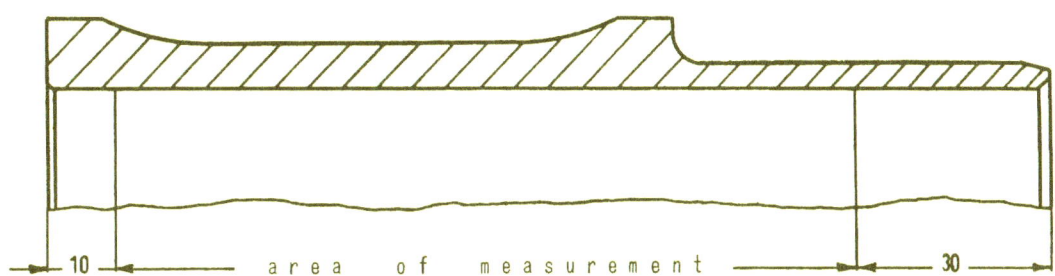

Clearance between cylinder barrel and piston	.055 to .074 mm
Wear limit	.12 mm
Elongation and taper of barrels { new	.01 mm
wear limit	.05 mm
Projection of barrels from cylinder block	.000 to .060 mm
Surface roughness of barrel bore	20 to 40 microinches RMS

Compression and oil scraper rings

Height of grooves in piston for compression rings { normal	1.775 to 1.790 mm
chromium-plated	1.785 to 1.800 mm
Height of groove in piston for oil scraper ring	4.015 to 4.030 mm
Thickness of compression rings	1.728 to 1.740 mm
Thickness of oil scraper ring	3.978 to 3.990 mm
End play of rings in grooves { compression rings { normal	.035 to .062 mm
chromium-plated	.045 to .072 mm
oil scraper rings	.025 to .052 mm
Gap of rings to be inspected in ring gauge or in cylinder barrels	.300 to .450 mm

Crankshaft

Diameter of main journals	standard	59.960 to 59.973 mm
	1st undersize	59.706 to 59.719 mm
	2nd undersize	59.452 to 59.465 mm
Diameter of crankpins	standard	49.987 to 50.000 mm
	1st undersize	49.733 to 49.746 mm
	2nd undersize	49.479 to 49.492 mm
Thickness of main bearings	standard	1.829 to 1.835 mm
	1st oversize	1.956 to 1.962 mm
	2nd oversize	2.083 to 2.089 mm
Diameter of seat for main bearings in crankcase		63.657 to 63.676 mm
Length of central journal	standard	30.000 to 30.035 mm
	1st oversize	30.127 to 30.162 mm
	2nd oversize	30.254 to 30.289 mm
Thickness of thrust rings for central journal	standard	2.311 to 2.362 mm
	1st oversize	2.374 to 2.425 mm
	2nd oversize	2.438 to 2.489 mm
End play of crankshaft		.111 to .228 mm
Radial clearance between journals and main bearings		.014 to .058 mm
Fillet radii	main journals & crankpins	1.7 to 2.1 mm
	pin on flywheel side	3.7 to 4.1 mm
Main journals & crankpins surface roughness		63 microinches RMS
Maximum elongation of main journals and crankpins		.007 mm
Maximum taper of main journals and crankpins measured on their full length		.010 mm
Maximum error of parallelism of main journals and crankpins measured on their full length		.015 mm
Maximum misalignment allowed between main journals		.010 mm
Maximum misalignment allowed between ₵ of the two pairs of crankpins and ₵ of main journals		.300 mm

Clutch

Pedal free travel	23 mm
Distance between **thrust ring** and the reference sleeve of tool C.6.0104 (for the use of this tool refer to Tool Bulletin no. 50 performing the items 1, 2 and 3)*	.75 to 1.25 mm
Squareness of the clutch driven plate assembled on gearbox direct drive shaft	.50 mm
Wear limit of driven plate thickness	6 mm
Spring rating — free length	43.5 to 45.5 mm
Spring rating — length under test load	29 mm
Spring rating — test load	45 to 49 Kg

* For adjustment use special tools A.5.0166 and A.2.0189 as per Tool Bulletin no. 151.

Gearbox

Transmission ratios — 1st gear	3.304 : 1
Transmission ratios — 2nd gear	1.988 : 1
Transmission ratios — 3rd gear	1.355 : 1
Transmission ratios — 4th gear	1.000 : 1
Transmission ratios — 5th gear	.791 : 1
Transmission ratios — Reverse gear	3.010 : 1
Maximum eccentricity of main shaft	.05 mm
End play between forks and sleeves — assembly	.15 to .34 mm
End play between forks and sleeves — wear limit	.85 mm

Gear	1st - 2nd - 3rd	5th - Rev.
Calibration of springs for striking rod balls — free length	15.2 mm	30.5 mm
Calibration of springs for striking rod balls — length under test load	10 mm	20 mm
Calibration of springs for striking rod balls — test load	2.88 to 3.12 Kg	4.32 to 4.68 Kg

Maximum end play of the main shaft gears — 1st speed gear	.170 to .245 mm
Maximum end play of the main shaft gears — 2nd & 3rd speed gear	.130 to .205 mm
Maximum end play of the main shaft gears — 5th speed gear & Rev.	.160 to .220 mm
Distance between outer planes of the engaging teeth of 3rd and 4th gears	42 to 42.2 mm
Distance, in neutral, of the rear band (propeller shaft side) of 5th speed sleeve from the rear edge of gear engaging teeth	12.9 mm

REAR AXLE AND SUSPENSION

Transmission-axle overall ratios-with final drive 41 : 9
- 1st gear .... 15.049 : 1
- 2nd gear .... 9.055 : 1
- 3rd gear .... 6.172 : 1
- 4th gear .... 4.555 : 1
- 5th gear .... 3.603 : 1
- Reverse .... 13.710 : 1

Maximum eccentricity of axle shaft .... .10 mm

Clearance between teeth of planetary gears .... .05 mm

Play between teeth of final drive .... .05 to .10 mm

Max factory end play between reaction trunnion and attachment to body .... 1 mm

Reference dimension on tool C.6.0101 for pinion-to-ring gear fitting .... 70 ± .0025 mm

Pre-load on pinion bearing .... 11.5 to 15.5 Kgcm

Total pre-load on final drive bearings .... 16.5 to 24.5 Kgcm

Checking of suspension springs

Colored marks: sky blue - sky blue

Free length .... 449 mm

Length under test load .... 252 mm

Test load .... 321 to 341 Kgs

Checking of shock absorbers on test bench

Calibration data (when cold)

	GIRLING		BIANCHI - ALLINQUANT	
	Extension	Compression	Extension	Compression
High speed	121 to 190 Kgs	27 to 42 Kgs	135 to 190 Kgs	50 to 80 Kgs
Low speed	13 to 32 Kgs	9 to 18 Kgs	19 to 55 Kgs	9 to 22 Kgs

FRONT SUSPENSION

Adjustment of clearance in wheel bearings

When performing regular servicing or whenever the removal of wheel hubs is required, adjust the bearing clearance as follows:

- Screw in the castellated nut and lock it to a torque of 2 to 2.5 Kgm while at the same time revolving the wheel hub to set the bearings properly in their seats to prevent the rollers from brinelling the races.
- Slacken the castellated nut, then again apply torque up to .5 - 1 Kgm.
- Back up the nut by a quarter turn and insert the split pin; if the nut slot and the hole in the axle are not aligned, screw in the nut of the minimum required to line up the hole and the next slot. Tap one or twice on the stub axle end to settle the bearings.
- Make sure the bearing retainer plate is not blocked by inserting the tip of a screwdriver in the plate holes: the plate should be easily rotated.
- If the plate is blocked, unscrew the nut by one slot and tap again on the stub axle end.

Wheel bearing lubricating instructions

The quantity of lubricating grease should be about 65 grammes for each hub; do not exceed such a quantity to avoid bearing overheating, grease leakage, etc.

The grease should be well distributed inside the bearings and into side recesses.

Subsequently, at the regular schedule, remove the hub cover and pack the outboard bearing.

Ball joints

Maximum allowed end play of lower ball joint in its socket . . . . .5 to 1 mm

N o t e - Ball joints require no regular lubrication being provided with special grease seals which retain the grease packed in by factory on assembly.

Checking of suspension springs

Colored marks: sky blue - sky blue

Free length . . . . 312.5 mm
Length under test load . . . . 200 mm
Test load . . . . 911.8 to 968.2 Kgs

Checking of shock absorbers on test bench

Calibration data (when cold)

	GIRLING		BIANCHI - ALLINQUANT	
	Extension	Compression	Extension	Compression
High speed	210 to 310 Kgs	27 to 52 Kgs	150 to 190 Kgs	55 to 80 Kgs
Low speed	30 to 52 Kgs	9 to 22 Kgs	25 to 55 Kgs	9 to 22 Kgs

BRAKES

Disc

Whenever a brake unit is overhauled or replaced check the disc for true rotation with the disc fitted to the car.

Use a dial gauge and check that runout does not exceed .15 mm. Should the reading exceed this value, then the installation of disc on stub axle must be carefully examined; if the run out persists, replace the disc.

If the disc is scored, the grinding of the surfaces is allowed providing not to exceed an undersize of 1 mm, equalized on both faces, i.e. .5 mm each face.

Friction pads

	Front	Rear
Thickness when new	16 mm	17.5 mm
Wear limit	8 mm	10 mm

Calipers

On replacement of disc or caliper measure the running clearance between caliper and disc on each side; the difference should not exceed .5 mm.

To centralize the caliper about the disc, insert shims between caliper and mounting flange as required.

Hand brake

It is mechanically-operated and acts on the rear service brake pads.

The adjustment is performed by acting on the nut of control cable located between intermediate levers and calipers. After the adjustment, make sure that levers of rear calipers to which the cable is connected are all the way outward. In such a position the cable must not be tight but slightly slackened. Furthermore the brake pads must not contact the disc.

N.B. - For repair and maintenance instructions refer to: "Disc Brake System for GIULIA T.I. model" publication no. 930.

WHEEL ALIGNMENT

Checking of wheel angles and car "trim" under static load

Put the car under static load, with shock absorbers and stabilizer rod connected, with full tank or equivalent, with spare wheel, tool kit and the tires inflated to the prescribed pressures.

Before checking, slightly move the car up and down so as to settle the suspensions.

Front seats { 1 weight of 45 Kgs on each seat
2 weights of 25 Kgs on flooring where feet rest

Rear seats { 2 weights of 45 Kgs on seat
2 weights of 25 Kgs on flooring where feet rest

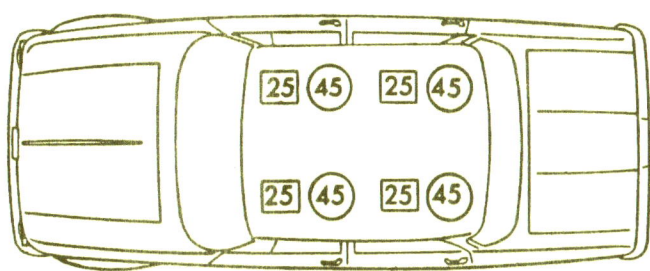

FRONT TRIM

Distance of lower wishbone of front suspension from a reference level

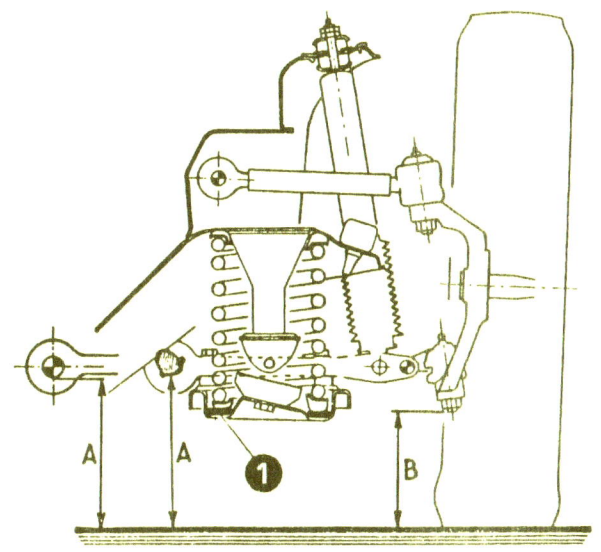

A - B - { for elongated-cross-section shaft   34 ± 5 mm
for round-cross-section shaft   38 ± 5 mm

Note - Dimension "A" must be measured in correspondence of the lower line of wishbone shaft as shown.

To adjust, add shims in position "1".

Shims are available in the following thicknesses:

.... 3.5 mm
.... 7 mm
.... 10.5 mm

Distance of rear axle from rubber buffers

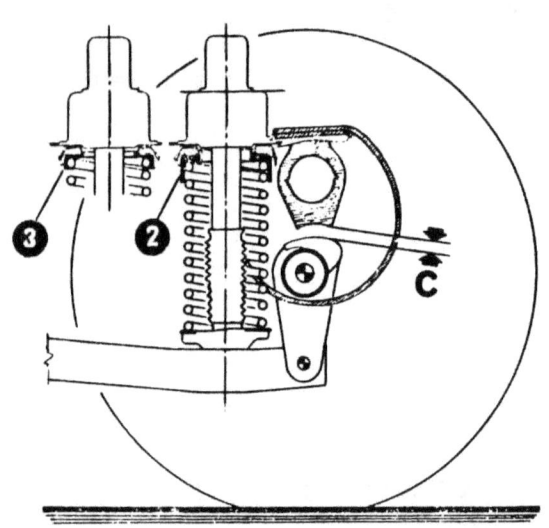

C = 10 ± 5 mm

<u>Note</u> - To adjust remove the seat "3" and add shims in "2" as shown.

Shims are available in the following thicknesses:

. . . . 6.5 mm
. . . . 11.5 mm
. . . . 16.5 mm
. . . . 21.5 mm

In the conditions as specified above, check the wheel angles.

Caster angle: $\alpha = 1° 30' \pm 30'$

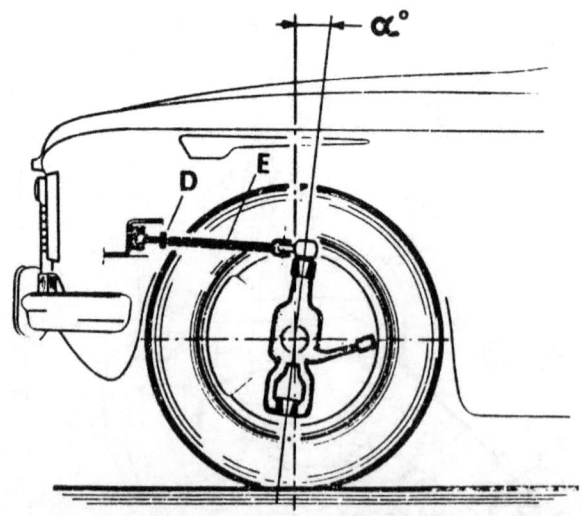

The difference in caster angle between R.H. and L.H. wheel must not exceed 0° 20'.

To adjust, loosen jam nut "D" and rotate rod "E".

Small adjustments of the caster angle allow to correct slight drift tendency of the car.

<u>N.B.</u> - Before checking the caster angle shake the front end of car in order to allow the rubber bushing on the front slanting arm to set properly.

Front wheel camber

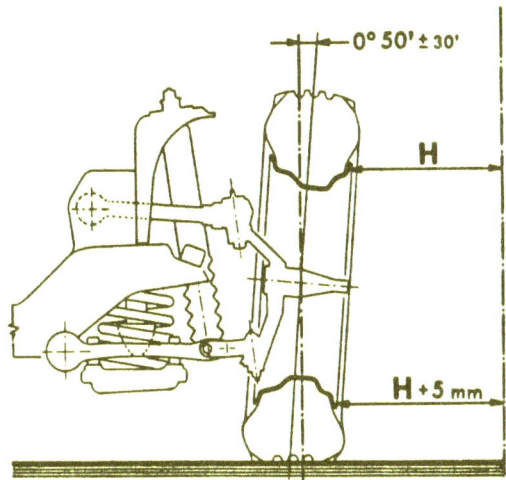

Not adjustable.
Make a check of the chassis, if necessary.

Front wheel toe-in

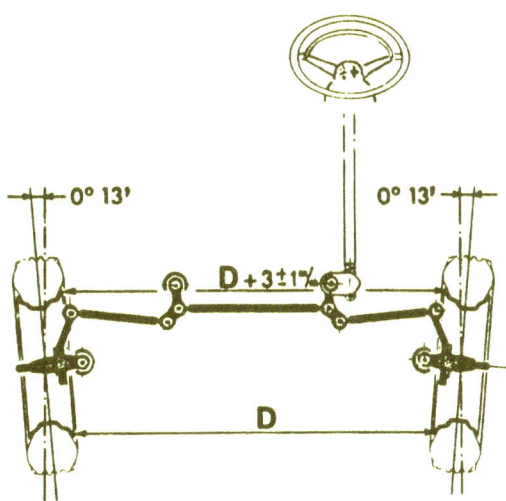

Rod length:

    side . . . . 272 to 288 mm
    track . . . . 544 to 552 mm

With the toe-in as specified, the length of rods as measured between ball joint centers should fall within the limits shown. If these values cannot be restored, the cause will probably be found in distortion resulting from a collision.

Modifications from chassis no.	862001 (L.H.D.)
	722501 (R.H.D.)

PRINCIPAL CHARACTERISTIC DATA

Wheel track	front	1324 mm
	rear	1274 mm
Curb weight (full tank)		1040 Kg

REFILLINGS

Engine (sump & filter)	to max. level (for regular changing)	5.800 Kg (5.75 qts)
	to min. level	4.000 Kg (3.95 qts)

- The total amount of oil in the circuit (sump, filter, passages) is 6.550 Kg (6.5 qts)

CARBURETION

Two Weber 40 DCOE 33 carburettors

Venturi	30
Main jet	120
Main mixer	F 9
Main air metering jet	200
Idling jet (170 axial passage)	50 F 14
Idling air metering jet	120
Choke jet	65 F 5
Choke air metering jet	200
Acceleration pump jet (axial spray)	35
Acceleration pump inlet valve with by-pass	60
Acceleration pump stroke	14 mm
Delevery of acceleration pump (per 20 pump strokes for each barrel)	3 to 5 cc
Needle valve with spring (spring preload 50 grs)	150
Weight of float	26 grs
Distance of fuel level from float chamber flange (with a pressure of 2 mts H_2O upstream the needle valve)	29 to 29.5 mm
Idling speed	600 to 700 rpm

Two Solex C 40 DDH carburettors

Venturi	30
Main jet	125
Main mixer	4 holes diameter 1.5 mm
Main air metering jet	140
Idling jet	45
Idling air metering jet	130
Choke jet	140
Choke air metering jet (1.3 mixture hole)	600
Acceleration pump jet	35
Delivery of acceleration pump (per 20 pump strokes for each barrel)	5 to 7 cc
Needle valve	1.60
Spacer under needle valve	1 mm
Weight of float	14 grs
Distance of fuel level (with a pressure of 2 mts H2O upstream the needle valve) (for level measurement remove the mixer tube and have the gauge passing through the hole)	16 mm

N o t e - WEBER & SOLEX carburettors are alternative supply.

VALVE TIMING

Checking of valve opening and closing angles

Closing of intake valve	lift of cup		.20 mm
	corresponding to an angle	after BDC of	42° 10' ± 1° 30'
Closing of exhaust valve	lift of cup		.15 mm
	corresponding to an angle	after TDC of	18° 10' ± 1° 30'

ANGLE VALUES OF THE ACTUAL DIAGRAM OF VALVE TIMING SYSTEM WITH COLD ENGINE
(clockwise rotation direction of the crankshaft seen from the front side)

Opening of intake valve	before TDC	36° 50'
Closing of intake valve	after BDC	60° 30'
Opening of exhaust valve	before BDC	54° 10'
Closing of exhaust valve	after TDC	29° 50'
Induction stroke		277° 20'
Exhaust stroke		264°

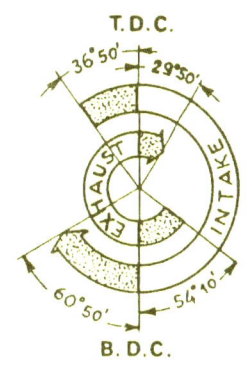

ELECTRICAL SYSTEM

Voltage .... 12 V
Battery .... 60 Ah

	BOSCH	MARELLI
Generator	EG (R) 14 V 25 A 29	DN 62 E
Voltage regulator	VA 14 V 25 A	SD 368 A 300/12
Starting motor	EF (R) 12 V 0.7 PS	MT 54 B
Coil	TK 12 A 19	BZR 200 D
Ignition distributor	JF 4	S 103 A
Windshield wiper	WS 13/11 S 1 A	TGE 93 BX

DRY TIGHTENING TORQUE SPECIFICATIONS

FRONT FRAME

	Kgm.
Nut securing upper wishbone front arm to rear arm	3.8 to 4.7
Nut securing upper wishbone rear arm to body	11 to 13.65
Nuts securing lower arm shaft to cross-member	5.6 to 5.9
(To tighten these nuts use tool A.5.0161 and torque to 5.2 to 5.5 Kgm.)	
Nuts securing steering arm to steering knuckle	4 to 4.5
Nut securing lower ball joint to wishbone	8.2 to 9.2
Nuts securing splash shields to steering knuckle	.8 to 1
Screws securing caliper to steering knuckle	7.5 to 8.5

ATE BRAKES

Brake bleed screw	.2 to .35
Caliper joining bolts	2.9 to 3.4
Inlet fitting to caliper { with gasket	.8 to 1.1
{ without gasket	1 to 1.5

MAJOR INSPECTION SPECIFICATIONS

VALVES AND VALVE GUIDES

(Valves added)

	Intake	
	ATE	GARRONE
Valve { Poppet dia.	41.000 to 41.200 mm	41.000 to 41.150 mm
{ Stem dia.	8.962 to 8.987 mm	8.972 to 8.987 mm
{ Total length	106.8 mm	107 mm

Projection of intake valve guides from their recesses in the cylinder head .... 13.800 mm
Projection of exhaust valve guides from their recesses in the cylinder head .... 16.800 to 17.000 mm

VALVE SPRINGS

(alternative springs added)

	Free length	Length under test load	Test load
Inner spring	47 mm	26 mm	22.2 to 23.1 Kg
Outer spring	52 mm	27.5 mm	35.9 to 37.3 Kg

PISTONS AND BARRELS

Diameter of pistons to be measured to square with the hole for piston pin and at a distance of L = 17 mm from the lower border of skirt.

For cylinder classification purpose, use the minimum diameter recorded.

	Class A - BLUE	Class B - PINK	Class C - GREEN
BORGO piston (new construction)	77.945 to 77.955 mm	77.955 to 77.965 mm	77.965 to 77.975 mm
Cylinder barrel bore	77.985 to 77.994 mm	77.995 to 78.004 mm	78.005 to 78.014 mm

Clearance between cylinder barrel and BORGO new-construction piston .... .039 to .049 mm

COMPRESSION AND OIL CONTROL RINGS

(for BORGO new-construction piston)

Height of grooves in piston for compression rings
- chromium-plated .... 1.535 to 1.555 mm
- standard .... 1.775 to 1.795 mm

Height of groove in piston for oil scraper ring .... 4.015 to 4.035 mm

Thickness of compression rings
- chromium-plated .... 1.478 to 1.490 mm
- standard .... 1.728 to 1.740 mm

Thickness of oil scraper ring .... 3.978 to 3.990 mm

End play of rings in grooves
- compression rings
  - chromium-plated .... .045 to .077 mm
  - standard .... .035 to .067 mm
- oil scraper rings .... .025 to .057 mm

CRANKSHAFT

End play of crankshaft .... .076 to .263 mm

CLUTCH

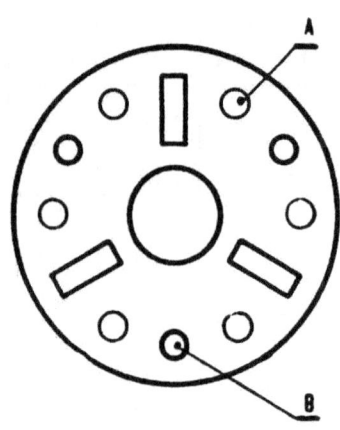

Rating of springs A
- free length ..... 43 to 46 mm
- length under test load 29.2 mm
- test load ...... 44.5 to 49.5 Kg

Rating of springs B
- free length ..... 39.5 to 42.5 mm
- length under test load 29.2 mm
- test load ...... 55 to 61 Kg

GEARBOX

Clearance between gear bushing and mainshaft
- 1st speed gear .... .125 to .170 mm
- 2nd & 3rd speed gear .... .095 to .140 mm
- 5th speed gear .... .065 to .107 mm

FRONT SUSPENSION

Free length of spring	292 mm	312.5 mm
Length under test load	200 mm	200 mm
Test load	911.8 to 968.2 Kg	911.8 to 968.2 Kg
	WHITE - BLUE	BLUE - BLUE
	alternative	

Shock absorbers

	ALLINQUANT	
	Extension	Compression
High speed	150 to 190 Kg	55 to 80 Kg
Low speed	25 to 55 Kg	9 to 22 Kg

BRAKES (ATE make)

Disc

When a brake disc is replaced it is necessary to check it for run-out after installation:

- use a dial indicator and the special tool A.2.0151 which is mounted to the caliper by means of the pad retaining pins.

Maximum permissible run out as measured at the swept surface should not exceed .22 mm.

Note - run-out readings can be misleading if bearing clearance is not as specified; therefore, check and adjust if necessary, according to factory instructions.

If the disc is scored, see I.S. 0.00.055/3; the grinding of the surfaces is allowed providing not to exceed an undersize of 1 mm, equalized on both faces, i.e. .5 mm each face; disc wear limit: front 10 mm - rear 8.5 mm thick.

Inspection specifications after regrinding of disc surfaces:

- Max. out of parallelism with disc mounting plane: .05 mm;
- Max. out of flat: .025 mm and max. difference in thickness: .038 mm as measured along any radial line;
- Max. out of flat: .025 mm and max. difference in thickness: .015 mm as measured along any circular line;
- The surface should show no sign of scoring or porosity.

The surface roughness should be:

- 26 microinches as measured circularly;
- 36 microinches as measured radially.

Friction pads

	Front	Rear
Thickness when new	15 mm	
Wear limit	7 mm	

Calipers

On replacement of disc or caliper, measure the running clearance between caliper and disc on each side; the difference should not exceed .5 mm.

To centralize the caliper about the disc, insert shims between caliper and mounting flange as required.

Hand brake

It is mechanically operated and acts on the rear wheels through suitable shoes which spread apart against a drum machined in the disc casting.

For a brief description of repair and maintenance instructions refer to:

ATE DISC BRAKES - Publication no. 1202

Note - When reassembling the operating levers, a slight quantity of grease AGIP F.1 Gr SM or SHELL Retinax AM is to be applied to the pivot points and rubbing surfaces of levers.

WHEEL ALIGNMENT

Distance of lower wishbone of front suspension from a reference level

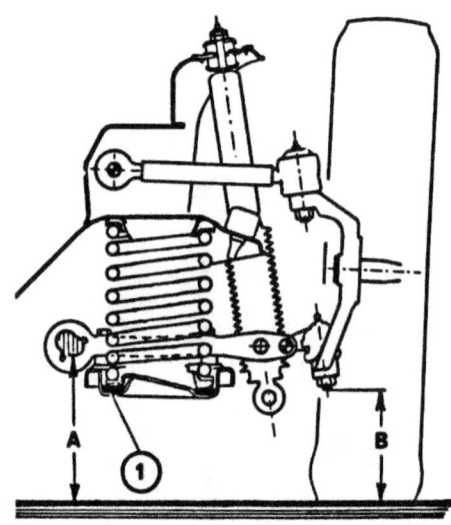

A - B = 34 ± 5 mm

Dimension "A" must be measured in correspondence of the lower line of wishbone shaft as shown.

To asjust, add shims in "1".

Shims are available in the following thicknesses:

3.5 - 7 - 10.5 mm

Distance of rear axle from rubber buffers

C = 36 ± 5 mm

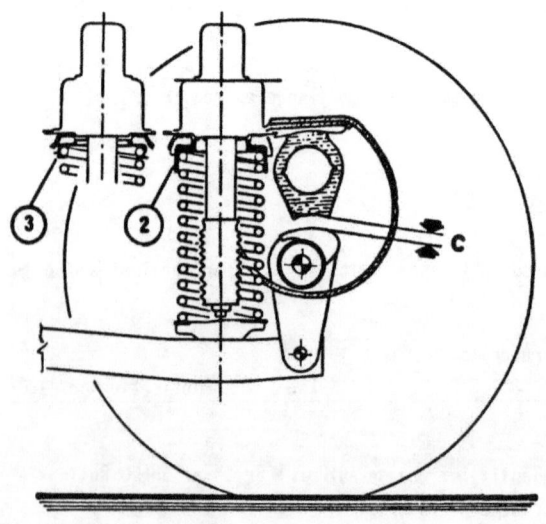

N o t e - To adjust, remove the seat "3" and add shims in "2" as shown.

Shims are available in the following ticknesses:

6.5 - 11.5 - 16.5 - 21.5 mm

In the condition as specified check the wheel angles.

Front wheel camber

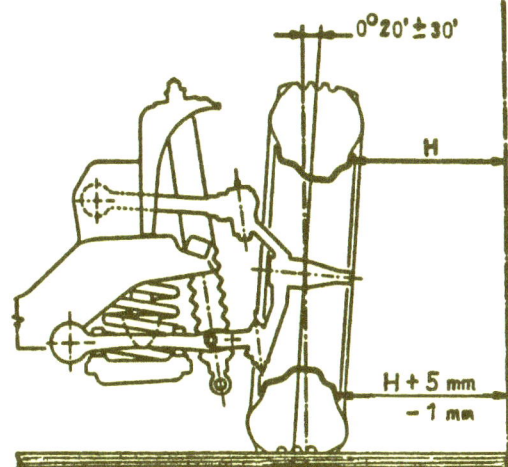

Difference in camber angle between R.H. and L.H. wheel = 0° 40'

N o t e - Not adjustable. Check the chassis and suspension arms if necessary.

Front wheel toe-in

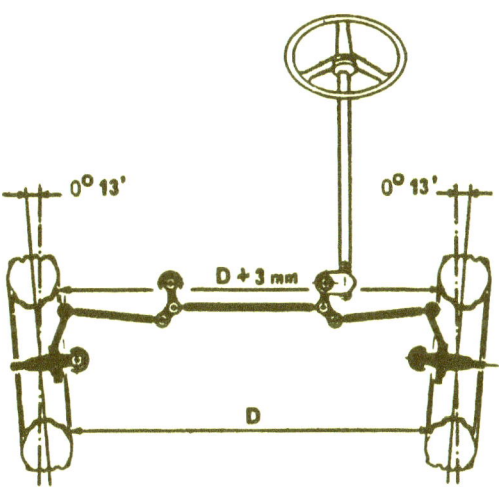

Rod length:

    side . . . . 264 to 280 mm
    track . . . . 530 to 550 mm

With the toe-in as specified, the length of rods as measured between ball joint centers should fall within the limits shown. If these values cannot be restored, the cause will probably be found in distortion resulting from a collision.

Variants from chassis no.	880001 (L.H.D.)
	724001 (R.H.D.)

PRINCIPAL CHARACRERISTIC DATA

Max. power at 5500 rpm	DIN	102 HP
	SAE	116 HP
Wheel track	front (with 165 x 14 tyres)	1314 mm (51.7 in.)
	rear (with 165 x 14 tyres)	1264 mm (49.7 in.)
Overall length		4160 mm (164 in.)

TYRES - Inflation pressure (when cold) - Kg/cm^2

		Front	Rear
155 x 15	Michelin ZX	1.6 *	1.7 *
		1.7 **	2 **
	Kleber Colombes V 10 GT	1.6 *	1.7 *
		1.9 **	2.2 **
165 x 14	Ceat Drive D 2 - Continental - Pirelli cinturato SR (under all conditions)	1.5	1.6
	Michelin ZX (under all conditions)	1.7	1.8
	Kleber Colombes V 10	1.7 *	2 *
		1.9 **	2.2 **

* With reduced load and touring riding
** With full load and top range of speed

REFILLINGS

Steering box	Burman	.360 Kg
	ZF	.120 Kg

ELECTRICAL EQUIPMENT

	BOSCH
Coil	K 12 V
Alternator	K 1 (R,L) 14 V 35 A 20
Voltage regulator	AD 1/14 V
Windshield wiper	WS 4902 AR 5 A (0)

BULB'S WATTAGE

Inner headlights (high beams)	40/45 asymmetric
Outer headlights (high & low beams)	40/45 asymmetric
Tail lights - parking & stop	5/21
Front direction indicators	21
Tail direction indicators	21
Reversing light	21
Front parking lights	5 globular
Number plate light	5 globular
Engine compartment light	5 cylindrical
Courtesy light	5 cylindrical
Light in luggage compartment	5 cylindrical
Side direction indicators	3 tubular
Instrument light	3 tubular
Light for cigarette lighter	3 tubular
Tell-tale for blower	3 tubular
Tell-tale for alternator	3 tubular
Tell-tale for fuel reserve	3 tubular
Tell-tale for direction indicators	3 tubular
Tell-tale for parking light	3 tubular
Tell-tale for high beams	3 tubular

TIGHTENING TORQUE SPECIFICATIONS

	Kgm.	Manner of tightening
Nut of alternator pulley	3.5 to 4	dry
Nut of gearbox layshaft	4.5 to 5.5	"
Nut of gearbox inner swivel	3.25 to 3.65	"
Bolt joining gearbox output shaft yoke to prop. shaft yoke	5.5 to 5.7	"
Oil drain plug on sump bottom	7 to 8	"
Plug on oil filter	3.5 to 4	"

REAR FRAME

	Kgm.	Manner of tightening
Nuts securing radius rods to body	9 to 10	"
Nuts securing radius rods to rear axle tubes	12.5 to 14	"
Nut securing reaction triangle to rear axle	11.5 to 13	"
Nut securing reaction triangle to body	4.8 to 5.5	"
Nut attaching the joining flange to front shaft	9 to 11	"
Bolts joining flanges of front shaft and sliding yoke	3.2 to 3.5	"
Screws securing rear brake caliper to support (ATE brakes)	5.5 to 6.5	"
Bolts joining differential yoke to prop. shaft yoke	3.2 to 3.5	"
Nuts securing rear axle tubes to differential carrier	2.4	"
Bolts for rebound strap butt joints	0.5	"
Nut securing link to radius rod bolt	3.3 to 3.5	"

CLUTCH

The clutch is of the hydraulically-operated single plate dry type. The clutch pedal acts on a master cylinder supplied with the same type of fluid as the brake system.

When the clutch pedal is depressed, the fluid under pressure actuates the piston in the cylinder "4" connected to the clutch disengagement lever "5".

The pressure plate is controlled by means of diaphragm spring "6".

The clutch pedal free travel "A" should be about 30 - 32 mm. When owing to wear on the clutch disc facing, the pedal free travel is reduced to 17 - 19 mm the free travel must be restored.

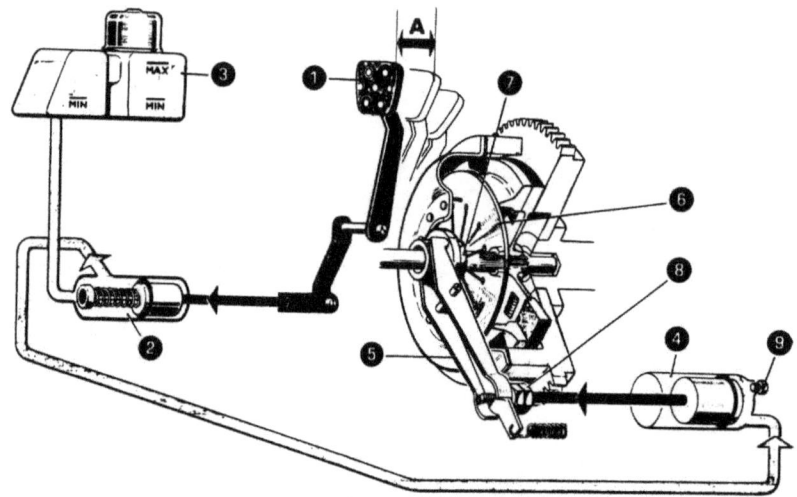

A Pedal free travel
B Disengagement lever free travel

1 Pedal
2 Master cylinder
3 Clutch & brake fluid reservoir
4 Slave cylinder
5 Disengagement lever
6 Diaphragm spring
7 Throwout bearing
8 Adjusting nuts
9 Air bleed screw

Adjustment

Measure with a rule the free travel "B" at the end of push rod of cylinder "4" depressing the clutch pedal until the throwout bearing "7" contacts the spring "6"; the travel "B" should be about 2 - 2.5 mm.

If the travel is shorter, act on the adjusting nut "8".

At the same time make sure that, by pressing the pedal as far as it will go, the push rod can move through a total travel of 13.5 - 14.2 mm. If any component of the system has been removed, thoroughly bleed the circuit. To check as specified use special tool no. C.6.0146 (see Tool Bulletin no. 135).

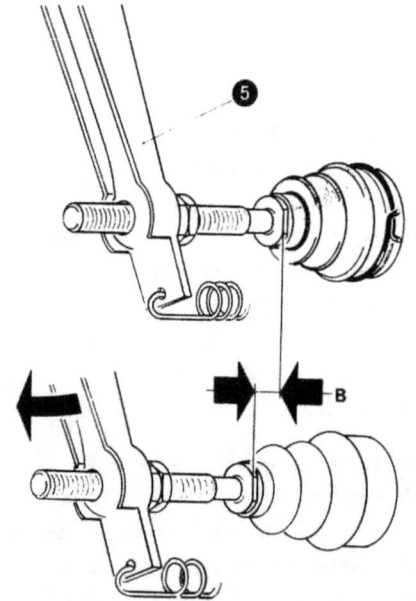

Inspection specifications

Wear limit of driven plate thickness . . . .   6.5 mm
Squareness of driven plate as mounted on gearbox output
    shaft . . . .   0.50 mm

GEARBOX

Calibration of striking rod ball springs
- free length . . . .   35.8 mm
- length under test load . . . .   17.2 mm
- test load . . . .   7.680 to 8.320 mm

BRAKE SYSTEM

The ATE brake system consists of four caliper type disc brakes operated by an assisted master cylinder. The friction pads of the front and rear brakes are directly actuated by the cylinders integral with the calipers.

The brakes are self-adjusting.

A pressure regulating valve controls the braking power to rear brakes. Such a regulator shall not be tampered with; specifically do not attempt to act on the adjusting nut as it is factory sealed.

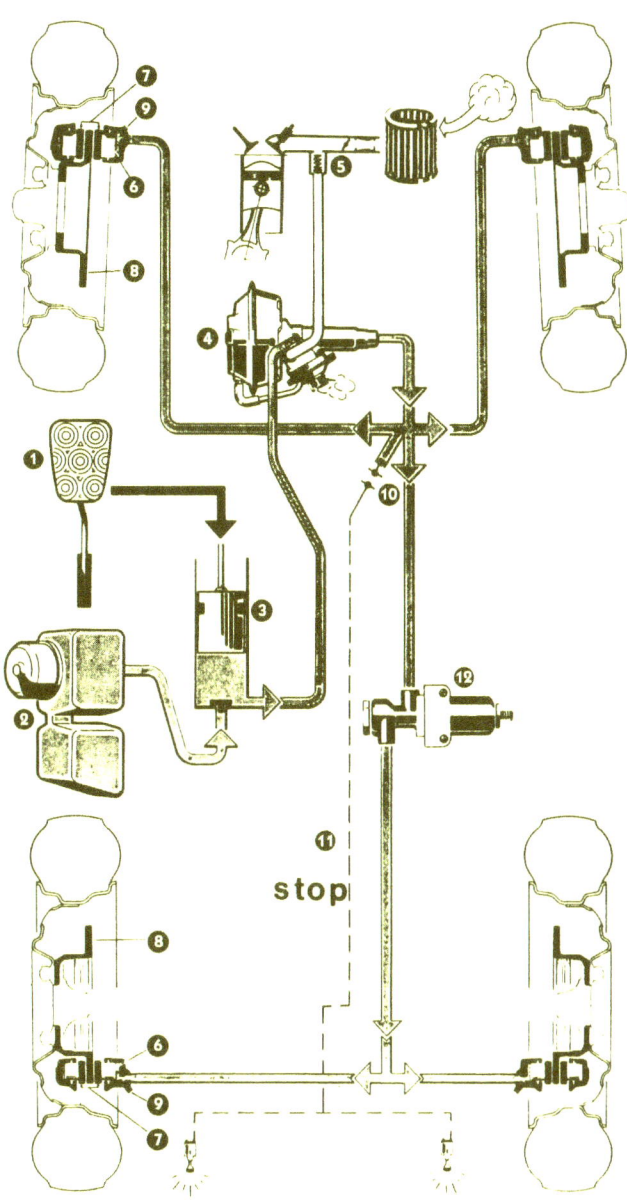

1	Brake pedal	7	Friction pads
2	Reservoir	8	Discs
3	Master cylinder	9	Bleed screws
4	Vacuum servo	10	Stop light switch
5	Vacuum connection	11	Stop light cable
6	Pistons	12	Pressure regulating valve

FRONT WHEEL TOE-IN (for L.H.D.)

Lock steering wheel in the central position i.e. with the spokes symmetrically disposed in relation to the vertical. Starting with the track rod "1" on the steering box side, place the corresponding wheel so that the toe-in is 1.5 mm. Measure the length thus obtained of the track rod and adjust the rod "2" on the other side to a length 5 mm shorter. Bring the first wheel to a 1.5 mm toe-in by adjusting the centre track rod "3".

$$A \begin{cases} \text{for 15" wheels} = 0° 13' \\ \text{for 14" wheels} = 0° 14' \end{cases}$$

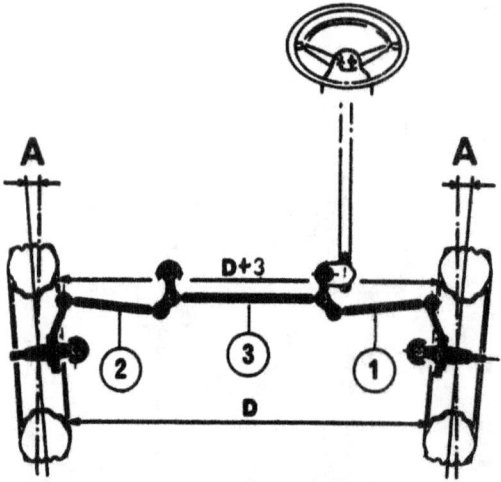

Rod length:

side	264 to 280 mm
track	530 to 550 mm

With the toe-in as specified, the length of rods as measured between ball joint centers should fall within the limits shown. If these values cannot be restored, the cause will probably be attributable to distortion of the body resulting from a collision.

N o t e - For R.H.D. the side rods maintain the same length (symmetrical adjustment).

1750 Berlina
1750 GT Veloce
1750 Spider Veloce

**technical characteristics
and
principal inspection specifications**

C O N T E N T S

T E C H N I C A L   C H A R A C T E R I S T I C S

PRINCIPAL CHARACTERISTIC DATA . . . . Page 2
    Performance . . . . " 2
    Tires . . . . " 3
    Refillings . . . . " 3
    Prescribed oils and lubrificants . . . . " 3
    Carburetion . . . . " 4
    Idling adjustment . . . . " 4
    Float level adjustment . . . . " 5
    Valve timing . . . . " 6
    Ignition . . . . " 6
    Spark plugs . . . . " 6
    Cooling system . . . . " 7
    Electrical equipment . . . . " 10
    Bulb's wattage . . . . " 10
    Tightening torque specifications . . . . " 10

M A J O R   I N S P E C T I O N   S P E C I F I C A T I O N S

Camshafts . . . . Page 12
Valves and valve guides . . . . " 12
Valve seats . . . . " 12
Valve cups . . . . " 13
Valve springs . . . . " 13
Connecting rods . . . . " 13
Piston pins . . . . " 13
Piston pin holes . . . . " 13
Pistons and piston rings . . . . " 14
Cylinder barrels . . . . " 14
Crankshaft . . . . " 15
Clutch . . . . " 16
Gearbox . . . . " 17
Rear axle and suspension . . . . " 18
Front suspension . . . . " 19
Brakes . . . . " 20

WHEEL ALIGNMENT

Checking of wheel angles and car "trim" under static load . . . . Page 22

1750 GT VELOCE and 1750 SPIDER VELOCE VARIANTS . . . . Page 25

TECHNICAL CHARACTERISTICS

PRINCIPAL CHARACTERISTIC DATA

Number of cylinders	4
Bore	80 mm. (3.15")
Stroke	88.5 mm. (3.48")
Total cylinder capacity	1779 cc.
Max. power at 5,500 rpm	SAE 132 HP
Front track	1324 mm. (52.1")
Rear track	1274 mm. (50.1")
Wheelbase	2570 mm. (101")
Min. turning circle	11100 mm. (437")
Overall length	4390 mm. (173")
Overall width	1565 mm. (61.7")
Overall height (unladen)	1430 mm. (56.3")
Dry weight with tools and jack	1110 Kg. (2447 lbs)
Number of seats	5
Tires 165 x 14	PIRELLI cinturato SR / KLEBER COLOMBES V 10 / MICHELIN X
Fuel consumption per 100 Km (CUNA standard)	11.6 lt. (25 mpg G.B. - 20.8 mpg U.S.)

(For best engine performance, the use of premium-grade fuel is advised)

With 43 : 10 final drive

Gear	Max. Speeds					
	Running in				After running in	
	up to 1000 Km (600 mi.)		1000 to 3000 Km (600 to 1900 mi)			
	Km/h	mph	Km/h	mph	Km/h	mph
1st	27	17	34	21	44.5	28
2nd	46	29	56	35	74	46
3rd	67	42	82	51	109	68
4th	91	57	111	69	146	91
5th	115	71	141	88	180	112
Rev.	-	-	-	-	48	30

Oil pressures with hot engine:
- min. pressure at idling speed .... .5 - 1 Kg/cm^2 (7 - 14 psi)
- min. pressure at top speed .... 3.5 Kg/cm^2 (50 psi)
- max. pressure at top speed .... 4.5 - 5 Kg/cm^2 (65 - 70 psi)

WARNING: Check that alternator warning light goes off as soon as the engine exceeds idling speed.

Tires

Inflation pressure (with tire cold)

	Front wheels		Rear wheels	
	Kg/cm²	psi	Kg/cm²	psi
PIRELLI cinturato SR - 165 x 14 (all conditions)	1.5	21.3	1.6	22.7
KLEBER COLOMBES V 10 - 165 x 14 — With reduced load & occasional bursts of max. speed	1.7	24	2	28.5
KLEBER COLOMBES V 10 - 165 x 14 — With full load and continuous max. speed	1.9	27	2.2	31
MICHELIN X - 165 x 14 — With reduced load & occasional bursts of max. speed	1.8	25.6	1.8	25.6
MICHELIN X - 165 x 14 — With full load and continuous max. speed	1.95	27.7	2.2	31

Refillings

			G. B.		U. S.	
ALFA ROMEO coolant mixture		9.7 lts	2.1	gals	2.5	gals
Fuel reserve 6 to 7 lts (1.3 - 1.5 gals G.B.) (1.6 - 1.8 gals U.S.)		46 lts	10.1	gals	12.1	gals
Oil	Engine (sump & filter)* — to max. level (regular changing)	6.00 Kgs	5.95	qts	7.1	qts
Oil	Engine (sump & filter)* — to min. level	4.00 Kgs	3.95	qts	4.75	qts
Oil	Gearbox	1.65 Kgs	3.2	pts	3.8	pts
Oil	Differential	1.25 Kgs	2.5	pts	3.0	pts
Oil	Steering box	.25 Kgs	.5	pts	.6	pts

- The total amount of oil in the circuit (sump, filter, passages) is 6.500 Kg. (6.5 qts G.B. - 7.8 qts U.S.)

* It is recommended to top up with the same type of oil as that in the engine.

Prescribed oils and lubricants

	Classification API - SAE - NLGI	Recommended commercial equivalent	
		A G I P	S H E L L
Engine	SAE 20 W/40 API MS	** F.1 Supermotoroil Multigrade 20 W/40	Super Motor Oil
Gearbox - Differential - Steering box	SAE 90 EP	F.1 Rotra Hypoid SAE 90	Spirax 90 EP
Propeller shaft universal joints and sliding yoke	NLGI 1	F.1 Grease 15	Retinax G
Front wheel bearings	NLGI 2/3	F.1 Grease 33 FD	Retinax AX
Brake & clutch fluid		ATE "Blau H"	

** For steady temperatures below 0°C (32°F) we advise the use of F.1 Supermotoroil Multigrade 10 W/40.

SAE - Society of Automotive Engineers
API - American Petroleum Institute
NLGI - National Lubricating Grease Institute

In countries where the recommended lubricants are not available it is possible to replace them with products of other leading Companies provided that in accordance with the prescribed specifications.

Carburetion

2 Carburettors WEBER 40 DCOE 32

Venturi	32 mm (1 3/16")
Main jet	125
Main mixture tube	F 9
Main air metering jet	200
Idling jet (axial passage 170)	50 F 14
Idling air metering jet	120
Choke jet	65 F 5
Choke air passage	200
Choke mixture passage	100
Acceleration pump jet	35
Acceleration pump inlet valve	80
Travel of acceleration pump control rod	14 mm (.55")
Delivery of acceleration pump every 20 strokes (for each barrel)	4 ± 1 cc.
Needle valve seat dia.	150
Float weight	26 grs
Distance of fuel level from float chamber flange (with a pressure of 2 mts (6'6") H$_2$O upstream the needle valve)	29 ± .5 mm (1.12 to 1.16")

Idling adjustment

F Adjusting screw for minimum opening of throttle

M Idling mixture adjusting screw.

S Screw for synchronizing throttles of the two carburettors

T Joint for control linkage (to pedal)

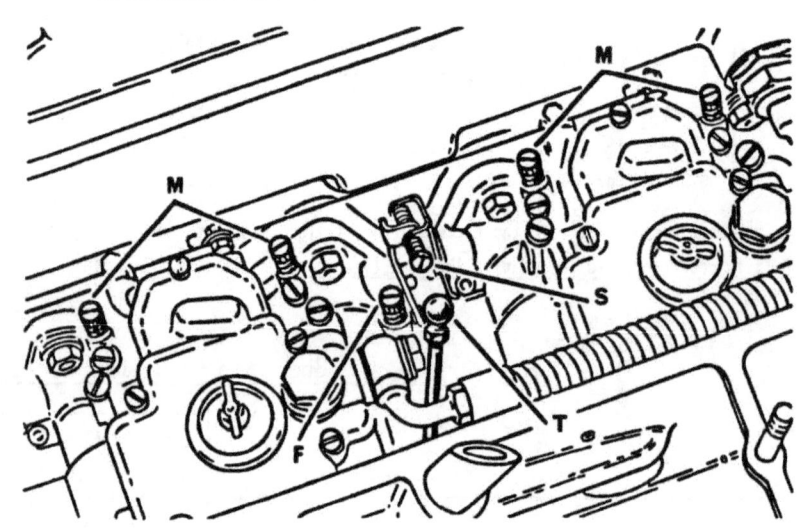

PREPARATORY STEPS

- Check the ignition timing and inspect the electric system (spark plugs, distributor, coil, etc.) for proper operation.
- Remove the air filter element and clean it thoroughly.
- Check the flexible mounts between carburettors and intake manifold for tightness.

ALIGNING THE THROTTLE VALVES

- Detach the control linkage "T" from carburettors.
- Slacken the screws "F" and "S" almost fully.
- Operate the throttles a few times to make sure there is no binding.
- Fully depress the throttle control lever of rear carburettor so that the throttles are fully closed; then screw in the screw "S" until contact is made.

IDLING

- Back up the screw "M" of half a turn.
- Tighten the screw "F" to contact, then screw it in one more turn to ensure feeding of engine.
- Connect the accelerator control linkage "T" to carburettors.
- Start the engine and warm it up.
- If necessary, back up the screw "F" very slowly until the engine runs at about 600 to 700 rpms.

Float level adjustment

WEBER 40 DCOE 32 carburettor

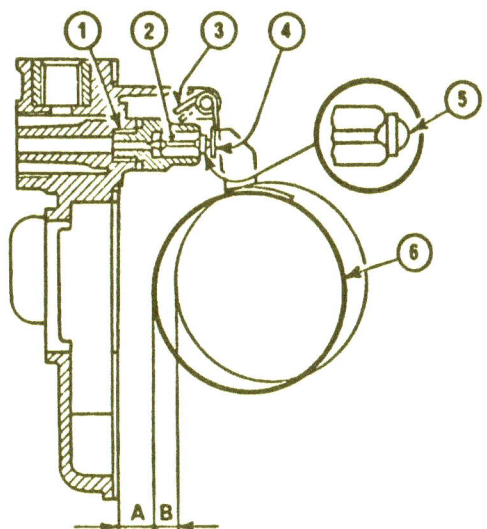

Check the level of fluid in float chamber as follows:

- Make sure the float weight is as specified (26 grs - .9 oz), that there are no leaks or indentations and that float can rotate frely about the pivot pin.

- The float weight must not be altered; consequently haphazard repairs (tinning, etc.) are detrimental to proper float operation.

- Check that needle valve (1) is well screwed into its seating and that the spring-loaded ball (5) part of the needle (2) is not jammed.

- Hold the carburettor cover in a verical position as shown in the figure so that the float (6) does not depress the ball (5)

- With the cover vertical and the float tongue (4) in light contact with the ball, the two floats should be at a distance A = 8.5 mm (.33") from the cover mating surface with the gasket fitted and well stuck to the cover.

- When the level has been set, check that the travel (B) of the float is 6.5 mm (.26"); if necessary, adjust the position of float pivot tail (3).

- The adjustment described above will correspond to a fuel level of 29 + .5 mm (1.12 to 1.16") from the upper face of the float chamber (with a pressure of 2 mts - 6'6" H_2O upstream the needle valve).

- If distance (A) is not as specified, slightly bend the float tongue (4) until the correct distance is obtained; inspect the working surface of the float tongue for any sign of nicks wich may restrict the free movement of needle (2).

- Then fit the carburettor cover and check that the float can move freely without rubbing against the walls of the float chamber.

C A U T I O N - The float level should be checked whenever the float or the needle valve has been changed. In the latter case it is also advisable to replace the gasket and make certain the new valve is securely screwed into its seating.

CHECKING OF VALVE OPENING AND CLOSING ANGLES

Clearance (with cold engine) between the unlobed profile of cams and the valve cup ceiling
- intake .... .475 to .500 mm (.0187 to .0197")
- exhaust .... .525 to .550 mm (.0206 to .0216")

Opening of intake valve
- lift of cup .... .20 mm (.008")
- corresponding to an angle (before TDC) .... 18° 30' ± 1° 30'

Closing of intake valve
- lift of cup .... .20 mm (.008")
- corresponding to an angle (after BDC) .... 42° 30' ± 1° 30'

Opening of exhaust valve
- lift of cup .... .15 mm (.006")
- corresponding to an angle (before BDC) .... 42° 30' ± 1° 30'

Closing of exhaust valve
- lift of cup .... .15 mm (.006")
- corresponding to an angle (after TDC) .... 18° 30' ± 1° 30'

ANGLE VALUES OF THE ACTUAL DIAGRAM OF VALVE TIMING SYSTEM WITH COLD ENGINE
(clockwise rotation direction of the crankshaft seen from the front side)

opening of intake valve (before TDC) .... 36° 50'
closing of intake valve (after BDC) .... 60° 50'
opening of exhaust valve (before BDC) .... 54° 10'
closing of exhaust valve (after TDC) .... 30° 10'
induction stroke .... 277° 40'
exhaust stroke .... 264° 20'

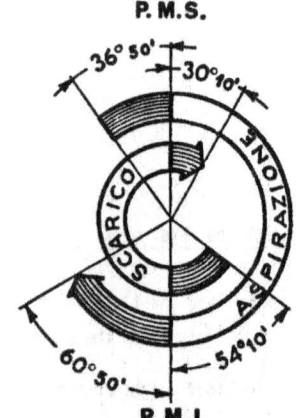

IGNITION

Firing order: 1 - 3 - 4 - 2 (no. 1 cylinder is that at the fan side)

VALUES OF ADVANCE OF IGNITION DISTRIBUTOR

Opening of contact points of ignition distributor S = .35 to .40 mm (.014 to .016")
The distributor is correctly fitted when the oiler is toward the engine.

Fixed advance F Before TDC	Maximum advance M Before TDC
3° ± 1°	43° +0° −3° at 5300 rpm

P - T.D.C.
F - Fixed advance
M - Maximum advance

SPARK PLUGS

Lodge 2HL

COOLING SYSTEM

The cooling circuit is provided with a compensating reservoir containing a special ALFA ROMEO Coolant Mixture which gives full protection against freezing down to -20°C (-5°F).

TO ENSURE THE EFFICIENT OPERATION OF THE COOLING SYSTEM, THE FOLLOWING PROCEDURE SHOULD BE OBSERVED.

Occasionally, check level of coolant in the reservoir: this should be done exclusively with a cold engine as with a hot engine the level may increase remarkably, even after stopping the engine.

The level of mixture in the reservoir should never fall below the "Min" or exceed the "Max".

To top up the reservoir use the specified Coolant Mixture.

If too frequent a topping up is required, check the cooling system for damage.

Should sudden and excessive leaks be experienced from the system, the use of fresh water is provisionally allowed. To replenish the circuit follow the directions given on next page.

IMPORTANT NOTE

Never remove radiator plug unless absolutely necessary; in any case, to avoid severe injuries, wait that the liquid is cooled down to ambient temperature.

Changing the coolant mixture

Every 18,750 mi - 30,000 Kms (or once a year whichever comes first) flush the circuit and renew the coolant mixture. (See page 8).

WARNING

In places where the temperature falls below -20°C (-5°F) the antifreeze mixture can be made stronger by varying its concentration.

To this end, a certain amount of mixture shall be drained off the circuit and replaced by the same quantity of "ALFA ROMEO Antifreeze" drawn from suitable containers.

The quantities of antifreeze to be added to radiator and reservoir depending on the lowest anticipated temperature are the following:

Temperature	Quantity of ALFA ROMEO coolant Mixture to be replaced with an equal quantity of "ALFA ROMEO Antifreeze"		
	Radiator	Reservoir	Total
-26°C - -16°F	800 cc	200 cc	1 lt
-35°C - -30°F	1,600 cc	400 cc	2 lts
-44°C - -48°F	2,400 cc	600 cc	3 lts

Draining and replenishing the system

Proceed as follows:

Draining

- Remove radiator filler plug "1".
- Unscrew the drain plug "3" and the bleed screw "7" on manifold.
- Turn on the heater cock "6".
- Turn on the bleed cock "5" on crankcase; let liquid drain off and empty the reservoir "8" by detaching pipe "9". Then turn off the cock "5", reconnect pipe "9" to reservoir and retighten drain plug "3".

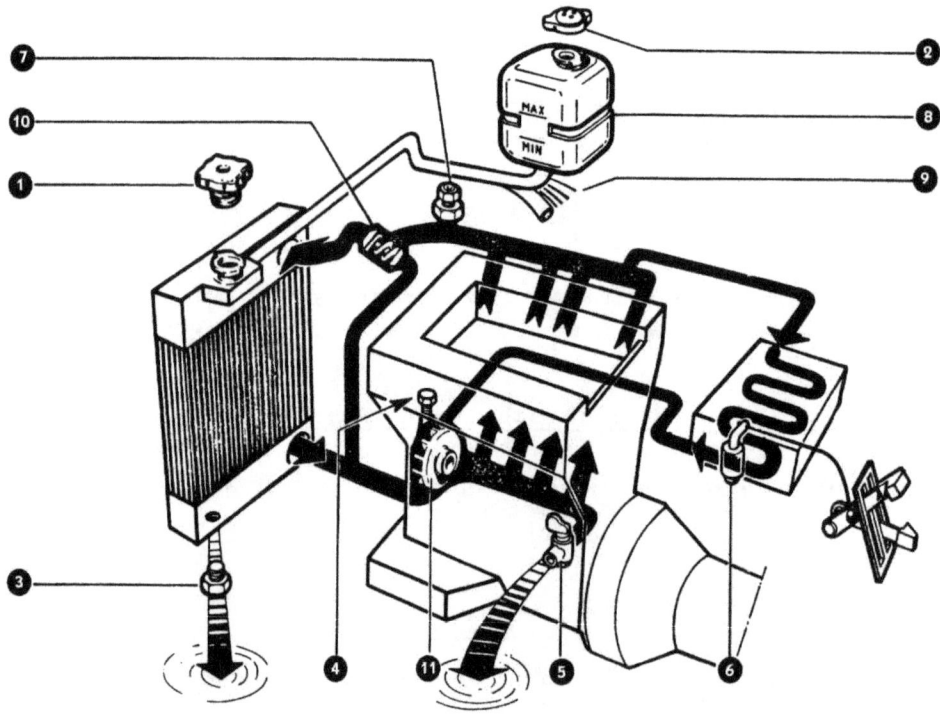

1 Radiator plug
2 Reservoir filler plug
3 Radiator drain plug
4 Bleed screw on pump
5 Bleed cock on crankcase
6 Heater cock
7 Bleed screw on manifold
8 Reservoir
9 Supply line from reservoir
10 Thermostat
11 Centrifugal pump

Replenishing

- Remove radiator and reservoir filler plug and turn on the heater cock.
- Open the bleed screw "7" on manifold and "4" on pump.
- Pour coolant mixture through radiator filler port until coolant escapes from bleed screw "4"; then screw in the latter. Go on in adding mixture until it appears at the bleed screw "7" on manifold.
- With the bleed screw on manifold opened and no plug on filler port of radiator, start the engine and keep it running for a few seconds in order to bleed air completely.
- Close the bleed screw on manifold.
- Add mixture to radiator filler port until full.
- Add mixture also to reservoir until "Max" level is reached.
- Put plugs on reservoir and radiator.

Checking cooling system for proper operation after topping up

After the system has been fully replenished or even topped up owing to drainings for mixture change or for repair, it is advisable to check the system for proper operation as follows:

a) with the circuit closed and the heater cock opened, run the engine until the coolant mixture has reached a temperature of about 80-85°C and keep on idling the engine; in this condition the thermostat opens thus allowing possible air bubbles trapped in the circuit to pass in the radiator and then in the reservoir.

b) let the engine cool down to room temperature in order to allow the mixture in the reservoir to compensate for the air bled off as said above.

c) remove the filler plug and check that radiator is full.

d) fill the reservoir up to "Max" mark.

N.B. - If, when opening the filler plug as in c) above, the radiator is not full, repeat the procedure, keeping the engine running for a longer time at operating temperature (thermostat opened) to bleed all the air from the circuit.
Should the trouble persist, air instead of coolant from reservoir is likely to enter the circuit through some leaking component (radiator filler plug included) in this case, inspect the circuit accordingly, then again repeat the checking procedure.

Electrical equipment

	BOSCH
Voltage	12 Volts
Battery	60 Amp.h
Alternator	K1 (R,L) 14 V 35 A 20
Voltage regulator	AD 1/14 V
Starting motor	EF (R) 12 V 0,7 PS
Coil	K 12 V
Ignition distributor	JF 4 (R)
Windshield wiper (2-speed)	WS 13/11 S 1 A

Bulb's wattage

Inner headlights (high beams)	40/45 asymmetric
Outer headlights (high & low beams)	40/45 asymmetric
Tail lights - parking & stop	5/20
Front direction indicators	20
Tail direction indicators	20
Back-up light	20
Front parking lights	5 globular
License plate light	5 globular
Engine compartment light	5 cylindrical
Courtesy light	5 cylindrical
Light in luggage compartment	5 cylindrical
Lighting on instruments	3 tubular
Tell-tale for blower	3 tubular
Tell-tale for alternator	3 tubular
Tell-tale for parking lights	3 tubular
Tell-tale for high beams	3 tubular
Tell-tale for fuel reserve	3 tubular
Tell-tale for choke	1.2 tubular
Tell-tales for direction indicators	1.2 tubular
Tell-tale for low oil pressure	1.2 tubular

Tightening torque specifications

ENGINE - GEARBOX UNIT	Kgm.	lb. ft	Manner of tightening
Cylinder head nuts — Inspection — when cold	7.2 to 7.4	52.1 to 53.5	Slacken without lubricating
Cylinder head nuts — Inspection — when hot	7.6 to 7.7	55.0 to 55.7	Tighten without slackening the nut
Cylinder head nuts — after repairing — when cold	7.2 to 7.4	52.1 to 53.5	Retighten with lube
Cylinder head nuts — after repairing — when hot	7.6 to 7.7	55.0 to 55.7	Lock without slackening
If the cylinder head gasket has been replaced retighten after the first 300 mi. (500 Km.)	7.2 to 7.4	52.1 to 53.5	Slacken by a quarter turn and retighten when cold
Spark plugs	2.5 to 3.5	18.1 to 25.3	With graphite grease, when cold
Nuts of the camshaft caps	2 to 2.25	14.5 to 16.3	in oil
Nuts of the connecting rod caps	5 to 5.3	36.2 to 38.3	" "
Nuts of main bearing caps	4.7 to 5	33.9 to 36.1	" "
Screws of flywheel on crankshaft	4.2 to 4.5	30.4 to 32.5	" "
Nut of alternator pulley	3 to 3.5	21.7 to 25.3	d r y
Nut of gearbox main shaft yoke	11.9 to 12	86 to 86.8	"
Nut of gearbox layshaft	4.5 to 5.5	32.6 to 39.7	"
Nut of gearbox half-casing	1.8	13	"
Bolts joing gearbox output shaft yoke to prop. shaft yoke	4 to 4.5	29 to 32.5	"
Nut of gearbox inner swivel	3.25 to 3.65	23.6 to 26.4	"
REAR FRAME			
Screws securing ring gear to differential case	4.5 to 5	32.6 to 36.1	"
Ringnut securing yoke on final drive pinion shaft	8 to 14	50 to 101.2	"
Nuts securing bearing housing to real axle tubes	4.8 to 5.5	34.8 to 39.7	"
Nuts securing radius rods to body	10 to 11.5	72.4 to 83	"
Nuts securing radius rods to rear axle tubes	11.5 to 13	83 to 94	"
Nut securing reaction triangle to body	4.8 to 5.5	34.8 to 39.7	"
Nut securing reaction triangle to rear axle	11 to 15	79.6 to 108.5	"
Nut securing link to radius rod bolt	5.2 to 5.9	37.6 to 42.6	"
Screws securing rear brake caliper to support (ATE brakes)	2.3 to 2.8	16.7 to 20.2	"
Nuts securing wheels	6 to 8	43.4 to 57.8	"
Bolts joining differential yoke to prop. shaft yoke	3.5 to 4	25.3 to 28.9	"
Bolts for rebound strap butt joints	.5	3.6	"
Nuts securing rear axle tubes to differential carrier	2.4	17.4	"
FRONT FRAME			
Nut securing steering wheel to column	5 to 5.5	36.1 to 39.7	"
Screws securing Burman steering box cover	2.3 to 2.5	16.7 to 18	"
Screws securing steering box & bellcrank bracket to body	4.8 to 5.5	34.8 to 39.7	"
Nuts of steering linkage ball joints	4.8 to 5.5	34.8 to 39.7	"
Nut securing steering arm to box	12.5 to 14	90.5 to 101.2	"
Nut securing shock absorber to suspension arms	8.2 to 9.2	59.3 to 66.5	"
Screws securing upper wishbone front arm to body	2.3 to 2.8	16.7 to 20.2	"
Nut securing upper wishbone front arm to rear arm	4 to 4.5	29 to 32.5	"
Nut securing upper wishbone rear arm to body	12.5 to 14	83 to 94	"
Nuts securing lower wishbone shaft to cross-member (To tighten these nuts use tool A.5.0161 and torque to 5.2 to 5.5 (37.6 to 39.7)	5.6 to 5.9	94 to 130	"
Nuts securing steering arm to steering knuckle	4 to 4.5	29 to 32.5	"
Nut securing upper wishbone rear arm to steering knuckle	7.5 to 8.5	54.3 to 61.4	"
Nut securing lower ball joint to wishbone	8.2 to 9.2	59.3 to 66.5	"
Nut securing lower ball joint to steering knuckle	7.5 to 8.5	54.3 to 61.4	"
Nuts securing caliper to steering knuckle	7.5 to 8.5	54.3 to 61.4	"
Screws securing brake splash shields	.8 to 1	5.8 to 7.2	"
Nuts securing wheels & brake discs	6 to 8	43.4 to 57.8	"
ATE BRAKES			
Bleed screw	.2 to .35	1.5 to 2.5	"
Caliper joining bolt	2.9 to 3.4	21 to 24.6	"
Inlet fitting to caliper — with gasket	.8 to 1.1	6 to 8	"
Inlet fitting to caliper — without gasket	1 to 1.5	7.2 to 10.8	"

MAJOR INSPECTION SPECIFICATIONS

Camshafts

Diameter of journals . . . . A = 26.959 to 26.980 mm (1.0614 to 1.0622")
Diameter of journal bearings . . . . B = 27.000 to 27.033 mm (1.0630 to 1.0642")
Clearance between journals and bearings . . . . B-A =   .020 to .074 mm (.0008 to .0028")
End play of camshaft in thrust bearing . . . . C =   .065 to .182 mm (.0026 to .0071")

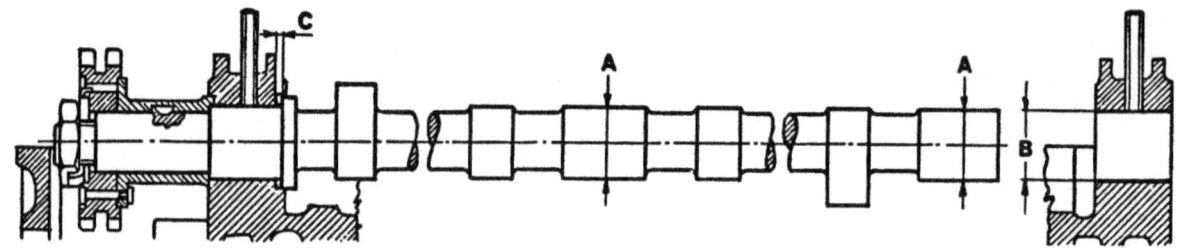

Valves and valve guides

		INTAKE			EXHAUST (sodium cooled)
		LIVIA H	ATE	GARRONE	LIVIA C
Valves	Diameter of valve poppet . . . . . O	41.000 to 41.150 mm (1.614 to 1.620")	41.000 to 41.200 mm (1.614 to 1.622")	41.000 to 41.150 mm (1.614 to 1.620")	37.000 to 37.150 mm (1.4567 to 1.4625")
	Diameter of valve stem . . . . . . M	8.972 to 8.987 mm (.3532 to .3538")			8.935 to 8.960 mm (.3518 to .3527")
	Total length . . L	106.900 to 107.150 mm (4.2087 to 4.2186")	106.800 mm (4.2047")	107.000 mm (4.2126")	106.300 mm (4.1850")

N.B.: ATE - LIVIA - GARRONE intake valves are alternate supply.

Valve guide { Outside diameter with guide removed . . . . E = 14.033 to 14.044 mm (.5528 to .5529")
              { Inside diameter with guide assembled in cylinder head D = 9.000 to 9.015 mm (.3544 to .3549")
Projection of intake valve guides from their recesses in cylinder head . 13.800 to 14.000 mm (.543 to .551")
Projection of exhaust valve guides from their recesses in cylinder head . 16.800 to 17.000 mm (.662 to .669")
Clearance between guide assembled in cylinder { intake . . . . .013 to .043 mm (.0005 to .0031")
  head and valve stem . . . . { exhaust . . . . .040 to .080 mm (.0016 to .0031")

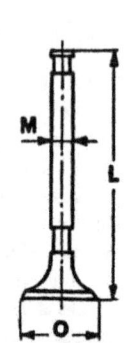

Valve seats

Diameter of valve guide seat in cylinder head F = 13.990 to 14.018 mm (.5508 to .5519")
Interference between seat and valve guide E-F =   .015 to .054 mm (.0006 to .0021")

		Intake	Exhaust
Outer diameter of the valve seat insert . . . . H	standard .	42.597 to 42.632 mm (1.6771 to 1.6784")	38.597 to 38.632 mm (1.5196 to 1.5209")
	oversized .	42.897 to 42.932 mm (1.6889 to 1.6902")	38.897 to 38.932 mm (1.5314 to 1.5327")
Diameter of recess in the cylinder head for valve seat insert . . . . G	standard .	42.532 to 42.557 mm (1.6744 to 1.6754")	38.532 to 38.557 mm (1.5169 to 1.5179")
	oversized .	42.832 to 42.857 mm (1.6862 to 1.6872")	38.832 to 38.857 mm (1.5288 to 1.5298")

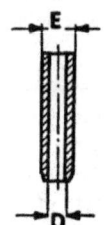
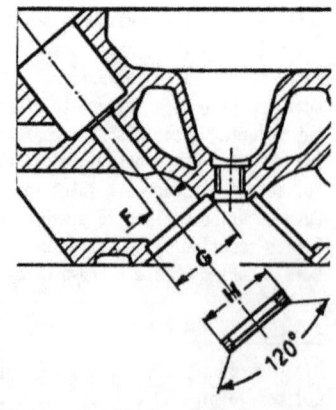

Interference between valve seat insert and recess in cylinder head . . . . H-G   .100 to .040 mm (.0039 to .0010")

Valve cups

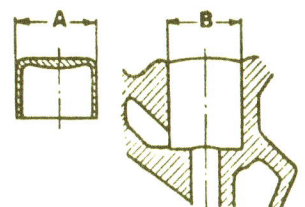

Diameter of cup . . . . A	standard . .	34.973 to 34.989 mm (1.3769 to 1.3775")
	oversized . .	35.173 to 35.189 mm (1.3848 to 1.3854")
Diameter of cup seat in cylinder head . . . . B	standard . .	35.000 to 35.025 mm (1.3780 to 1.3789")
	oversized . .	35.200 to 35.225 mm (1.3859 to 1.3868")
Clearance between seat and cup		.011 to .052 mm (.0005 to .0020")

Valve springs

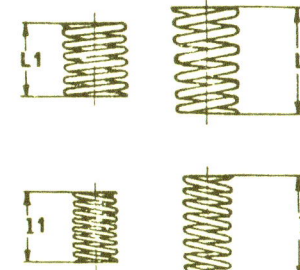

	Free length	Length under test load	Test load
Inner spring l	46.50 mm (1.83") 47.35 mm (1.88") 47.00 mm (1.85")	l1 - 26 mm (1.02")	22.3 to 23.1 Kg. 49.9 to 51.1 lbs
Outer spring L	51.30 mm (2.02") 52.80 mm (2.08") 52.00 mm (2.05")	L1 - 27.5 mm (1.08")	35.67 to 37.13 Kg. 78.6 to 81.8 lbs 35.87 to 37.33 Kg. 79.1 to 82.3 lbs

Connecting rods

Length between ₵ of big end and ₵ of small end of connecting rod . . . . D =	156.950 to 157.050 mm (6.1792 to 6.1830")
Inner diameter of the big end of connecting rod . . . . E =	53.695 to 53.708 mm (2.1140 to 2.1144")
Inner diameter of bushing in the small end of rod . . . . C =	22.005 to 22.015 mm (.8664 to .8667")
Thickness of connecting rod bearings F { standard	1.829 to 1.835 mm (.0720 to .0722")
1st oversize	1.956 to 1.962 mm (.0770 to .0772")
2nd oversize	2.083 to 2.089 mm (.0820 to .0824")
Radial clearance between crankpins and bearings for big end of connecting rod . .	.025 to .063 mm (.0010 to .0024")
Maximum out of parallelism between ₵ of big end hole and ₵ of small end hole . .	.078 mm (.0031")

Piston pins

O.D. of pin I { black	21.994 to 21.997 mm (.86590 to .86602")
white	21.997 to 22.000 mm (.86605 to .86614")
Clearance between con. rod small end bore and piston pin { black	.008 to .021 mm (.0003 to .0008")
white	.005 to .018 mm (.0002 to .0007")

Piston pin hole

BORGO piston H { black	22.000 to 22.002 mm (.86614 to .86621")
white	22.003 to 22.005 mm (.86626 to .86633")

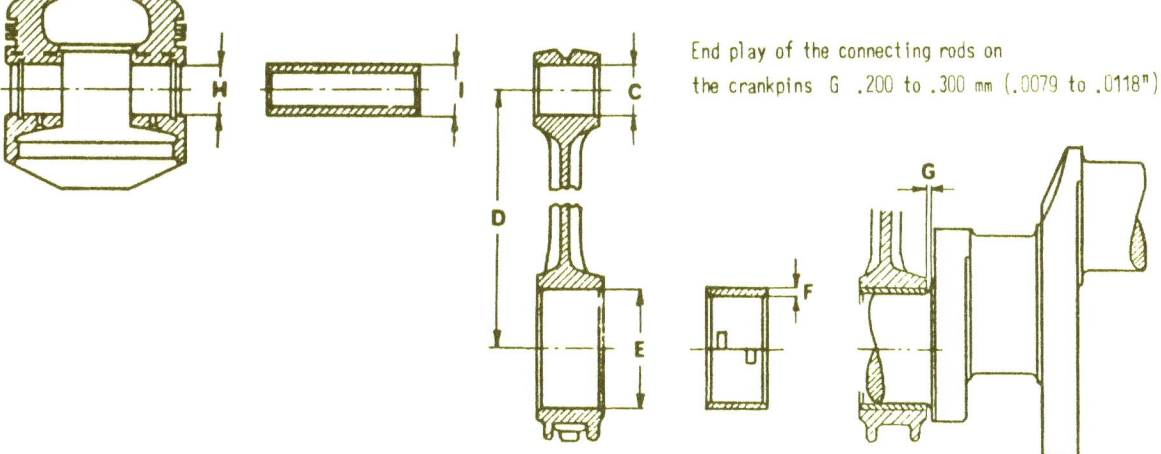

End play of the connecting rods on the crankpins G .200 to .300 mm (.0079 to .0118")

Pistons and piston rings

Diameter of pistons to be measured to square with the hole for piston pin and at a sistance of L = 15 mm (.591") from the lower border of skirt.

	Class A (Blue)	Class B (Pink)	Class C (Green)
BORGO piston diameter	79.945 to 79.955 mm (3.1475 to 3.1479")	79.955 to 79.965 mm (3.1479 to 3.1483")	79.965 to 79.975 mm (3.1483 to 3.1487")

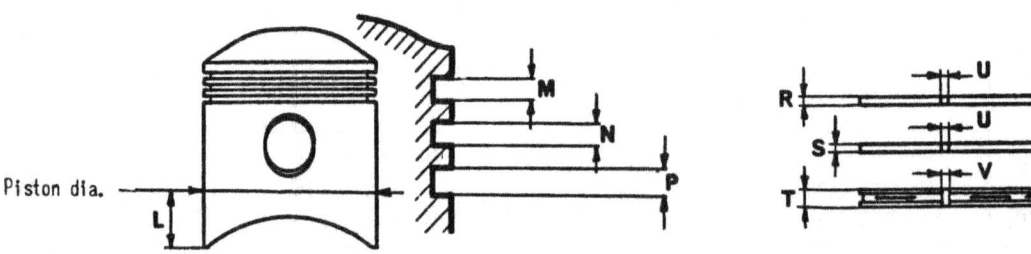

Height of grooves in piston for compression rings	chromium-plated	M = 1.525 to 1.545 mm (.0601 to .0609")
	normal	N = 1.775 to 1.795 mm (.0699 to .0706")
Height of groove in piston for oil scraper ring		P = 4.015 to 4.035 mm (.1581 to .1588")
Thickness of compression rings	chromium-plated	R = 1.478 to 1.490 mm (.0582 to .0586")
	normal	S = 1.728 to 1.740 mm (.0681 to .0685")
Thickness of oil scraper ring		T = 3.978 to 3.990 mm (.1567 to .1571")
End play of rings in grooves	compression rings chromium-plated	.035 to .067 mm (.0014 to .0026")
	normal	.035 to .067 mm (.0014 to .0026")
	oil scraper ring	.025 to .057 mm (.0010 to .0022")
Gap of compression rings to be inspected in ring gauge or in cylinder barrels		U = .300 to .450 mm (.0118 to .0177")
Gap of oil scraper rings to be inspected in ring gauge or in cylinder barrels		V = .250 to .400 mm (.0100 to .0157")

Cylinder barrels

	Blue	Pink	Green
Cylinder barrel bore	79.985 to 79.994 mm (3.1490 to 3.1493")	79.995 to 80.004 mm (3.1494 to 3.1497")	80.005 to 80.014 mm (3.1498 to 3.1501")

Clearance between cylinder barrel and piston . . . . .030 to .049 mm (.0012 to .0019")

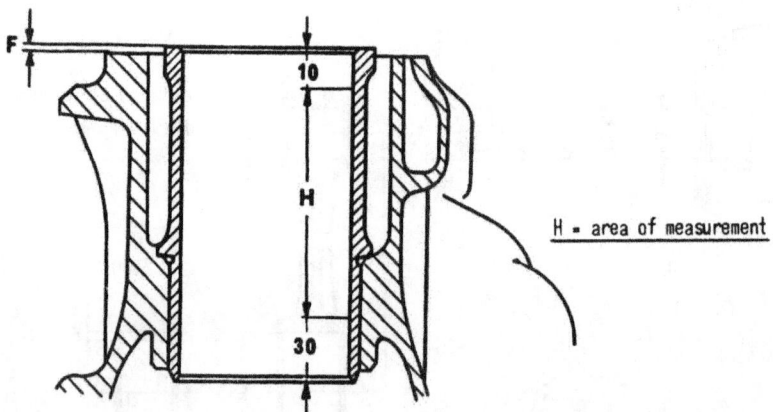

H = area of measurement

Projection of barrels from cylinder block . . . . F = .000 to .060 mm (.0000 to .0024")
Surface roughness of barrel bore . . . . 20 to 40 microinches RMS

Crankshaft

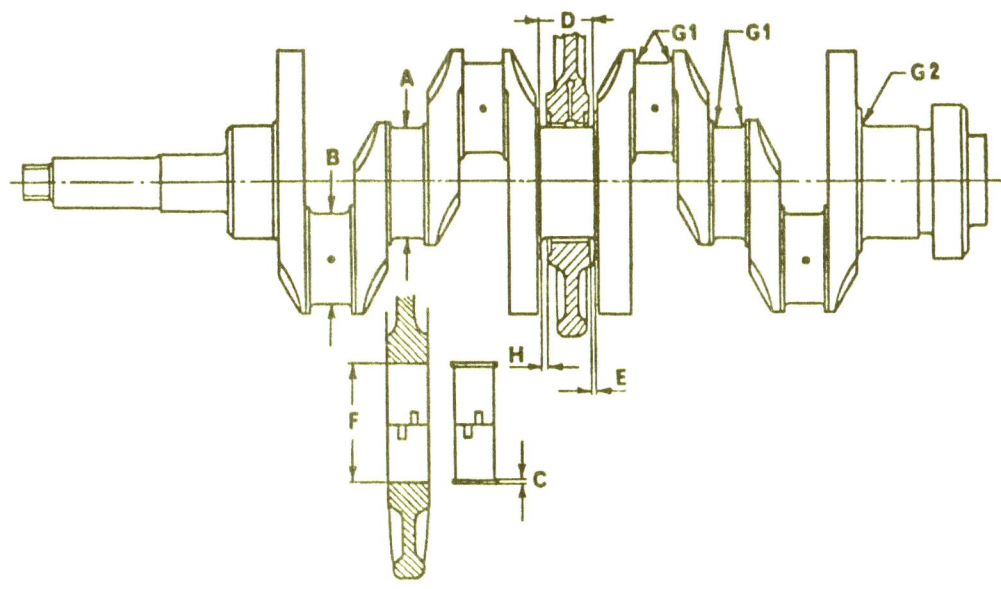

Diameter of main journals A	standard		59.960 to 59.973 mm (2.3606 to 2.3611")
	1st undersize		59.706 to 59.719 mm (2.3506 to 2.3511")
	2nd undersize		59.452 to 59.465 mm (2.3407 to 2.3411")
Diameter of crankpins B	standard		49.987 to 50.000 mm (1.9680 to 1.9685")
	1st undersize		49.733 to 49.746 mm (1.9581 to 1.9585")
	2nd undersize		49.479 to 49.492 mm (1.9480 to 1.9485")
Thickness of main bearings C	standard		1.829 to 1.835 mm (.0720 to .0722")
	1st oversize		1.956 to 1.962 mm (.0770 to .0772")
	2nd oversize		2.083 to 2.089 mm (.0820 to .0822")
Diameter of seat for main bearings in crankcase		F =	63.657 to 63.676 mm (2.5062 to 2.5069")
Length of central journal D	standard		30.000 to 30.035 mm (1.1811 to 1.1824")
	1st oversize		30.127 to 30.162 mm (1.1861 to 1.1874")
	2nd oversize		30.254 to 30.289 mm (1.1911 to 1.1924")
Thickness of thrust rings for central journal E	standard		2.311 to 2.362 mm (.0910 to .0929")
	1st oversize		2.374 to 2.425 mm (.0935 to .0954")
	2nd oversize		2.438 to 2.489 mm (.0960 to .0980")
End play of crankshaft		H =	.076 to .263 mm (.003 to .010")
Radial clearance between journals and main bearings			.014 to .058 mm (.0005 to .0022")

Note - Radial clearance = main bearing ID - (twice bearing thickness + journal OD)

Fillet radii	main journals & crankpins	G1	1.7 to 2.1 mm (.07 to .08")
	pin on flywheel side	G2	3.7 to 4.1 mm (.15 to .16")
Main journals & crankpins surface roughness			63 microinches RMS
Maximum elongation of main journals and crankpins			.007 mm (.00027")
Maximum taper of main journals and crankpins measured on their full length			.01 mm (.00039")
Maximum error of parallelism of main journals and crankpins measured on their full length			.015 mm (.00059")
Maximum misalignment allowed between main journals			.01 mm (.00039")
Maximum misalignment allowed between ₵ of the two pairs of crankpins and ₵ of main journals			.300 mm (.0118")

CLUTCH

The clutch is of the hydraulically-operated single plate dry type. The clutch pedal acts on a master cylinder supplied with the same type of fluid as the brake system.

When the clutch pedal is depressed, the fluid under pressure actuates the piston in the cylinder "4" connected to the clutch disengagement lever "5".

The pressure plate is controlled by means of diaphragm spring "6".

The clutch pedal free travel "A" should be about 1 1/4" (30-32mm). When owing to wear on the clutch disc facing, the pedal free travel is reduced to 3/4" (17-19 mm) the free travel must be restored.

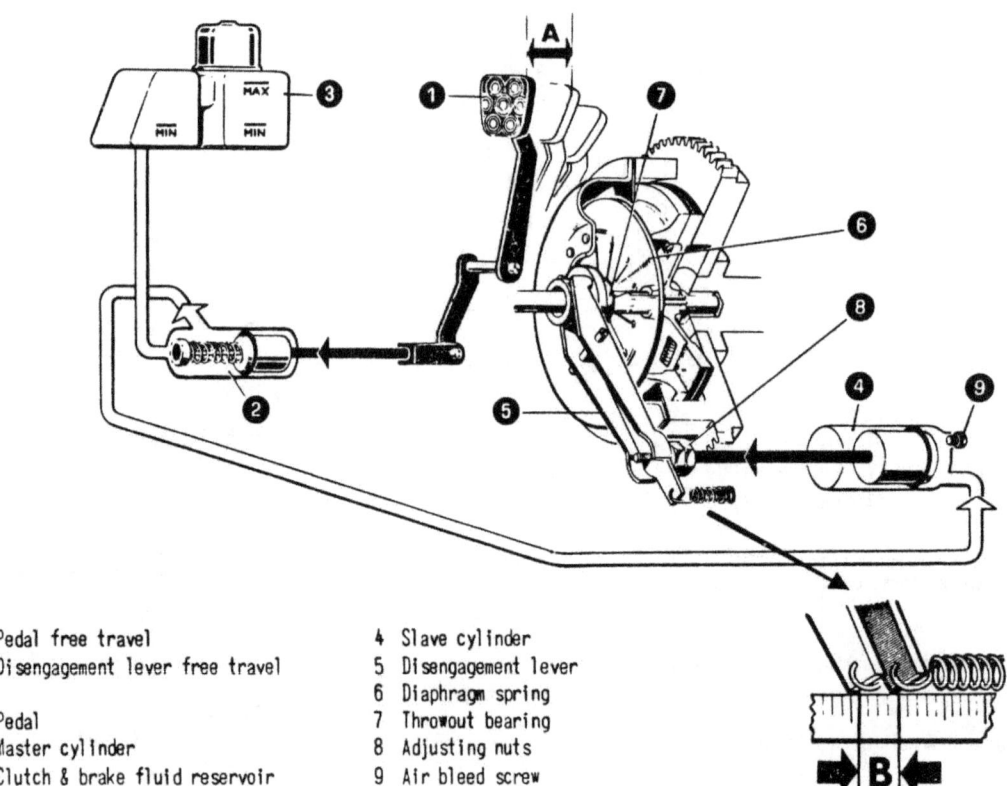

A Pedal free travel
B Disengagement lever free travel

1 Pedal
2 Master cylinder
3 Clutch & brake fluid reservoir
4 Slave cylinder
5 Disengagement lever
6 Diaphragm spring
7 Throwout bearing
8 Adjusting nuts
9 Air bleed screw

Adjustment

Measure with a rule the free travel "B" at the end of lever "5" pushing the lever by hand until the throwout bearing "7" contacts the spring "6"; the travel "B" should be about .08" (2 mm) corresponding to a clearance of .04" (1 mm) between bearing "7" and diaphragm spring "6". If the travel is shorter, act on the adjusting nut "8".

At the same time make sure that, by pressing the pedal as far as it will go, the actuating rod can move through a total travel of 3/4" (18-19 mm). If any component of the system has been removed, thoroughly bleed the circuit.

Inspection specifications

Thickness of driven plate when new under a load of 480 Kg (1058 lbs) . . . . 8.9 mm (.35")
Wear limit of driven plate thickness under a load of 480 Kg (1058 lbs) . . . . 7 mm (.27")

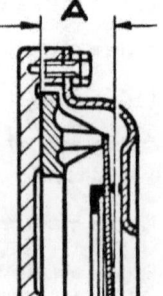

A = 33.1 to 35.1 mm (1.30 to 1.38")

To check dimension "A" use the special tool C.6.0139.

GEARBOX

Transmission ratios	1st gear	3.30 : 1
	2nd gear	1.99 : 1
	3rd gear	1.35 : 1
	4th gear	1.00 : 1
	5th gear	.79 : 1
	Rev.	3.01 : 1

Maximum eccentricity of main shaft .... .050 mm (.020")

End play between forks and sleeves	assembly	.150 to .340 mm (.006 to .013")
	wear limit	.850 mm (.033")

Calibration of striking rod ball spring	free length	35.8 mm (1.41")
	length under test load	17.2 mm (.69")
	test load	7.680 to 8.320 mm (16.97 to 18.3 lbs)

Maximum end play of mainshaft gears	1st speed gear	.170 to .245 mm (.0067 to .0096")
	2nd & 3rd speed gears	.130 to .205 mm (.0052 to .0081")
	5th speed gear & Rev.	.160 to .220 mm (.0063 to .0087")

Radial clearance between gear bushings and mainshaft	1st speed gear	.125 to .170 mm (.0049 to .0067")
	2nd & 3rd speed gears	.095 to .140 mm (.0038 to .0055")
	5th speed gear	.065 to .107 mm (.0026 to .0041")

Distance between outer planes of the engaging teeth of 3rd and 4th gears .... 42.000 to 42.200 mm (1.65 to 1.66")

Distance, in neutral, of the rear band (propeller shaft side) of 5th speed sleeve from the <u>r e a r</u> edge of gear engaging teeth .... 12.9 mm (.508")

REAR AXLE AND SUSPENSION

Transmission-axle overall ratios with 43 : 10 final drive
- 1st gear . . . . 14.20 : 1
- 2nd gear . . . . 8.55 : 1
- 3rd gear . . . . 5.82 : 1
- 4th gear . . . . 4.30 : 1
- 5th gear . . . . 3.40 : 1
- Rev. . . . . . . 12.94 : 1

Maximum eccentricity of axle shafts	.10 mm (.004")
Play between teeth of planetary gears	.05 mm (.002")
Play between teeth of final drive	.05 to .10 mm (.002 to .004")
Reference dimension on tool C.6.0101 for pinion-to-ring gear fitting	70 ± .0025 mm (2.7559 ± .0001")
Maximum end play between reaction trunnion and attachment to body	1 mm (.04")
Pre-load on pinion bearing	11.5 to 15.5 Kgcm (10 to 13.5 in. lbs)
Total preload on final drive bearings	16.5 to 24.5 Kgcm (14.4 to 21.3 in. lbs)

Checking of shock absorbers on test bench - Calibration data (when cold)

	BIANCHI	
	Extension	Compression
High speed	135 to 190 Kgs (298 to 418 lbs)	50 to 80 Kgs (111 to 176 lbs)
Low speed	19 to 55 Kgs (42 to 121 lbs)	9 to 22 Kgs (20 to 48 lbs)

Checking of suspension springs

Free length	467 mm (18.4")
Length under test load	252 mm (10")
Test load	349 to 371 Kgs (770 to 815 lbs)

FRONT SUSPENSION

Adjustment of clearance in wheel bearings

When performing regular servicing or whenever the removal of wheel hubs is required, adjust the bearing clearance as follows:

1) Screw in the castellated nut and lock it to a torque of 2.5 Kgm (18 ft-lbs) while at the same time revolving the wheel hub to set the bearings properly in their seats;
2) Unscrew the nut half a turn or more;
3) Lightly tap on the stub axle end with a mallet in order to return the outboard bearing in its proper position even in the case a slight interference between bearing cone and stub axle exists;
4) Lock the nut in place to 1.5 Kgm (10.8 ft-lbs);
5) Unscrew the nut of a quarter turn;
6) If the hole in the axle is aligned with a slot in the castellated nut insert the cotter pin; if not, screw in the nut by the minimum angle needed to line up the hole and the next slot;
7) Again tap lightly on stub axle end to restore the same condition as under step 3;
8) The end play so obtained on stub axle should fall between .02 - .12 mm (.0008 - .0047").

Wheel bearing lubricating instructions

The quantity of lubricating grease should be about 65 grammes (2½ ozs) for each hub; do not exceed such a quantity to avoid bearing overheating, grease leakage, etc.

The grease should be well distributed inside the bearings and into side recesses.

Subsequently, at the regular schedule, remove the hub cover and pack the outboard bearing.

Ball joints

End play of lower ball joint in its socket .... 1 mm (.04")

N o t e - Ball joints require no regular lubrication being provided with special grease seals which retain the grease packed in by factory on assembly - Only if strictly needed (joints squealing) grease with SHELL Retinax A or AGIP F.1 Grease 30 (See I.S. 1.05.097/1).

Checking of suspension springs

	R.H. side	L.H. side
Free length	345 mm (13.6")	355 mm (14")
Length under test load	214 mm (7.9")	214 mm (7.9")
Test load	902 to 958 Kgs (1986 to 2110 lbs)	970 to 1030 Kgs (2138 to 2271 lbs)

Checking of shock absorbers on test bench

Calibration data (when cold)

	ALLINQUANT	
	Extension	Compression
High speed	150 to 190 Kgs (331 to 418 lbs)	55 to 80 Kgs (121 to 176 lbs)
Low speed	25 to 55 Kgs (56 to 121 lbs)	9 to 22 Kgs (20 to 48 lbs)

BRAKE SYSTEM

The ATE brake system consists of four caliper type disc brakes operated by an assisted master cylinder.
The brakes are self-adjusting.
A pressure regulator controls the braking power to rear brakes. Such a regulator shall not be tampered with; specifically do not attempt to act on the adjusting nut as it is factory sealed.

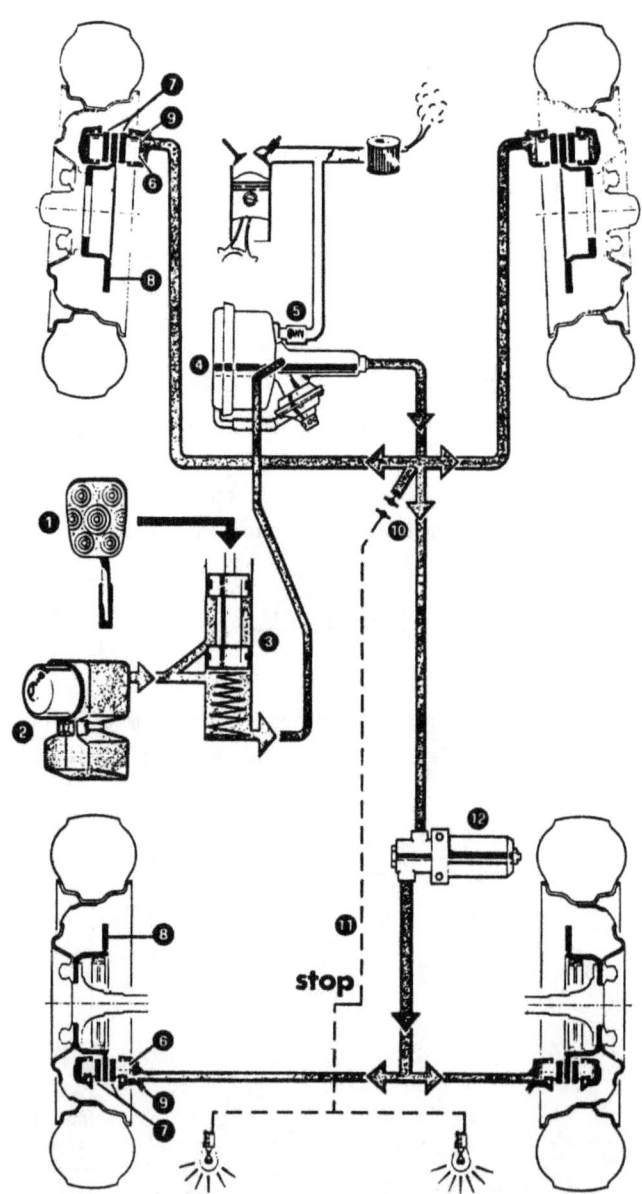

1 Brake pedal
2 Reservoir
3 Master cylinder
4 Vacuum servo
5 Vacuum connection
6 Pistons
7 Friction pads
8 Discs
9 Bleed screws
10 Stop light switch
11 Stop light cable
12 Pressure regulator

ATE BRAKES

Disc

When a brake disc is replaced it is necessary to check it for run-out after installation:

- use a dial indicator and the special tool A.2.0151 which is mounted to the caliper by means of the pad retaining pins.

Maximum permissible run out as measured at the swept surface should not exceed .22 mm (.0086").

N o t e - run-out readings can be misleading if bearing clearance is not as specified; therefore, check and adjust if necessary, according to factory instructions.

If the disc is scored, see I.S. 0.00.055/3; the grinding of the surfaces is allowed providing not to exceed an undersize of 1 mm (.0394"), equalized on both faces, i.e. .5 mm (.0197") each face; disc wear limit: front 11.5 mm (.452") rear 8.5 mm (.335") thick.

Inspection specifications after regrinding of disc surfaces:

- Max. out of parallelism with disc mounting plane: .05 mm (.0020");
- Max. out of flat: .025 mm (.0010") and max. difference in thickness: .038 mm (.0015") as measured along any radial line;
- Max. out of flat: .025 mm (.0010") and max. difference in thickness: .015 mm (.0006") as measured along any circular line;
- The surface should show no sign of scoring or porosity.

The surface roughness should be:

- 26 microinches as measured circularly;
- 36 microinches as measured radially.

Friction pads

	Front	Rear
Thickness when new	15 mm (.590")	
Wear limit	7 mm (.275")	

Calipers

On replacement of disc or caliper, measure the running clearance between caliper and disc on each side; the difference should not exceed .5 mm (.0197").

To centralize the caliper about the disc, insert shims between caliper and mounting flange as required.

Hand brake

It is mechanically operated and acts on the rear wheels through suitable shoes which spread apart against a drum machined in the disc casting.

For a brief description and repair and maintenance instructions refer to:

ATE DISC BRAKES (Publication no. 1202)

N o t e - When reassembling the operating levers, a slight quantity of grease AGIP F1 Gr SM or SHELL Retinax AM is to be applied to the pivot points and rubbing surfaces of levers.

WHEEL ALIGNMENT

Checking of wheel angles and car "trim" under static load

Put the car under static load, with shock absorbers and stabilizer rods disconnected, with full tank or equivalent with spare wheel, tool kit and the tires inflated as specified.

Before checking, slightly move the car up and down so as to settle the suspensions.

Front seats
- 1 weight of 45 Kgs on each seat
- 2 weights of 25 Kgs on flooring where feet rest

Rear seats
- 2 weights of 45 Kgs on seat
- 2 weights of 25 Kgs on flooring where feet rest

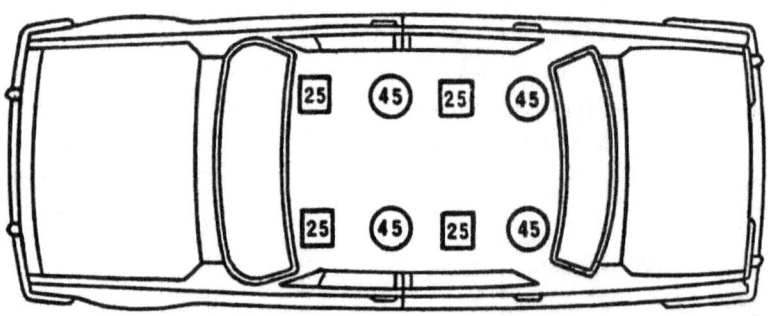

Distance of lower wishbone of front suspension from a reference level

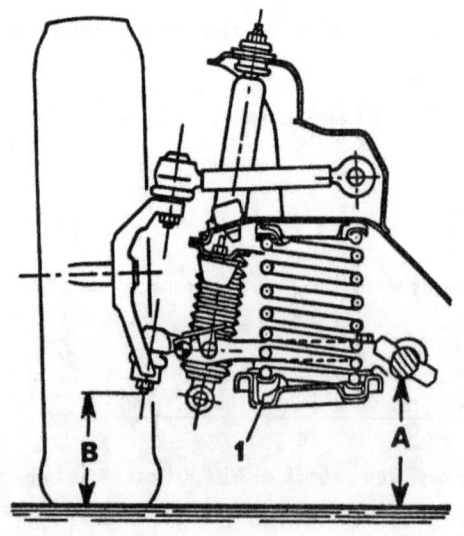

$A - B = 34 \pm 5$ mm $(1.34 \pm .20")$

Dimension "A" must be measured in correspondence of the lower line of wishbone shaft as shown.

To adjust add shims in "1".

Shims are available in the following thicknesses:
3.5 mm (.14") - 7 mm (.28") - 10.5 mm (.42")

Distance of rear axle from rubber buffers

$$C = 36 \pm 5 \text{ mm} (1.42 \pm .20")$$

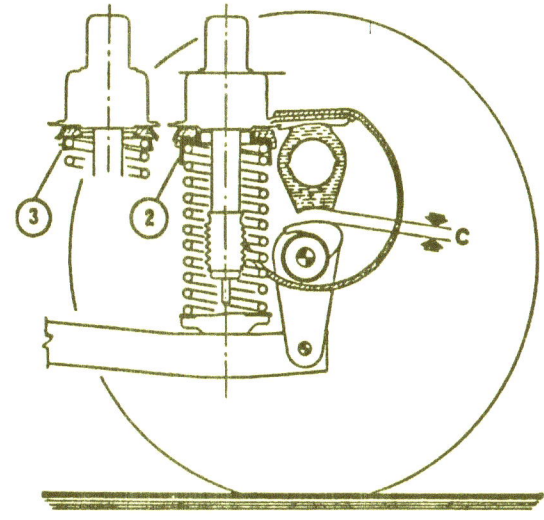

Note - To adjust, remove the seat 3 and add shims in 2 as shown.

Shims are available in the following ticknesses:

6.5 mm (.26")
11.5 mm (.45")
16.5 mm (.65")
21.5 mm (.85")

In the conditions as specified check the wheel angles.

Caster angle: $\alpha = 1° \pm 30'$

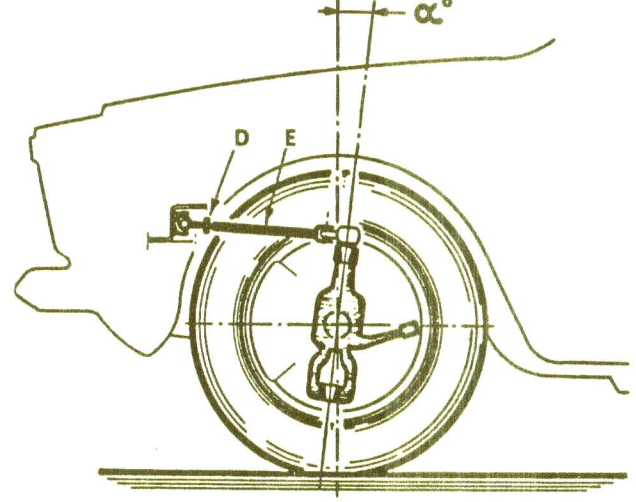

The difference in caster angle between R.H. and L.H. wheel must not exceed 0°20'.

To adjust, loosen jam nut "D" and rotate rod "E".

Note - Small adjustments of the caster angle allow to correct slight drift tendency of the car.

The caster angle should be checked under static load and alignment conditions as specified and with shock absorbers disconnected at an end.

N.B. - Before checking the caster angle shake the front end of car in order to allow the rubber bushing on the front slanting arm to set properly.

Front wheel camber

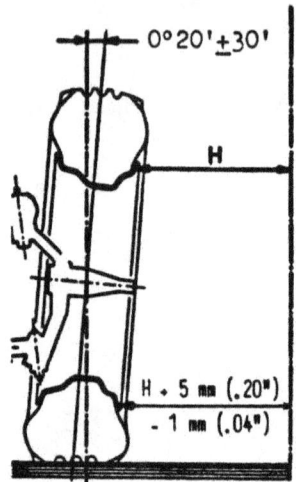

Difference in camber angle between R.H. and L.H. wheel - 0° 40'

N o t e - Not adjustable. Check the chassis and suspension arms if necessary.

Front wheel toe-in

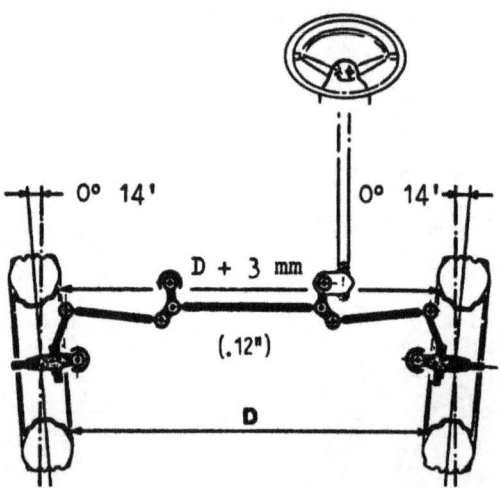

Rod length:

    side . . . . 264 to 280 mm (10.4 to 11")
    track . . . . 530 to 550 mm (20.86 to 21.65")

With the toe-in as specified, the length of rods as measured between ball joint centers should fall within the limits shown. If these values cannot be restored, the cause will probably be attributable to distortion of the body resulting from a collision.

"1750 GT Veloce and 1750 Spider Veloce" VARIANTS

PRINCIPAL CHARACTERISTIC DATA

Number of cylinders	4
Bore	80 mm. (3.15")
Stroke	88.5 mm. (3.48")
Total cylinder capacity	1779 cc
Max. power at 5,500 giri/min.	SAE 132 HP
Front track	1324 mm. (52.1")
Rear track	1274 mm. (50.1")
Wheel base — GT Veloce	2350 mm. (92.7")
Wheel base — Spider Veloce	2250 mm. (88.6")
Min. turning circle — GT Veloce	10700 mm. (420.1")
Min. turning circle — Spider Veloce	10500 mm. (413.4")
Overall length — GT Veloce	4080 mm. (161")
Overall length — Spider Veloce	4250 mm. (167.3")
Overall with — GT Veloce	1580 mm. (62.2")
Overall with — Spider Veloce	1630 mm. (64.2")
Overall height (unladen) — GT Veloce	1315 mm. (51.8")
Overall height (unladen) — Spider Veloce (with top)	1290 mm. (50.8")
Curb weight (full tank)	1040 Kg. (2293 lbs)
Number of seats — GT Veloce	2 + 2
Number of seats — Spider Veloce	2
Tires 165 x 14	PIRELLI cinturato HR / KLEBER COLOMBES V 10 GT / MICHELIN X A S
Fuel consumption per 100 Km. (CUNA standard)	11.4 lt. (24.6 mpg. GB) (20.6 mpg. US)

(For best engine performance, the use of premium-grade fuel is advised)

With 41 : 10 final drive

Gear	Max. Speeds					
	Running in				After running in	
	up to 1000 Km (600 mi.)		1000 to 3000 Km (600 to 1900 mi)			
	Km/h	mph	Km/h	mph	Km/h	mph
1st	27	17	34	21	47	29
2nd	46	29	56	35	77	48
3rd	67	42	82	51	114	71
4th	91	57	111	69	154	96
5th	115	71	141	88	190	118
Rev.	-	-	-	-	51	32

Tires

Inflation pressures (with tire cold)

	Front wheels		Rear wheels	
	Kg/cm²	psi	Kg/cm²	psi
PIRELLI cinturato HR - 165 x 14	1.7	24.1	1.8	25.6
KLEBER COLOMBES V 10 GT - 165 x 14	1.7	24.1	1.8	25.6
MICHELIN X A S - 165 x 14	1.4	19.9	1.7	24.1

N o t e - The pressures given apply to all conditions.

Electrical equipment

	BOSCH	
	1750 GT Veloce	1750 Spider Veloce
Two-speed windshield wiper	WS 13/11 T 1 A	WS 13/11 T 3 A

Bulb's wattage

1750 GT Veloce

Inner headlights (high beams)	45/40 asymmetric
Outer headlights (low beams)	45/40 asymmetric
Tail lights - parking & stop	5/20
Front direction indicators	20
Tail direction indicators	20
Back-up light	20
Front parking lights	5 globular
License plate light	5 globular
Engine compartment light	5 cylindrical
Courtesy light	5 cylindrical
Lighting on instruments	3 tubular
Tell-tale for blower	3 tubular
Tell-tale for alternator	3 tubular
Tell-tale for fuel reserve	3 tubular
Tell-tale for low oil pressure	3 tubular
Tell-tale for direction indicators	1.2 tubular
Tell-tale for parking lights	1.2 tubular
Tell-tale for high beams	1.2 tubular

1750 Spider Veloce

Headlamps (high & low beams)	45/40 asymmetric
Tail lights - parking & stop	5/20
Front direction indicators	20
Tail direction indicators	20
Back-up light	20
Front parking light	5 globular
Side direction indicator	5 globular
License plate light	5 globular
Engine compartment light	5 cylindrical
Courtesy light (in rearview mirror)	5 cylindrical
Glove box light	5 cylindrical
Ash tray light	5 cylindrical
Lighting on instruments	3 tubular
Tell-tale for alternator	3 tubular
Tell-tale for blower	3 tubular
Tell-tale for fuel reserve	3 tubular
Tell-tale for direction indicators	1.2 tubular
Tell-tale for low oil pressure	1.2 tubular
Tell-tale for parking lights	1.2 tubular
Tell-tale for high beams	1.2 tubular

REAR AXLE AND SUSPENSION

Transmission-axle overall ratios - with 41 : 10 final drive
- 1st gear .... 13.54 : 1
- 2nd gear .... 8.15 : 1
- 3rd gear .... 5.55 : 1
- 4th gear .... 4.10 : 1
- 5th gear .... 3.24 : 1
- Reverse .... 12.34 : 1

Checking of shock absorbers on test bench - Calibration data (when cold)

	BIANCHI	
	Extension	Compression
High speed	135 to 190 Kgs (298 to 418 lbs)	50 to 80 Kgs (111 to 176 lbs)
Low speed	19 to 55 Kgs (42 to 121 lbs)	9 to 22 Kgs (20 to 48 lbs)

Checking of suspension springs

	1750 GT Veloce	1750 Spider Veloce
Free length	437 mm (17.2")	429 mm (16.9")
Length under test load	252 mm (10")	252 mm (10")
Test load	268.7 to 285.3 Kgs (592.5 to 635 lbs)	265 Kgs (584 lbs)
Colored marks	Blue-Blue / Blue-White	White-White / White-Blue

FRONT SUSPENSION

Checking of shock absorbers on test bench

Calibration data (when cold)

	ALLINQUANT	
	Extension	Compression
High speed	150 to 190 Kgs (330 to 420 lbs)	55 to 80 Kgs (121 to 175 lbs)
Low speed	25 to 55 Kgs (55 to 121 lbs)	9 to 22 Kgs (20 to 48 lbs)

Checking of suspension springs

	1750 GT Veloce	1750 Spider Veloce
Free length	303 mm (11.9")	317 mm (12.5")
Length under test load	200 mm (7.8")	200 mm (7.8")
Test load	778 to 828 Kgs (1715 to 1826 lbs)	820.6 to 871.4 Kgs (1809.4 to 1920.5 lbs)
Colored marks	White-White / Blue	White-Blue / Blue-Blue

WHEEL ALIGNMENT

Checking of wheel angles and car "trim" under static load

Put the car under static load, with shock absorbers and stabilizer rods disconnected, with full tank or equivalent, with spare wheel, tool kit and the tires inflated as specified.

Before checking, slightly move the car up and down so as to settle the suspensions.

Static load { 2 weights of 45 Kgs (100 lbs) on front seats
2 weights of 25 Kgs (55 lbs) on flooring where feet rest

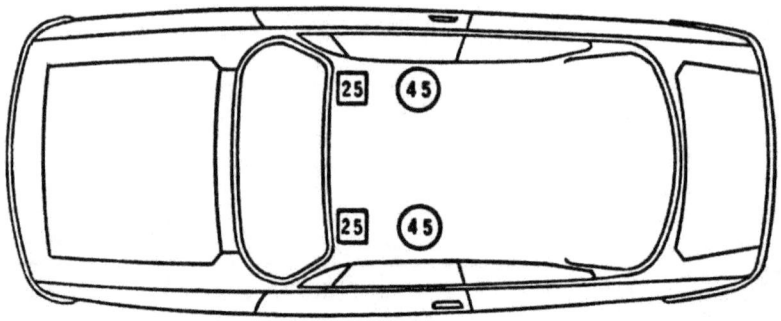

Distance of lower wishbone of front suspension from a reference level

$A - B = 24 \pm 5$ mm $(.94 \pm .2")$ (See figure on page 22)

Distance of rear axle from rubber buffers

$C = 41 \pm 5$ mm $(1.62 \pm .2")$ for 1750 GT Veloce

$C = 33 \pm 5$ mm $(1.30 \pm .2")$ for 1750 Spider Veloce   (See figure on page 23)

The importance of using the Alfa Romeo Factory 'Mechanical Repair' publications in conjunction with this Manual

As noted in the introduction to this manual, in addition to the 'Technical' publications, Alfa Romeo also issued a series of 'Mechanical Repair' publications that were focused on the overhaul and service of various mechanical and electrical components. The intention was that these two separate publications were to be used in conjunction with each other in order to provide both technical and mechanical data for a particular model. Consequently, we feel it is important that the reader is made aware of the associated workshop manual that compliments this technical manual

Alfa Romeo Giulia Workshop Manual 1962-1975 All Models 1300cc, 1600cc, 1750cc & 2000cc
ISBN 9781588502254

This 338 page manual was compiled using data from seven of the individual factory 'Mechanical Repair' publications plus a number of additional pages of maintenance, repair, overhaul and wiring diagrams that were not included in the original factory publications. Consequently, it provides a generic 'Workshop Manual' for the repair and overhaul of the 1965-1971 Giulia series of automobiles. However, as the 1962-1975 series of Alfa models shared many of the same mechanical components, these 'Mechanical Repair' publications are also of use to owners of both the earlier and later models. The combination of the manual above, when used in conjunction with this manual, will provide a comprehensive 'Workshop Manual' for the carbureted series of Alfa Giulia.

The additional pages in this workshop manual include maintenance and repair information on:

Drum brakes, hydraulic braking system, Dunlop disc brakes and additional information on ATE disc brakes. Front hubs, shock absorbers and stabilizer rod, ZF steering box, Burman steering box, steering linkage and steering adjustments. Electrical components including control box, regulator, generator, starter motor, windscreen wiper motor (both Bosch & Marelli), lamps and lighting and wiring diagrams for 14 different models.

The factory 'Mechanical Repair' publications included in this compilation are:

(1) Engine, Clutch & Gearbox Manual for the 1600 Giulia TI, Sprint GT & TI Super.

(2) Propeller Shaft, Rear Axle & Suspension for the Giulia 1300, 1300TI the Giulia 1600 TI Super, Sprint GT, GTC, TI, Super, Sprint GT Veloce & Spider 1600.

(3) ATE Disc Brakes all Models, as appropriate.

(4) Wheel, Suspension & Front End Geometry, for all Giulia and 1750 Models plus 2000 models amendment.

(5) Electrical for the 1600 Giulia Super, 1750 Berlina, 1750 GT Veloce & 1750 Spider Veloce.

(6) Air Conditioning all Models, as appropriate.

(7) Body, for all Giulia and 1750 Models

Alfa Romeo Giulia Technical Manual for 1969 and onwards SPICA Fuel Injected Models
ISBN 9781588502278

Owners of SPICA fuel injected equipped cars are directed to the above publication which combines six of the appropriate factory 'Technical' publications into a single manual for the 1750cc and 2000cc series of SPICA fuel injected Giulia models.

Technical Characteristics and Principal Inspection Specifications Manual for:

(1) 1750 Berlina, 1750 GT Veloce & 1750 Spider Veloce (1969 publication)

(2) 2000 Berlina, 2000 GT Veloce & 2000 Spider Veloce (1973 publication)

Instruction and Maintenance Manuals for Fuel Injection Models USA:

(3) 1750 All Models USA (1969 publication)

(4) 1750 All Models USA (1971 publication)

(5) 2000 All Models USA (1972 publication)

(6) 2000 All models USA including Alfetta (1975 publication)

While copies of the original factory publications can be sourced on the secondary market, they are scarce and relatively expensive. Consequently, we are pleased to be able to offer these reasonably priced alternatives to Alfa Romeo Giulia owners worldwide.

VELOCEPRESS MANUALS - MOTORCYCLE

1930'S BRITISH MOTORCYCLE CARBS & ELEC COMPONENTS (BOOK OF)
1930'S BRITISH MOTORCYCLE ENGINES (OVERHAUL & MAINTENANCE)
1930'S BRITISH MOTORCYCLE GEARBOXES & CLUTCHES (BOOK OF)
AJS 1932-1948 SINGLES & TWINS 250cc THRU 1000cc (BOOK OF)
AJS 1945-1960 SINGLES 350cc & 500cc MODELS 16 & 18 (BOOK OF)
AJS 1955-1965 SINGLES 350cc & 500cc (BOOK OF)
ARIEL 1932-1939 PREWAR MODELS (BOOK OF)
ARIEL 1933-1951 (WORKSHOP MANUAL)
ARIEL 1939-1960 4 STROKE SINGLES (BOOK OF)
ARIEL 1958-1964 LEADER & ARROW (BOOK OF)
BMW R26 R27 (1956-1967) FACTORY WORKSHOP MANUAL
BMW R50 R50S R60 R69S (1955-1969) FACTORY WORKSHOP MANUAL
BRIDGESTONE 90 SERIES FACTORY WSM & PARTS CATALOGUE
BRIDGESTONE 175 SERIES FACTORY WSM & PARTS CATALOGUE
BSA BANTAM ALL MODELS FROM 1948 ONWARDS (BOOK OF)
BSA SINGLES & V-TWINS UP TO 1927 (BOOK OF)
BSA SINGLES & V-TWINS UP TO 1935 (BOOK OF)
BSA SINGLES & V-TWINS 1936-1939 (BOOK OF)
BSA SINGLES & V-TWINS 1936-1952 (BOOK OF)
BSA OHV & SV SINGLES 250-600cc 1945-1954 (BOOK OF)
BSA OHV & SV SINGLES 250cc 1954-1970 (BOOK OF)
BSA OHV SINGLES 350 & 500cc 1955-1967 (BOOK OF)
BSA TWINS 1948-1962 (BOOK OF)
BSA TWINS 1962-1969 (SECOND BOOK OF)
CYCLEMOTOR (BOOK OF)
DOUGLAS 1929-1939 PREWAR ALL MODELS (BOOK OF)
DOUGLAS 1948-1957 POSTWAR ALL MODELS FACTORY SHOP MANUAL
DUCATI 160cc, 250cc & 350cc OHC MODELS FACTORY SHOP MANUAL
HONDA 50 ALL MODELS UP TO 1970 INC MONKEY & TRAIL (BOOK OF)
HONDA 90 ALL MODELS UP TO 1966 (BOOK OF)
HONDA 125-150cc TWINS C/CS/CB/CA FACTORY WORKSHOP MANUAL
HONDA 250-305 TWINS C/CS/CB FACTORY WORKSHOP MANUAL
HONDA C100 SUPER CUB FACTORY WORKSHOP MANUAL
HONDA C110 SPORT CUB 1962-1969 FACTORY WORKSHOP MANUAL
HONDA TWINS & SINGLES 50cc THRU 305cc 1960-1966 (BOOK OF)
HONDA TWINS ALL MODELS 125cc THRU 450cc UP TO 1968 (BOOK OF)
J.A.P. ENGINES 1927-1952 & MOTORCYCLES 1934-1952 (BOOK OF)
LAMBRETTA 1947-1957 ALL 125 & 150cc MODELS (BOOK OF)
LAMBRETTA 1957-1970 LI & TV MODELS (SECOND BOOK OF)
MATCHLESS 1931-1939 ALL MODELS 250cc THRU 990cc (BOOK OF)
MATCHLESS 1945-1956 350 & 500cc SINGLES (BOOK OF)
MATCHLESS 1955-1966 350 & 500cc SINGLES (BOOK OF)
NEW IMPERIAL ALL SV & OHV FROM 1935 ONWARDS (BOOK OF)
NORTON 1932-1939 PREWAR MODELS (BOOK OF)
NORTON 1932-1947 (BOOK OF)
NORTON 1938-1956 (BOOK OF)
NORTON 1955-1963 MODELS 19, 50 & ES2 (BOOK OF)
NORTON 1955-1965 DOMINATOR TWINS (BOOK OF)
NORTON 1957-1970 TWINS FACTORY WORKSHOP MANUAL
NSU PRIMA 1956-1964 ALL MODELS (BOOK OF)
NSU QUICKLY 1953-1963 ALL MODELS (BOOK OF)
PANTHER 1932-1958 LIGHTWEIGHT MODELS 250 & 350cc (BOOK OF)
PANTHER 1938-1966 HEAVYWEIGHT MODELS 600 & 650cc (BOOK OF)
RALEIGH MOPEDS 1960-1969 (BOOK OF)
RALEIGH MOTORCYCLES 1919-1933 (BOOK OF)
ROYAL ENFIELD 1934-1946 SINGLES & V TWINS (BOOK OF)
ROYAL ENFIELD 1937-1953 SINGLES & V TWINS (BOOK OF)
ROYAL ENFIELD 1946-1962 SINGLES (BOOK OF)
ROYAL ENFIELD 1958-1966 250cc & 350cc SINGLES (SECOND BOOK OF)
ROYAL ENFIELD 736cc INTERCEPTOR FACTORY WORKSHOP MANUAL
RUDGE 1933-1939 (BOOK OF)
SUNBEAM 1928-1939 (BOOK OF)
SUNBEAM 1946-1957 S7 & S8 (BOOK OF)
SUZUKI 50cc & 80cc UP TO 1966 (BOOK OF)
SUZUKI T10 1963-1967 FACTORY WORKSHOP MANUAL
SUZUKI T20 & T200 1965-1969 FACTORY WORKSHOP MANUAL
TRIUMPH 1935-1939 PREWAR MODELS (BOOK OF)
TRIUMPH 1935-1949 (BOOK OF)
TRIUMPH 1937-1951 (WORKSHOP MANUAL)
TRIUMPH 1945-1955 FACTORY WORKSHOP MANUAL
TRIUMPH 1945-1958 TWINS (BOOK OF)
TRIUMPH 1956-1969 TWINS (BOOK OF)
VELOCETTE 1925-1970 ALL SINGLES & TWINS (BOOK OF)
VESPA 1951-1961 (BOOK OF)
VESPA 1955-1963 125 & 150cc & GS MODELS (SECOND BOOK OF)
VESPA 1955-1968 GS & SS (BOOK OF)
VESPA 1963-1972 90, 125 & 150cc (THIRD BOOK OF)
VILLIERS ENGINE UP TO 1959 INC. 3 WHEELERS (BOOK OF)
VILLIERS ENGINE UP TO 1969 (BOOK OF)
VINCENT 1935-1955 (WORKSHOP MANUAL)

VELOCEPRESS TECHNICAL BOOKS – MOTORCYCLE

CATALOG OF BRITISH MOTORCYCLES (1951 MODELS)
INDIAN PONYBIKE, BOY RACER & PAPOOSE ILL PARTS LIST & SALES LIT
MOTORCYCLE ENGINEERING (P.E. Irving)
SPEED AND HOW TO OBTAIN IT (Motor Cycle Magazine UK)
TUNING FOR SPEED (P.E. Irving)

VELOCEPRESS MANUALS - THREE WHEELER'S

BSA THREE WHEELER (BOOK OF)
VINTAGE MORGAN THREE WHEELER (BOOK OF)

VELOCEPRESS MANUALS - AUTOMOBILE

ALFA ROMEO GIULIA WORKSHOP MANUAL 1300 TO 2000cc 1962-1975
ALFA ROMEO GIULIA TECH MANUAL CARBURETED CARS FROM 1962
ALFA ROMEO GIULIA TECH MANUAL FUEL INJECTED CARS FROM 1969
AUSTIN-HEALEY 6-CYLINDER WORKSHOP MANUAL
AUSTIN-HEALEY SPRITE & MG MIDGET WORKSHOP MANUAL 1958-1971
BMW 600 LIMOUSINE FACTORY WORKSHOP MANUAL
BMW 600 LIMOUSINE OWNERS HAND BOOK & SERVICE MANUAL
BMW 2000 & 2002 1966-1976 WORKSHOP MANUAL
BMW ISETTA FACTORY WORKSHOP MANUAL
CORVAIR 1960-1969 WORKSHOP MANUAL
CORVETTE V8 1955-1962 WORKSHOP MANUAL
FIAT 500 FACTORY WORKSHOP MANUAL 1957-1973
FIAT 600, 600D & MULTIPLA FACTORY WORKSHOP MANUAL 1955-1969
JAGUAR E-TYPE 3.8 & 4.2 SERIES 1 & 2 WORKSHOP MANUAL
JAGUAR MK 7, 8, 9 & XK120, 140, 150 WORKSHOP MANUAL 1948-1961
METROPOLITAN FACTORY WORKSHOP MANUAL
MGA & MGB OWNERS HANDBOOK & WORKSHOP MANUAL
MG MIDGET TC, TD, TF & TF1500 WORKSHOP MANUAL
PORSCHE 356 1948-1965 WORKSHOP MANUAL
PORSCHE 911 2.0, 2.2, 2.4 LITRE 1964-1973
PORSCHE 912 WORKSHOP MANUAL
TRIUMPH TR2, TR3, TR4 1953-1965 WORKSHOP MANUAL
VOLKSWAGEN TRANSPORTER, TRUCKS & WAGONS 1950-1979 WSM
VOLVO 1944-1968 ALL MODELS WORKSHOP MANUAL

VELOCEPRESS TECHNICAL BOOKS - AUTOMOBILE

FERRARI 250/GT SERVICE AND MAINTENANCE
FERRARI GUIDE TO PERFORMANCE
FERRARI OWNER'S HANDBOOK
FERRARI TUNING TIPS & MAINTENANCE TECHNIQUES
HOW TO BUILD A FIBERGLASS CAR
HOW TO BUILD A RACING CAR
HOW TO RESTORE THE MODEL 'A' FORD
MASERATI OWNER'S HANDBOOK
OBERT'S FIAT GUIDE
PERFORMANCE TUNING THE SUNBEAM TIGER
SOUPING THE VOLKSWAGEN
SOLEX CARBURETORS (EMPHASIS ON UK & EU AUTOMOBILES)
SU CARBURETORS (EMPHASIS ON UK AUTOMOBILES)
WEBER CARBURETORS (EMPHASIS ON ALFA & FIAT)

VELOCEPRESS BOOKS & GUIDES - AUTOMOBILE

ABARTH BUYERS GUIDE
COMPLETE CATALOG OF JAPANESE MOTOR VEHICLES
FERRARI 308 SERIES BUYER'S AND OWNER'S GUIDE
FERRARI BERLINETTA LUSSO
FERRARI BROCHURES AND SALES LITERATURE 1946-1967
FERRARI BROCHURES AND SALES LITERATURE 1968-1989
FERRARI OPP, MAINTENANCE & SERVICE H/BOOKS 1948-1963
FERRARI SERIAL NUMBERS PART I - ODD NUMBERS TO 21399
FERRARI SERIAL NUMBERS PART II - EVEN NUMBERS TO 1050
FERRARI SPYDER CALIFORNIA
HENRY'S FABULOUS MODEL "A" FORD
MASERATI BROCHURES AND SALES LITERATURE

VELOCEPRESS BOOKS – RACING

CARRERA PANAMERICANA - MEXICAN ROAD RACE (BOOK OF)
DIALED IN - THE JAN OPPERMAN STORY
IF HEMINGWAY HAD WRITTEN A RACING NOVEL
LE MANS 24 (THE BOOK THAT THE FILM WAS BASED ON)
VEDA ORR'S NEW REVISED HOT ROD PICTORIAL

AUTOBOOKS WORKSHOP MANUALS & BROOKLANDS ROAD TEST PORTFOLIOS

FOR A COMPLETE LISTING OF THE AUTOBOOKS & BROOKLANDS TITLES THAT WE CURRENTLY HAVE AVAILABLE, PLEASE VISIT OUR WEBSITE.

For a detailed description of any of the above titles please visit
www.VelocePress.com

www.ingramcontent.com/pod-product-compliance
Lightning Source LLC
Chambersburg PA
CBHW060249240426
43673CB00047B/1900